Upper–Intermediate

Student's Book

New Headway

English Course

Liz & John Soars

This book is dedicated to the memory of John Haycraft, founder of the International House organization, who inspired so much in so many in the field of English Language teaching.

Oxford University Press

Contents   LANGUAGE INPUT

SKILLS DEVELOPMENT

Stop and Check 2   Teacher's Book p 149

Stop and Check 3   Teacher's Book p 152

SKILLS DEVELOPMENT

● Reading	● Speaking	● Listening	● Writing
Letters between Sean and his grandmother – an exercise on verb patterns pp 68, 70 'The family who turned back the clock' – a family who give up all domestic appliances for three days p 72	Discussion – domestic life fifty years ago – things you couldn't live without p 72 Discussion – the pros and cons of television p 75	A song – *Fast car*, by Tracy Chapman p 75 `T7.5`	Contrasting ideas *whereas* *However* *although* Writing about an invention you couldn't live without p 75
'Jane Austen, the hottest writer in Hollywood' – the famous English novelist who is enjoying a revival p 82	Talking about the lives of famous people p 81 Discussion – the lives of women past and present p 83	One side of a phone conversation p 80 `T8.1` An interview with Tim Rice, who wrote the lyrics to *Jesus Christ Superstar*, and Paul Nicholas, who played Jesus p 85 `T8.7`	Writing a fan letter p 86
'Mysteries of the universe' – puzzles that have plagued human beings for thousands of years p 91	General knowledge quiz p 89 Discussion – retelling a story from another point of view p 95	'Saying *I won't*' – a radio programme about people who change their mind at the altar p 95 `T9.6` A song – *Waiting at the church* p 95 `T9.7`	Joining sentences Conjunctions *whenever unless* Adverbs *anyway actually* p 96
'Living history' – the 100-year-old lady who lives in the past p 98 'People and their money' – who's rich and who's poor these days? (jigsaw) p 103	Giving a short talk about your first friend or teacher p 100 Attitudes to money p 102 Homelessness p 105	Homelessness – interviews with people who live on the streets, and those who try to help them p 105 `T10.4`	Writing about a period in history p 106
'Whose life's perfect anyway?' – two people's lives p 109 'Things we never said' – a short story about a failed relationship, by Fiona Goble p 112	Roleplay – two lovers tell each other the truth p 113 Acting out a dramatic scene p 116	A radio play, based on the text 'Things we never said' p 111 `T11.4` 'Family secrets' – two people talk about a secret in their lives p 115 `T11.5`	Writing a play with stage directions p 116
'Michelangelo' – one of the world's greatest artists p 118 'It blows your mind!' – eye-witness accounts of the first atomic explosion p 121	Discussion – famous photos of the twentieth century p 124 Discussion – how the atomic bomb changed history p 123	Children's jokes p 124 `T12.4` Various people describe great events of the twentieth century p 125 `T12.5`	Describing a career Word order and focus of attention p 126

Phonetic symbols (inside back cover)

There's no place like home

The tense system
Dates, numbers, spelling

Test your grammar

1 Work in pairs. Which time expressions from the box can be used with the sentences below? Make sure the sentences sound natural.

> when I was born   never   tonight
> in the 1960s   rarely   for a year
> for ages   ages ago   the other day
> in a fortnight's time   recently
> during a blizzard   always   later
> since I was a child

a My parents met in Warsaw.
b My father speaks Polish.
c They were working in Germany.
d I was born in Berlin.
e My grandparents have lived in Hong Kong.
f I wrote to my grandmother.
g I'm going to work in Peru.
h My brother's flying to Rome on business.
i I've been learning Spanish.
j I'll see you.

2 Make similar sentences with time expressions to talk to a partner about yourself and your family. Tell the rest of the class some things about your partner.

3 Ask your teacher questions.

Where/you born?
... you travel/much?
How long/you/teach/English?
... brothers or sisters?

LANGUAGE IN CONTEXT

Letters home

1 **T 1.1** Look at these extracts of three letters home. Who wrote them? Who to? Where is the writer of the letter? What is she/he doing there? Who are the other people mentioned?

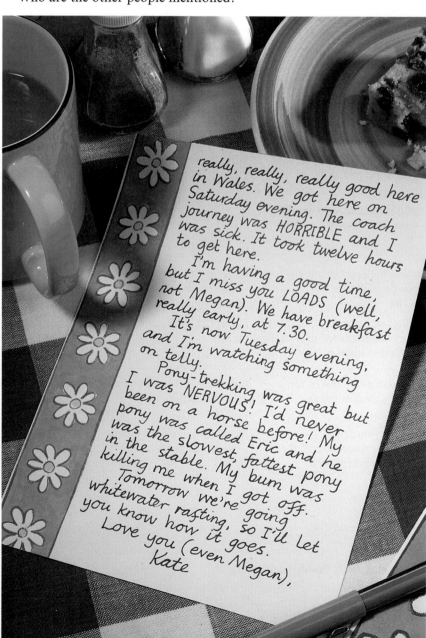

> really, really, really good here in Wales. We got here on Saturday evening. The coach journey was HORRIBLE and I was sick. It took twelve hours to get here.
> I'm having a good time, but I miss you LOADS (well, not Megan). We have breakfast really early, at 7.30.
> It's now Tuesday evening, and I'm watching something on telly.
> Pony-trekking was great but I was NERVOUS! I'd never been on a horse before! My pony was called Eric and he was the slowest, fattest pony in the stable. My bum was killing me when I got off.
> Tomorrow we're going whitewater rafting, so I'll let you know how it goes.
> Love you (even Megan),
> Kate

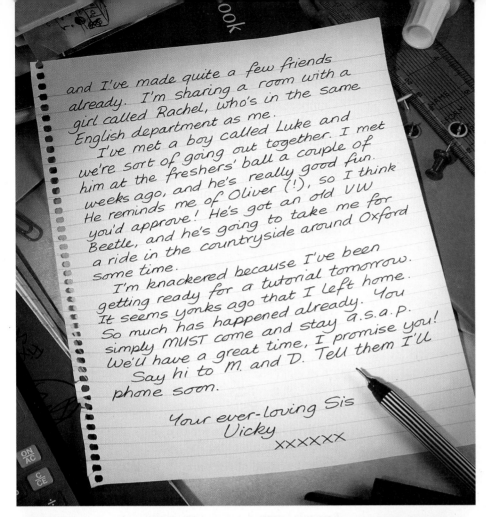

and I've made quite a few friends already. I'm sharing a room with a girl called Rachel, who's in the same English department as me.

I've met a boy called Luke and we're sort of going out together. I met him at the freshers' ball a couple of weeks ago, and he's really good fun. He reminds me of Oliver (!), so I think you'd approve! He's got an old VW Beetle, and he's going to take me for a ride in the countryside around Oxford some time.

I'm knackered because I've been getting ready for a tutorial tomorrow. It seems yonks ago that I left home. So much has happened already. You simply MUST come and stay a.s.a.P. We'll have a great time, I promise you! Say hi to M. and D. Tell them I'll phone soon.

Your ever-loving Sis
Vicky
xxxxxx

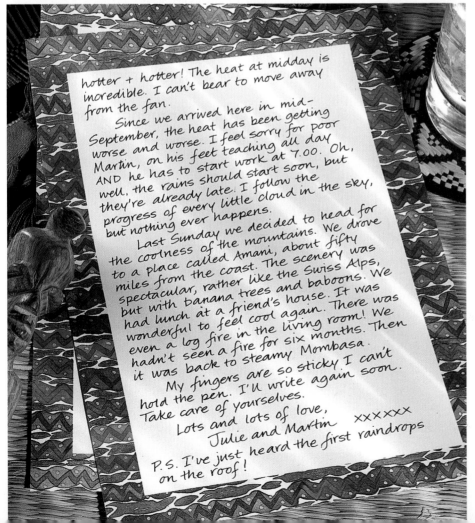

hotter + hotter! The heat at midday is incredible. I can't bear to move away from the fan.

Since we arrived here in mid-September, the heat has been getting worse and worse. I feel sorry for poor Martin, on his feet teaching all day, AND he has to start work at 7.00. Oh, well, the rains should start soon, but they're already late. I follow the progress of every little cloud in the sky, but nothing ever happens.

Last Sunday we decided to head for the coolness of the mountains. We drove to a place called Amani, about fifty miles from the coast. The scenery was spectacular, rather like the Swiss Alps, but with banana trees and baboons. We had lunch at a friend's house. It was wonderful to feel cool again. There was even a log fire in the living room! We hadn't seen a fire for six months. Then it was back to steamy Mombasa.

My fingers are so sticky I can't hold the pen. I'll write again soon. Take care of yourselves.

Lots and lots of love,
Julie and Martin   xxxxxx

P.S. I've just heard the first raindrops on the roof!

2 Complete the questions and answers.

Kate

a How long _____ Kate _____ in Wales?
_____ three days.

b _____ a good time?
Yes, _____ enjoying it a lot.

c How long _____?
Twelve hours.

d What time _____?
At 7.30.

e _____ nervous?
Because _____ before.

f _____?
She's going whitewater rafting.

Vicky

a What _____ Vicky _____ at university?
English.

b How long _____ with Luke?
Two weeks.

c Where _____?
At a dance.

d What sort _____?
A VW Beetle.

e _____ tired?
Because _____.

Julie and Martin

a How long _____ in Mombasa?
_____ September.

b _____?
At 7.00.

c _____ Amani?
Because it's cooler.

d _____?
At a friend's house.

e What _____ just _____?
It _____ to rain.

T 1.2 Listen and check your answers.

● Grammar question

– Which tenses can you identify in the letters?

PRACTICE BANK

1 Forming the tenses

Complete the tense charts. Use the verb *work* for the active and *make* for the passive.

ACTIVE	Simple	Continuous
Present	He works	We
Past	She	I
Future	They	You
Present Perfect	We	She
Past Perfect	I	You
Future Perfect	They	He will have been working

PASSIVE	Simple	Continuous
Present	It is made	They
Past	It	It
Future	They	
Present Perfect	They	
Past Perfect	It	
Future Perfect	They	

> ⚠ Notice that not all the passive tenses are included. They are not normally used, and we avoid them by using the active.
> Our house <u>has been being decorated</u> for months. ✗
> *They've been decorating our house for months.* ✓

2 Discussing grammar

Work in pairs and discuss your answers.

Compare the verb forms in the pairs of sentences. Say which tense is used and why.

a Klaus **lives** in Berlin.
  Klaus **is living** with an English family while he's in London.

b You**'re** very kind. Thank you.
  You**'re being** very kind. What do you want?

c I**'ve got** a headache.
  I often **have** headaches.

d When we arrived, she **made** some coffee.
  When we arrived, she **was making** some coffee.

e What **were** you **doing** when you cut your finger?
  What **did** you **do** when you cut your finger?

f I**'ve lived** in Singapore for five years.
  I **lived** in Singapore for five years.

g When I arrived at the party, Peter **left**.
  When I arrived at the party, Peter **had left**.

h I **didn't teach** English very well.
  I **wasn't taught** English very well.

i You**'re annoying** me with all your questions.
  I can see you**'re annoyed**. What's the matter?

j How much **are** you **paying** to have the house painted?
  How much **are** you **being paid** to paint the house?

3 Auxiliary verbs and pronunciation

1 **T 1.3** Listen to the sentences. Identify the auxiliary verbs and the tense.

Examples
She's seen a lot of films recently.
has – Present Perfect

Are you being served?
are and being – Present Continuous passive

2 Where are the contractions? Practise saying the sentences, taking care with weak forms.

4 Reading

Read the text about an unusual home. Put the verbs in brackets into the correct tense. There are examples of active and passive sentences.

Example
Frank *has lived* (live) in his house for a year.

HOME IS WHERE YOU MAKE IT!

Frank Webb has a most unusual house, a former ladies' lavatory in Kew, south-west London.

As soon as Frank heard that someone (a)_____(try) to sell the ladies' loo, he wanted it. He was sure that he could make the building, which (b)_____(situate) next to the famous gardens at Kew, into a beautiful home. Now he's very busy – he (c)_____(convert) it into a one bedroom house.

'It might seem rather odd to want to live in a place which used to be a lavatory,' he said, 'but I (d)_____(think) it's really beautiful.'

He was divorced recently, and he needed somewhere to live. He knew he wanted something small but unique. 'A friend (e)_____(tell) me about it. I think she (f)_____(joke), but it was exactly what I (g)_____(search) for.'

He is 57. His 25-year-old daughter, Kathy, (h)_____(love) the place, too. She (i)_____(help) her father with the work for the past few weeks as she has been on holiday. He advises visitors not to go into the kitchen. 'It (j)_____(decorate) at the moment, and it looks awful.'

Since he bought the lavatory, several ladies (k)_____(knock) on the door, wanting to use it. He lets them use his own bathroom. When he first saw the building, it (l)_____(not use) for several years, so it was in quite a mess.

It (m)_____(build) in 1905. It is very solid, so he (n)_____(not have) to do any work on the walls or roof. He (o)_____(pay) £60,000 for it a year ago, and since then he (p)_____(spend) an extra £20,000 putting in an upper floor for the bedroom. **'I like the thought that my home has a history,' he says with great pride.**

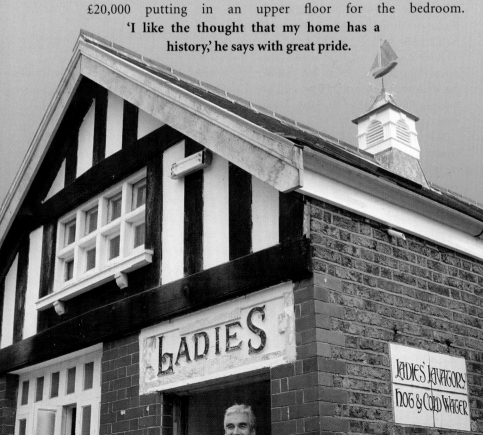

The tense system

1 English tenses have two elements of meaning: time and aspect. Time refers to when, and aspect refers to how the speaker sees the event.

Time	Aspect
Present Past Future	Simple Continuous Perfect

2 The simple aspect describes an event which is permanent, complete, habitual, or a simple fact.

*The River Danube **flows** through seven countries.*
*It **rained** yesterday.*
*He **goes** swimming every evening after work.*
*My daughter **will be** ten next week.*

3 The continuous aspect describes an event which is temporary, incomplete, or in progress.

*I'm **working** at home this week.*
*She's **writing** a book about the environment.*
*It **was raining** when I woke up this morning.*
*Don't phone me at 8.00. **I'll be having** dinner.*

4 The perfect aspect describes an event which relates to two different times. The event is completed at an indefinite time before another time.

*I've **read** that book. (Sometime before now)*
*Peter **had** already **left**. (Sometime before then)*
*I'll **have finished** my homework by 5.00. (Sometime before 5.00)*

5 English has an active and passive voice.

*She **speaks** three languages.*
*English **is spoken** all over the world.*
*You must **do** the homework tonight.*
*It must **be done** carefully.*

📖 **Grammar Reference: page 146.**

The great

Many people move to a new country in search of a new life. Do they always find what they are looking for? Here are the stories of two British families who decided to emigrate.

●READING AND SPEAKING

People who emigrate

Pre-reading task

Work in small groups and discuss the following questions.

1 Have any of your friends or family gone to live in a foreign country? Why? Do you know anyone who has come to live in your country from another country? Why? Do these people have any problems about living away from home?

2 Close your eyes and think about your country. What would you miss most about it if you went to live abroad? Write a list and compare it with the others in the group.

Reading

Read the introduction to the article. Divide into two groups.

Group A	Read about the **Clavy family**, who emigrated to **Canada**. (this page)
Group B	Read about the **White family**, who emigrated to **Greece**. (page 11)

Canada

The Clavy family and their two dogs, Bonzo and Doodah, moved from the suburbs of Birmingham to Canada two years ago. Marion, a full-time housewife,
5 **and Andy Clavy, a mechanical engineer with a machine supply company, now live with their two children, Matthew, 12, and Mark, 9, in Stony Plain, Alberta, not far from the Rocky Mountains.**

10 **Marion**: I still can't believe we're actually here. Do we really live in this big house, surrounded by fir trees, on four acres of land, just three hours' drive from the Rockies? It's the most spectacular
15 scenery I've ever seen. Not that life in Birmingham was that bad. We were comfortably well off, but Andy worked 12-hour days. He used to come home every night, have a shower, eat dinner,
20 then crash out. I thought, 'There must be more to life than this!' We rarely spent time together as a family.

Then Andy was made redundant and given a pay-out of more than £20,000, so
25 we took the plunge. We had always wanted to live in Canada, ever since we'd visited cousins here, so we applied. Our application took a nail-biting eighteen months to be accepted and it cost £2,000.
30 Then we sold our house, a semi with a pocket-handkerchief garden. Emigrating is an expensive business. It cost £1,000 just to fly the dogs here!

We didn't know a soul when we arrived
35 in Alberta, but in just a few months we had made plenty of Canadian friends. It took time for us to get used to the way they come into your house and use the

telephone and take drinks from the
40 fridge without asking. But I'm less English about such things now.

Moving to Canada has made us a lot closer as a family. We do sports together, visit friends' houses for barbecues, and
45 go sightseeing in the Rockies. The children love their schools. They think it's great not to have to wear a uniform. And the girls go mad for Matthew here because of his English accent – the phone
50 never stops ringing!

I don't miss much about England, except the castles and the greenness of the countryside, but now we have the Rocky Mountains. I certainly don't miss
55 the English weather. Even in the winter here, when the temperature is −45 degrees, the sun usually shines and the sky is blue.

Andy: Before we moved, I was always too
60 exhausted to do anything with Marion and the boys. Now I only work eight-hour days. Marion and I have much more time for each other. Business is a lot more relaxed, too. You don't wear suits and
65 ties, and nobody calls anybody 'Mr'. It's all first names and T-shirts and jeans. It took a few months to find a decent job, so for a while we had financial worries. But in the end I was lucky.
70 Unemployment here is quite high.

I don't miss anything about England except the cricket, and of course my family, but my parents have already visited us twice. My sisters are staying
75 with us at the moment and having a great time. Moving here is the best thing we've ever done.

escape

Greece

Hazel and Barry White left England five years ago with their baby daughter, Daisy. They moved from their basement flat in north London to a two-bedroom apartment overlooking the sea on the Greek island of Agastri. They earned about £18,000 between them in London, working in the hotel business. They have set up a watersports business in Greece.

Barry: Daisy was three months old when I decided we simply had to leave London. We weren't unhappy in London, we enjoyed our work. But we worried that our child couldn't run freely in the busy London streets. We wanted her to grow up carefree and in the sunshine.

Hazel and I had had a couple of holidays in Agastri and had made some Greek friends there. It's very beautiful and peaceful. In Greek, *agastri* means 'fishing hook', and the locals say, 'When you come to Agastri, you're hooked.' So we took the plunge, sold our flat, and moved. Our family and friends thought we were crazy.

A tourist sports business seemed a good way to earn a living in Greece, so with the money from our flat we bought waterskiing equipment and two speedboats. Later, I bought a *varka* or passenger boat for fishing trips and picnics round the island. Running the business hasn't been easy. Things are very bureaucratic here and sometimes this can be very frustrating. It took some time to get used to so many forms and officials, but I'm more patient now.

Also, I've found the Greek language very difficult. Fortunately, I understand more than I can speak, so I get by. But Daisy is more Greek than English now. She's absolutely bilingual and the only English child at her school. Living on Agastri is definitely better for her. She runs round the village and talks to everyone. Everyone knows her.

I don't miss England much, mainly family and friends. I do miss the theatre but we get good movies here. I also miss sausages, Stilton cheese, and white thick-sliced bread! But that's all. I think Hazel has found it more difficult than me.

Hazel: I didn't realize what a big culture shock it would be. It has taken me a long time to get used to the Greek way of life, especially on such a small island. Here the women aren't treated the same way as men. They are expected to stay at home more, and in the winter they hardly go out at all. But people are very kind and generous. In a way, the community is like a big happy family, which is great, especially for Daisy, but it also means that everyone knows everything about you.

I have a few Greek women friends, but the language barrier was very hard at first. I used to visit their homes for coffee and sit for hours not understanding a single word. Our life here has certainly tested my relationship with Barry. The business has had some bad times. There's such a huge difference between our winter and summer income, and money worries cause our tempers to fray! Next winter, I'm going back to London for a few months with Daisy – I miss my parents terribly. No doubt I'll be back here with Barry in the spring, but I'm not entirely sure. I sometimes have doubts about living here.

Comprehension check

1 Answer the questions about the family in your article.
a Why did they emigrate?
b Why did they go to that particular country?
c What are the changes in the way of life for the parents?
d What are the changes in the way of life for the children?
e Were there any initial difficulties?
f Have they had any money problems? Are they any better off now?
g Is the family happier?
h What do they miss about their life in England?
i How is the relationship between the husband and wife?
j Do they still think that moving was a wise decision?

2 Find a partner from the other group. Compare your answers.

3 Read about the other family. Which family do you think has made the more successful move? Would *you* like their new way of life?

Language work

1 Here are some sentences from the stories of two families. Can you work out the meaning of the words underlined?

Canada

a He used to come home every night, have a shower, eat dinner, and crash out. (l. 18–20)

b Andy was made redundant and given a pay-out of more than £20,000. (l. 23–4)

c Our application took a nail-biting eighteen months to be accepted. (l. 27–9)

d We didn't know a soul when we arrived. (l. 34)

Greece

e We wanted her to grow up carefree and in the sunshine. (l. 16–17)

f So we took the plunge, sold our flat, and moved. (l. 23–5)

g Things are very bureaucratic here and sometimes this can be very frustrating. (l. 34–6)

h Fortunately, I understand more than I can speak, so I get by. (l. 40–1)

i I didn't realize what a big culture shock it would be. (l. 54–5)

j Money worries cause our tempers to fray. (l. 75–6)

2 Use a question word in **A** and a verb in **B** to write some questions about the family you first read about.

Example
Why did they decide to emigrate?

Ask and answer the questions with a partner from the other group.

A	B
when where who	move live work be
what why how	go do miss visit
how long	decide feel have

Discussion

Write a list of as many disadvantages as you can think of for emigrating.
Compare your lists. For every disadvantage (–) try to find an opposing advantage (+).

Example
– *The language barrier – maybe you don't speak the language.*
+ *But this is an opportunity to learn a new language.*

● VOCABULARY AND PRONUNCIATION

HOUSE AND HOME

Compounds and dictionary work

> ! Words can combine to make new words. Look at the examples and note the different spellings. There are no rules.
>
> **life**   lifestyle   lifelong   life-size
>   life expectancy   life insurance

Work in pairs. Look at the texts on pages 10 and 11 and find some compound nouns and adjectives.

1 How many new words can you make by combining a word on the left with a word on the right?
Use your dictionaries to help with the meaning and the spelling.

home	work made trained wife sick
	plant proud town coming less
house	grown bound keeping warming

2 **T 1.4** Listen to the conversations. They contain examples of some of the compounds in Exercise 1. After each conversation, discuss these two questions.

Who is talking to who?   What exactly are they talking about?

3 Here are some lines from the conversations. Fill the gaps with a compound word.

a She's so cute. Is she _____ yet?

b Do you think you could possibly water my _____ for me?

c Don't worry, I know how _____ you are. I'll make sure everything stays clean and tidy.

d Let's give her a spectacular _____ party when she gets back.

e Not me. I'm the original happy _____, remember? Four kids, _____ cakes, _____ vegetables!

f We're having a _____ party on the 12th. Can you come?

g 'Yeah. Mind you, there's much more _____ to do!'
'That's a drag!'

h I never thought you'd be so _____.

4 Practise saying the lines in Exercise 3 with correct stress and intonation. Then use them to help you remember the conversations.
Act some of them out with your partner.

5 How many compounds can you make by combining a word from **A** with a word from **B**? There is sometimes more than one for each word in **A**. Use your dictionary to help.

A		B			
book	video	food	shop	table	mail
speed	radio	conditioned	software		
light	time	maker	perfect	recorder	
remote	junk	processor	bomb	headed	
word	food	consuming	limit	token	
air	computer	poisoning	bulb	boat	
		controlled	worm		

Compare your words in groups. Check the meanings.

● LISTENING

Hello Muddah, Hello Fadduh

Pre-listening task

You are going to listen to a song about an American boy who goes away to summer camp. First answer the questions.

1 Are there holiday camps for children in your country? What can the children do there?

2 Why might the children like these summer camps? Why might they be unhappy?

3 Look at the pictures and find the following:
  – a boy hiking – a bunk-bed
  – poison ivy – a search party
  – a forest – someone hugging another person
  – a bear – hail
  – an alligator

Check the verb *to disregard* in your dictionary.

Listening

The song is called *Hello Muddah, Hello Fadduh*. This is an exaggerated American pronunciation of *mother* and *father*. It also rhymes with *Camp Grenada*, which is the name of the camp where the boy is!

T 1.5 Listen and number the pictures 1–8.

Comprehension check

1 Let's say the boy's name is Chuck. How does Chuck's mood change during the song? How does he feel at the beginning, in the middle, and at the end? Why?

2 What happened to his friends …
   … Joe Spivey? … Leonard Skinner?
   … his bunk mate? … Jeffrey Hardy?

3 Chuck tries to persuade his parents to take him home in various ways. What are they?
   What does he say might happen to him at Camp Grenada?

4 A *sissy* is an informal word for a boy who isn't hard and aggressive. What do you know about the Greek writer, Homer, and his legendary hero, Ulysses (usually pronounced /'juːlisiːz/)? So why does the head coach read to the boys from *Ulysses*?

5 Do you think he likes his brother and Aunt Bertha?

6 How long has he been at the camp?

7 Why is everything better at the end?

Language work

The words in the boxes appear in the song. Write in the other parts of speech. Mark the stress.

Adjective	Noun	Verb
enter'taining		
	fun	
		de'velop
	'poison	
	'trainer	
		hate
		scare
		'organize
		'promise
	noise	
		mess
	play	

● WRITING AND SPEAKING

Looking forward to seeing you

Divide into two groups.

1 Each group reads one of the letters quickly. Answer the questions.

a Where was the letter written?
b Who is the guest? Who is the host?
c Which city is described? What is it like?
d What season is it?

Work with a student from the other group. Go through the answers together and compare the information in the two letters.

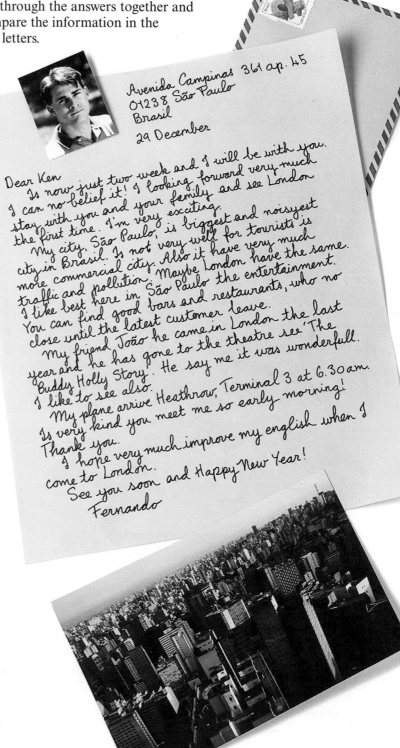

Avenida Campinas 361 ap. 45
01238 São Paulo
Brasil

29 December

Dear Ken
   Is now just two week and I will be with you. I can no belief it! I looking forward very much stay with you and your family and see London the first time. I'm very exciting.
   My city, São Paulo, is biggest and noisyest city in Brasil. Is not very well for tourists is more commercial city. Also it have very much traffic and pollution. Maybe London have the same.
   I like best here in São Paulo the entertainment. You can find good bars and restaurants, who no close until the latest customer leave.
   My friend João he came in London the last year and he has gone to the theatre see 'The Buddy Holly Story'. He say me it was wonderfull. I like to see also.
   My plane arrive Heathrow, Terminal 3 at 6.30 am. Is very kind you meet me so early morning! Thank you.
   I hope very much improve my english when I come to London.
   See you soon and Happy New Year!
   Fernando

Lindenstr. 15
5430 Basel
Switzerland

7 July

Dear Sophie

In just one week you are here with me in Switzerland. I want that you meet my family and I will show you my city. I hope you like. Basel is not a big city as London but it's everything very clean and very close the mountains, wich are beautifull. I am worry that you will find Basel a little bored. It is not excited as London becaus the street are very quiet after six o'clock the night. The peopel live in flats so they don't can do a lot of noises. There exists a museum but perhaps that isn't very interisting to look.

We have finished school the last week and I enjoy the holiday. My family don't speak english so you will practice a lot your german. I like also practice my english with you.

See you the next week! I come to the airport to meet you.

Love
Liliane

2 Both writers have made mistakes in their letters. Find the mistakes in your letter and correct them. What different kinds of mistakes are there?

3 Read the other letter. Do the two letters have any similar kinds of mistakes? Work as a group to write out a correct version of your letter on the board.

4 Write a similar letter. Imagine you are either expecting an English-speaking guest to stay with you in your country, or going to stay with a friend in an English-speaking country. Describe your home town briefly as part of your letter.

PostScript

Dates

Notice how we say and write dates.

'*the seventh of August*'   23 September 1982
'*January the tenth*'   19/8/96 (Americans write 8/19/96)

– What's the date today?
– When did this term start? When does it finish?
– What are some of the important dates in your life? Why?
– What are the most important dates in your country? Why?

Numbers

1   T 1.6   Listen to the conversations. What are the different ways of saying the number 0?

In British English, we always say *and* before the tens. In American English, *and* can be dropped.

456 (BE) four hundred and fifty-six; (US) four hundred fifty-six

2   T 1.7   Listen to the news broadcasts. They contain fifteen numbers. Write them down, and then practise them.

Spelling

We break up a longer word when we are spelling out loud.

Manchester   MAN – CHES – TER

Notice how we correct people when they make a spelling mistake!

Not p! B for ball!

Not n! M for mother!

Not s! F for Freddy!

Spell your surname to a partner.

Practice

You are all going to different parts of the world to learn English! Your teacher will give you a card to tell you where.

In pairs, ask and answer questions. Write down the information you hear.

a   Where are you going to?
b   What's your address?
c   When are you going?
d   Who are you staying with?
e   What's your telephone number?
f   How much money are you taking?

2 Been there, done that!

Present Perfect
Continuous verb forms
Exclamations

Test your grammar

Work in pairs. What is strange about these sentences?

a Amazing news! Columbus has discovered America!
b Man first walked on the moon.
c I travelled all my life.
I went everywhere.
d Peter! Hi! I didn't see you for ages!
e I've learnt English.
f 'Your face is all red.' 'I've run.'
g 'What's the matter?'
'I've been losing my passport.'
h I've been giving up smoking for years.
i Ouch! I've just stung a mosquito!

LANGUAGE IN CONTEXT

Present Perfect

1 Look at the pictures of two travellers. What differences can you see?

2 Read the first and last paragraphs of two articles about the travellers. Then match the sentences opposite with the correct person. Put DL or MW next to each line.

David Livingstone

Mick Watts

David Livingstone, African explorer

David Livingstone was one of the most important Victorian explorers. He spent thirty years travelling in Africa.

He died in 1873, in modern Zambia. His followers buried his heart at the foot of the tree where he died. His remains were buried at Westminster Abbey in London.

Mick Watts, backpacker in Asia

Mick Watts is in Melbourne. He is on a nine-month backpacking trip round Australia and south-east Asia.

He's looking forward to taking things easy for another week, then setting off again. 'Once you've got the travel bug, it becomes very hard to stay in the same place for too long,' he said.

a ☐ He flew into Bangkok five months ago. Since then, he has been to Kuala Lumpur, Singapore, Java, and Bali.

b ☐ With his wife, he travelled into regions where no Europeans had ever been.

c ☐ He's been staying in cheap hostels, along with a lot of other young people.

d ☐ The best part of the trip so far has been learning to scuba dive on the Great Barrier Reef.

e ☐ He went to the Kalahari Desert, the Zambezi River, and the Victoria Falls.

f ☐ He set out to discover the source of the River Nile on foot. He vanished, and some people thought he had died.

g ☐ 'I've had diarrhoea a few times, and I've been mugged once.' Apart from that, his only worry is the insects. He has been stung all over his body.

h ☐ His wife died of a fever.

i ☐ He has visited temples in Thailand, and seen giant turtles in Indonesia.

j ☐ He's been travelling mainly by public transport – bus, train, and ferry.

k ☐ The American journalist, Henry Morton Stanley, greeted him with the famous words, 'Dr Livingstone, I presume'.

T 2.1 Listen and check your answers. What other information do you learn about the two travellers?

3 Here are some contracted forms. Can you remember the sentences? Practise them.

he's been to …
he's visited …
he's seen …
I've had …
I've been mugged …
he's been stung …
he's been staying …
he's been travelling …

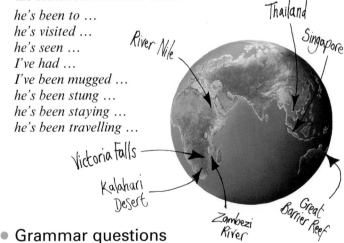

● Grammar questions

– What is the main tense in the sentences about David Livingstone? Why?

– What are the main tenses used in the sentences about Mick Watts? Why?

PRACTICE BANK

1 Questions and answers

1 Read the pairs of questions. First decide who each question is about, David Livingstone or Mick Watts. Then ask and answer the questions.

a Where did he go?
   Where has he been?

b How long has he been travelling?
   How long did he travel?

c How did he travel?
   How has he been travelling?

d Has he been ill?
   Where did he die?

e Did he have any problems?
   Has he had any problems?

2 Here are the answers to some questions. Write the questions.

About David Livingstone

a Medicine.
b To join a Christian mission.
c Soon after he arrived.
d A fever.
e Westminster Abbey.

About Mick Watts

f For five months. *(How long … away from home?)*
g Thailand, Malaysia, Singapore, Indonesia, and Australia. *(Which … ?)*
h In cheap hostels.
i A few times. *(How often … ?)*
j Yes, just once. *(Has he … ?)*

T 2.2 Listen and check your answers.

2 Discussing grammar

Work in pairs and discuss your answers.

1 Compare the use of tenses in the sentences. Say which tense is used and why.

a Charles Dickens wrote *Oliver Twist*.
   Ken Follett has written ten best-sellers.
   Ken Follett's been writing his autobiography for the past eighteen months.

b Have you ever tried Japanese food?
   Did you try *sushi* when you were in Japan?

c How many times has Kate been married?
   How many times was Tom married?

d She's been to Paris.
   She's gone to Paris.

e We've lived here all our lives.
We've been living with friends while we're looking for a flat.

f Who's eaten my chocolates?
Who's been eating my chocolates?

g I've been reading all morning.
I've read four chapters.

h Ouch! I've cut my finger.
I'm exhausted! I've been cutting the grass all morning.

2 Correct the mistakes.

a Sorry. Jack isn't in the office. He's been to lunch.
b How long have you been having your car?
c Tom Hanks hasn't made as many films as Charlie Chaplin has.
d Have you seen the football match on Saturday?
e Where have you bought your shoes? They're lovely!
f 'Why is your hair wet?' 'I've swum.'
g She's been smoking ten cigarettes since she arrived.

3 Speaking and listening

Work in pairs. Your teacher will give you some information about a large international company called *Virgo*. You will not have the same information as your partner. Ask and answer questions to complete the information.

Example

Student A	Student B
Originally, *Virgo* sold records. The company was founded in … (*When?*) The chairman and owner of *Virgo*, Jimmy Kramer, opened his first record shop in Oxford Street, London.	Originally, *Virgo* sold records. The company was founded in 1980. The chairman and owner of *Virgo*, Jimmy Kramer, opened his first record shop in … (*Where?*)

When was the company founded?

In 1980.

Where did Jimmy Kramer open his first record shop?

In Oxford Street, London.

4 Roleplay

You are going to interview Jimmy Kramer, the chairman of *Virgo*. Your teacher will give you some information. Work in groups to prepare the questions.

When you are ready, one half of the class will be the interviewers, and the other half will be Jimmy Kramer. (The teacher will give Jimmy some information.)

Conduct the interview. Begin by saying, '*Mr Kramer, it's very kind of you to agree to this interview. I wonder if I could ask you a few questions? First …*'

LANGUAGE REVIEW

Present Perfect

The Present Perfect relates a past action to the present.

1 It can express an action at an indefinite time before now.
I've been to Europe and America, but I've never been to Africa.
Peter's lost his wallet.
We're tired because we've been working hard.

If our attention moves to the exact time of the action, we must use past tenses.

I went to the States in 1995.
Peter lost his wallet this morning while he was shopping.
We started work at 8.00 this morning.

2 It can express an action that began in the past and continues into the future.
I've known Peter all my life.
We've been learning English for four years.

Present Perfect Simple versus Continuous

1 We use the continuous to emphasize the length of time that the activity has lasted, over hours, days, weeks, months, or years leading up to the present.
The Rolling Stones have been playing together for over 30 years.
I've been doing my homework for hours.

We use the simple when we see the action as a 'simple' whole.
The Rolling Stones have played in the biggest concert hall in the world.
I've done my maths and my English, but I haven't done my history yet.

2 The simple suggests a completed action, so we must use the simple if the sentence gives a definite number or quantity.
Ken Follett has been writing for years. He has written ten best-sellers.

Continuous verb forms

1 The continuous has the effect of lengthening an activity. The activity has duration, and we see the activity in progress.

*Sh! **I'm thinking**.*
*When I woke up, the sun **was shining**.*
***I've been studying** English for three years.*

2 The continuous can express a temporary activity or situation, not a permanent one.

***We're staying** with friends until we find somewhere of our own.*
***We've been living** with them for six weeks.*

📖 Grammar Reference: page 147.

● READING AND SPEAKING

Pre-reading task

Work in groups and discuss the following questions.

1 Look at the pictures of some famous tourist spots. How many do you recognize? Which countries are they in? Have you been to any of them?

2 As a tourist, have you ever:
- been on a package holiday?
- bought souvenirs?
  (*What? Where?*)
- taken lots of photographs?
  (*What of? Who of? Where?*)
- filmed your holiday with a camcorder?
  (*What? Who? Where?*)
- written your name in a visitors' book or on a wall or building?
  (*What? Where?*)

3 'Travel broadens the mind.'
Do you agree?

Death by tourism

Does tourism ruin everything that it touches?

by Arnold Baker

At the entrance to one of the ruined temples of Petra in Jordan, there is an inscription chiselled into the soft red rock. It looks as if it has been there for centuries. It could have been carved by one of King Herod's soldiers, when they were imprisoned in the town in 40 BC. But closer inspection reveals that it is not so ancient after all. It reads:

Shane and Wendy from Sydney were here. April 16th 1996.

The ruins of Petra were discovered in 1810 by a Swiss explorer, and a recent report has just concluded that 'they are in grave danger of being destroyed by the unstoppable march of tourism'. More than 4,000 tourists a day tramp through Petra's rocky tombs. They wear away the soft red sandstone to powder and (occasionally!) scratch their names into the rock.

It is not just Petra that is under threat of destruction. More than 600 million tourists a year now travel the globe, and vast numbers of them want to visit the world's most treasured sites: the Parthenon, the Taj Mahal, Stonehenge, the national parks of Kenya. The tourist industry will soon be the largest industry in the world, and it has barely reached its 50th birthday. Many places that once were remote are now part of package tours. Will nothing put a stop to the growth of tourism?

A brief history of tourism

The Romans probably started it with their holiday villas in the Bay of Naples.

In the 19th century, the education of the rich and privileged few was not complete without a Grand Tour of Europe's cultural sites.

Things started to change for ordinary people in 1845 when Thomas Cook, of Leicester, England, organized the first package tour.

By 1939, an estimated one million people were travelling abroad for holidays each year.

It is in the last three decades of the 20th century that tourism has really taken off. Tourism has been industrialized: landscapes, cultures, cuisines, and religions are consumer goods displayed in travel brochures.

Tourism today

The effects of tourism since the 1960s have been incredible. To take just a few examples:

- The **Mediterranean** shores have a resident population of 130 million, but this swells to 230 million each summer because of the tourists. This is nothing. The United Nations projects that visitors to the region could number 760 million by the year 2025. In Spain, France, Italy, and most of Greece, there is no undeveloped coastline left, and the Mediterranean is the dirtiest sea in the whole world.

- In the **Alps**, the cable cars have climbed ever higher. More and more peaks have been conquered. It is now an old Swiss joke that the government will have to build new mountains because they have wired up all the old ones. There are 15,000 cable car systems and 40,000 kilometres of ski-runs.

- **American national parks** have been operating permit systems for years. But even this is not enough for the most popular sites. By 1981, there was an eight-year waiting list to go rafting down the Grand Canyon's Colorado River, so now there is a lottery once a year to select the lucky travellers.

- In **Notre Dame** in Paris, 108 visitors enter each minute during opening hours. Thirty-five buses, having put down their passengers, wait outside, their fumes eating away at the stonework of the cathedral.

- Poor **Venice** with its unique, exquisite beauty. On one hot, historic day in 1987, the crowds were so great that the city had to be closed to all visitors.

- In **Barbados and Hawaii**, each tourist uses ten times as much water and electricity as a local inhabitant. Whilst feeling that this is unfair, the

locals acknowledge the importance of tourism to their economy overall.

• The prehistoric cave paintings at **Lascaux** in France were being slowly
105 ruined by the breath and bacteria from 200,000 visitors a year. The caves have now been closed to the public and a replica has been built. This is much praised for its likeness to the original.

110 **The future of tourism**

Will there be more replicas like in Lascaux? There already are. Heritage theme parks (mini-Disneylands!) are springing up
115 everywhere. Many of the great cities of Europe, such as Prague, Rome, and Warsaw, are finding that their historic centres are fast becoming theme parks – tourist ghettos, filled with clicking
120 cameras and whirring camcorders, abandoned by all local residents except for the souvenir sellers.

Until recently, we all believed that travel broadened the mind, but now
125 many believe the exact opposite: 'Modern travel narrows the mind'.

Reading

Work in pairs. Read the text quickly and discuss these questions.
– What do you understand by the title of the article?
– Which of the places in the pictures on page 19 are mentioned?
– What is said about them?
– Which other places are mentioned?
– Is the writer optimistic or pessimistic about the future of tourism?

Comprehension check

1 Are the following statements true (✓) or false (✗)? Correct the false ones with the right information and discuss your answers with a partner.

a An ancient inscription has been discovered at the entrance of a ruined temple in Petra.
b Nearly 1.5 million tourists a year visit Petra.
c The stone in Petra is so soft that the tourists' feet are destroying it.
d Tourism has been the world's largest industry since the 1960s.
e It is now possible to go everywhere in the world on a package holiday.
f In the 19th century, Thomas Cook organized tours of Europe's cultural sites for rich people.
g The number of foreign tourists has been growing gradually since 1939.
h There will be a huge increase in the numbers of tourists to the Mediterranean.
i The Swiss are considering ways of creating new mountains for skiers.
j Nowadays, you can only go rafting down the Colorado River if you win a lottery.
k The caves of Lascaux are going to be closed to the public and a replica is going to be built in Disneyland.
l Local people are moving away from many historic city centres.

2 What do the following numbers refer to?

40 BC   1810   600 million   1845   1939   230 million
eight-year   108   1987   ten times

Language work

1 Try to guess the meaning of the following words from the text.

chiselled (l. 3)	swells (l. 62)
tramp (l. 17)	clicking (l. 119)
treasured (l. 26)	whirring (l. 120)

2 Find a word in the text that has the same or similar meaning to the following:

shows (v)	unbelievable (adj)
reached a decision (v)	defeated and controlled (v)
serious (adj)	choose (v)
hardly (adv)	extremely beautiful or
distant and far away (adj)	delicate (adj)
having special rights and	admit, accept (v)
advantages (adj)	left (past participle)

Discussion

Work in groups of three. Discuss the following questions.

1 What are the favourite tourist spots in your country?
   Do you live near to any of them?
   Do they have any problems?

2 List as many advantages and disadvantages of tourism
   as you can think of. Compare your lists with the
   other groups.

3 There is an organization called 'Green Tourism'.
   Which in the following pairs do you think they will be
   in favour of? Which won't they approve of? Why?
   - package tourists or backpacking travellers?
   - using public transport or travelling by special
     tourist coach?
   - trekking in the Himalayas or wildlife safaris?
   - staying in five-star hotels or youth hostels?

● VOCABULARY

Hot Verbs (1): *take* and *put*

There are some very frequently used verbs in English,
such as *take, put, get, have, go, come, make,* and *do*.
They combine with other words in many different ways.

Read the examples with *take* and *put*.

Expressions with *take* and *put*
to take a few examples ...
She took a photo.
... put a stop to the growth of tourism ...

Phrasal verbs with *take* and *put*
Tourism has really taken off.
... buses, having put down their passengers
The waiter took away the plates.

Expressions with *take* and *put*

1 Which expressions go with *take* and which with *put*?
   Write *take* or *put* next to each expression.

   _____ my arm round sb   _____ drugs
   _____ three hours to get there _____ no notice
   _____ sb in charge of   _____ his work first
   _____ sb/sth for granted   _____ part
   _____ a plan into practice   _____ a risk
   _____ responsibility for sth   _____ place
   _____ pressure on sb   _____ my advice

2 Fill the gaps with one of the expressions from Exercise 1.
   Put the verb in the correct form.

a '_____ you ever _____?'
   'Well, things like aspirin, yes, but never anything illegal.'

b The wedding _____ in an old country church.
   It was lovely. But it was miles away from here!
   It _____.

c My mother was crying so I _____ her and told
   her not to worry.

d The older you get, the more you have to learn
   _____ for your own life. You have to look after
   everything yourself.

e I told you that boy was no good for you. You should
   have _____ and had nothing to do with him.

f The police _____ a very good _____ and
   they caught the thief at the airport.

g He's betting £10,000 on that horse. He _____
   a very big _____. He could lose the lot!

h Two thousand people _____ in a demonstration
   against experiments on animals yesterday.

i My boss has been _____ a lot of _____ me
   to finish the report by the end of the week.

j I tried to get the teacher's attention but she
   _____ of me at all. She just ignored me.

k Children just think that their mum and dad will always
   be there for them. They never say 'Thank you' or
   'How are you?' They just _____ their
   parents _____ .

l He never thinks about his home and family. He
   always _____.

m I was delighted to be _____ of the under-fives,
   because I love working with little children.

Phrasal verbs with *take* and *put*

1 As you know, there are lots of verbs
+ adverb or preposition in English!
They are called phrasal verbs, or
multi-word verbs.
Sometimes the same phrasal verb can
have several different meanings. What
are the different meanings of *take off*
in the following sentences?

*He **took off** his coat.*
*He **took** a day **off** work.*
*The football player was **taken off** at
half-time.*
*The plane **took off**.*
*The business **took off**.*

What are the different meanings of *put
down* in these sentences?

*The book was so good I couldn't **put**
it **down**.*
*Come to a party next Saturday. **Put** it
down in your diary.*
*She's always telling me I'm rubbish. I
hate the way she **puts** me **down**.*

2 Match a verb in **A** with a particle in **B** and a line in **C**. Look at
column **C** first and work backwards.

A	B	C
		your make-up in the morning/at night
	on	your father in looks
	someone down	a company by buying most of its shares
take	after	a meeting until next week
	away	by saying something cruel or unkind
	off	a CD so we can listen to some music
	out	to a shop because it's faulty
	up with	weight
	somebody out	for a couple of nights
put	something back	a fire/a cigarette
	over	to the cinema/for a meal
	somebody up	your clean clothes in the cupboard
		noisy neighbours without complaining

● LISTENING AND WRITING

Memories

Pre-listening task

Work in groups.

What are some of your earliest
memories? How old were you? Tell the
others about them. Try to bring in
some photos of when you were young.

Listening and note-taking

World traveller and lavender farmer

You are going to listen to a lady called Natalie Hodgson talking about her life. Look at the pictures from her family album. How old do you think she is in each picture? Which is the most recent picture?

Part One *Childhood*

T 2.3 Listen to the first part of the interview. <u>Underline</u> the correct answer or answers.

1 Natalie was born …
… just after the First World War/just before the First World War/just before the Second World War.

2 Her earliest memory is …
… her first birthday party/her third birthday party/ a cake with no candles on it.

3 When she was a child, she wanted to …
… become a glider pilot/fly the Atlantic/become a farmer/become a Member of Parliament.

4 In her life, she has been …
… a politician/a librarian/a glider pilot/a lavender farmer/an opera singer.

5 During her life, she has lived in …
… Paris/Berlin/Dresden/Lisbon/Wolverhampton/ Westminster/Shropshire.

6 She went abroad to …
… train to be an opera singer/learn foreign languages/ study Wagner's operas.

Part Two *The war years*

> Natalie had just got married and was living in London when the Second World War began. She had her first child whilst her husband was away in the war, and he didn't meet their son until he was four.

Read the questions. Listen to the second part of the interview, and take notes to answer the questions.

1 Where was Natalie immediately before the war? What memories does she have of that time?

2 What work did she do during and after the war? What was difficult about her job?

Part Three *The best is yet to come*

> After the war, Natalie and her husband moved to Shropshire. They had two more children. Her husband died in 1989, and it was then that she decided to become a lavender farmer.

Listen to the final part of the interview and take notes under the following headings:

– Home and family
– Travel and places visited
– Work
– Pastimes and hobbies
– The future

Compare your notes with the others in your group.

Language work

Here is a summary of Natalie's life. Put one word only into each gap.

Natalie Hodgson
World traveller and lavender farmer

Natalie Hodgson is now in her (a)_____. She was born in Coventry (b)_____ before the First World War. In 1934, when she was (c)_____ quite young, she went to live in Paris and Dresden, (d)_____ she was supposed to (e)_____ studying French and German, but she (f)_____ most of the time going to operas.

~

She (g)_____ married immediately before the Second World War, and she (h)_____ a son, (i)_____ didn't see his father (j)_____ he was four years old.

~

(k)_____ the war, she had a job broadcasting misinformation to the enemy, and after that she worked in naval intelligence and so she (l)_____ to take an oath of secrecy.

~

In 1953, she and her family (m)_____ to a large house in Shropshire, where she brought (n)_____ her three children. She (o)_____ start her lavender farm until after her husband died in 1989. She's now (p)_____ farming lavender for about ten years, and has created a highly (q)_____ business. She also (r)_____ bees.

~

Natalie has travelled a great (s)_____ in the course of her life. She still (t)_____ gliding and waterskiing, but probably the most remarkable thing about this lady is her belief that 'the best is yet to come'.

~

Writing

A biography

1 Word order. Put the adverbs or adverbial phrases in the correct place in the sentences.

a She goes waterskiing.
in summer, frequently
b She likes her garden in summer.
especially, very much
c She works with her bees.
hard, in the gardens, every day
d She goes gliding.
nowadays, occasionally, only
e She used to go to the opera.
in 1934, often, when she was in Dresden
f She enjoyed visiting the Grand Canyon.
ten years ago, thoroughly
g Her husband died.
suddenly, unfortunately, in 1989
h She enjoys looking after her grandchildren.
really, during their school holidays
i She has travelled.
abroad, throughout her life, to many countries
j She is fit enough to keep travelling. *still, fortunately*

2 Write a biography of an old person that you know who is still alive. A grandparent? A former teacher? A friend?
Start by making a few notes on each of the following aspects of the person's life:

– his/her childhood and education
– his/her achievements in life, both personal and professional
– his/her opinion of the world today
– his/her attitude to the past and the future

Expand your notes into four paragraphs.

● Exclamations

1 **T 2.4** You will hear several people talking about a variety of topics such as food, people, holidays. Reply to them, using an exclamation from **A** and a sentence from **B**. Draw a line.

A	**B**
a Mmm!	How disgusting!
b Wow!	I've dropped it!
c Hey, Peter!	That's crazy! What a stupid thing to say!
d Yuk!	Of course I'm listening to you.
e Whoops!	It's absolutely delicious!
f Ah!	Triplets! How amazing!
g Ouch!	What a shame!
h Uh?	I've just cut my finger.
i Uh-huh.	Come over here and sit with us.

2 What is the next line in the dialogue? Put a letter a–i next to the correct line.

- [ ] Don't worry. I'll get you a new one.
- [ ] That'll keep them busy!
- [ ] You must be so disappointed!
- [ ] Just the way I like it.
- [ ] You're talking about Keith whatsisname and some meeting or other.
- [ ] Did you eat any of it?
- [ ] I don't think it's very deep, but I'd better put a plaster on it.
- [ ] We'd really like you to join us.
- [ ] You know it's not true.

T 2.5 Listen and check your answers. Practise the dialogues, paying special attention to intonation. You could act some of them out and make them longer!

3 Put *What ...*, *What a ...*, or *How...* to complete the exclamations.

a _____ silly mistake!

b _____ brilliant idea!

c _____ ghastly weather!

d _____ utterly ridiculous!

e _____ terrific!

f _____ rubbish!

g _____ mess!

h _____ dreadful!

i _____ absolutely fabulous!

j _____ appalling behaviour!

k _____ hell of a journey!

l _____ terrible thing to happen!

Which are positive reactions? Which are negative?

4 Your teacher will read out some situations. Respond to them, using one of the exclamations.

5 In pairs, write a dialogue. Use some of the exclamations on this page. You could ask about ... a party, a meal, a film, a holiday, a sports event. Begin with the question.

> What was the ... like?

> Well, it was ...

Act out your dialogues to the class.

3

What happened was this ...

Narrative tenses
Expressing interest and surprise

1 Look at the picture, and read the situation.

> A man was travelling on a plane.
> He stood up, and fell over.

2 Read the questions. What tenses are used?

- Where was the plane flying to?
- Did the man have food poisoning?
- What had he eaten?
- Had he been drinking?

3 What else would you like to know? Write more questions.

LANGUAGE IN CONTEXT

Narrative tenses

1 **T 3.1** Listen to Mandy's story of what actually happened to the man on the plane. Answer the questions.

- What is Mandy's job?
- Why did the flight attendants think the man had fallen over?
- Why in fact had he fallen over?

2 Put the events of the story into their chronological order. Number them 1–9.

Mandy's story

5	The man stood up and fell over.
	The flight attendants helped him back into his seat.
	The man fell asleep.
	The man woke up.
	A bottle started leaking onto the man's head.
	They smelled alcohol on him.
	The man took off his wooden leg.
	The man explained what had happened.
	The flight attendants ran to help him.

3 Here are some weak forms. Can you remember the sentences? Practise them.

> it was in the night-time and ...
> they were trying to ...
> he managed to tell them what ...
>
> He'd been fast asleep, and ...
> he'd forgotten that ...
> I've no idea why ...

● Grammar question

- What are the three past tenses used in the story? Why are they used?

PRACTICE BANK

1 Discussing grammar

1 What is the correct verb form in these sentences? Put a ✓ or a ✗.

a The man fell over because he | wasn't wearing / didn't wear | his wooden leg.

b When he fell over, the flight attendants | were running / ran | to help him.

c I | read / was reading | Tolstoy's *War and Peace* on the flight.

d Mandy wasn't worried because she | saw / had seen | accidents like this before.

e The plane | had been flying / had flown | for a couple of hours when the incident | happened. / had happened.

f They thought he | had drunk. / had been drinking.

g As he was leaving, the man thanked Mandy for what she | was doing / had done | to help him.

2 Rewrite these stories, beginning with the last action.

Example
Peter got up at dawn. He was driving for ten hours. He got home. He was tired.
When Peter got home, he was tired because he had got up at dawn and had been driving for ten hours.

a Sally won £2,000 in a competition. She received a letter saying this. Last night she was celebrating.
b My flat was burgled. Someone stole my TV. I found this when I got home from work.
c Mick wasn't always poor. He had a successful business. Unfortunately, it went bust. Mick was a homeless beggar. (*Mick … but … business which …*)
d Jane and Peter were shopping all day. They spent all their money on clothes. They arrived home. They were broke.
e John's parents died. He had no relatives left in the UK. He decided to emigrate to Australia.

2 Gilly's story

1 Look at the picture of a girl called Gilly Woodward and read the caption.

ON FRIDAY… Gilly went shopping in Harrods.
ON SATURDAY… she wasn't allowed into the store.

2 Why do you think she wasn't allowed into Harrods on Saturday?

Example
Perhaps she'd stolen something on the Friday.

Compare your ideas with the rest of the class.

3 Read the full story and put the verb in brackets into the correct tense, active or passive.

GIRL BARRED FROM TOP STORE

As fashion-conscious Gilly Woodward left Harrods last Friday, she felt proud of the £90 designer jeans that she (a)_____ just _____ (buy). But when Gilly, 31, (b)_____ (return) to the store the next day to do some more shopping, she (c)_____ (bar) from entry because she (d)_____ (wear) the same jeans.

Gilly, now back home in Liverpool, (e)_____ (stay) with friends in London for a few days. She explained what (f)_____ (happen).

'I (g)_____ (walk) through the swing doors, when suddenly I (h)_____ (stop) by a large, uniformed security guard. He (i)_____ (point) at my knees, and said that my jeans (j)_____ (tear) and I couldn't enter. I tried to tell him that I (k)_____ (buy) them in Harrods the day before, and that the torn bits were fashionable. But he (l)_____ (not listen). He told me to get out. By this time, a crowd of people (m)_____ (gather). I (n)_____ (leave) immediately because I (o)_____ never _____ (feel) so embarrassed in my life.'

A spokesperson from Harrods said that the dress code (p)_____ (introduce) in 1989, and it states: no beachwear, no backpacks, no torn denims.

NO BEACHWEAR
NO BACKPACKS
NO TORN DENIMS

3 Listening to the news

1 **T3.2** You will hear the radio news. Listen to the first story. Tick (✓) the phrases you hear. Put a cross (✗) next to the phrases you *don't* hear. Correct them.

a have been found
b who were all from Glasgow
c have been climbing
d they are forced
e They were found
f They were recovering in hospital
g they said
h have warned walkers

2 **T3.3** Listen to the second news item. Here are the answers to some questions. Write the questions.

a The novelist, Saskia Lane.
b Last Sunday evening.
c Her ex-husband.
d In the bedroom of her apartment.
e She probably committed suicide.
f Since the break-up of her last marriage.
g Two years ago. It's called *Ex-wives of Manhattan*.
h She'd been married five times.
i Two. The daughter, and a son from a previous marriage.

3 **T3.4** Listen to the third news story. You will hear it first at normal speed, then at dictation speed. Write it down. <u>Underline</u> all the examples of the passive.

LANGUAGE REVIEW

Narrative tenses

Past Simple and Past Continuous

1 The Past Simple tells a story in chronological order.
   *I **woke** up this morning, **had** a shower, and **went** to work.*

2 The Past Continuous gives activities duration, and we see the activity in progress. It refers to longer, 'background' events.
   *When I woke up, the sun **was shining** and the birds **were singing**.*
   *While I **was having** a shower, the doorbell rang.*

Past Perfect and Past Perfect Continuous

1 The Past Perfect is used to make clear that one action in the past was completed *before* another past action.
   *When we arrived at the party, Andy **had** already **left**.*
   Compare *When we arrived at the party, Andy **left**.*

2 The Past Perfect Continuous expresses longer activities that happened over a period of time. All verbs in continuous tenses express duration.
   *They **had been walking** for nearly three hours when they saw the village in the distance.*

Passive

The uses are the same as in the active.
*His first book **was published** in 1872.*
*She thought she **was being followed**.*
*She was upset because her car **had been stolen**.*

📖 Grammar Reference: page 148.

● READING AND LISTENING

Pre-reading task

1 Look at the pictures and read the biographical information about a famous English writer.

HARDY, Thomas

Born 2 June 1840, near Dorchester, in Dorset, England
Died 11 January 1928, in Dorchester

Thomas Hardy was the son of a stonemason. After leaving the local school, he became an architect and went to work in London. However, he missed the Dorset countryside so much that he returned there in 1867 and began writing novels and poetry. In 1872, *Under the Greenwood Tree* was published. This was the first of many of his novels describing characters and scenes from country life. His first major success was the novel *Far from the Madding Crowd*, in 1874. After this, his stories became increasingly gloomy and tragic. His characters suffer terribly in a cruel and uncaring world. In *The Mayor of Casterbridge* (1886), the main character, Michael Henchard, is eventually destroyed because, as a young man, he had sold his wife and child to another man at a fair.

Other famous novels include *Tess of the D'Urbervilles* and *Jude the Obscure*. All his stories are about ordinary people caught up in situations over which they have no control. Many of them have been made into popular films.

2 Work in pairs. Use the prompts to ask and answer questions about Thomas Hardy.

- When/where/born/die?
- What/father/do?
- What/after school?
- Why/return/Dorset?
- When/begin/novels?
- What/*Under the Greenwood Tree* describe?
- When/first big success?
- … stories optimistic/pessimistic?
- Who/Michael Henchard? What/do?
- … *Mayor of Casterbridge* /happy ending?

Reading (1)

Look at the picture and read the caption. Then read the extract from Chapter 1 of *The Mayor of Casterbridge* below. Answer the questions.

Extract 1

The Man Who Sold His Wife

The conversation took a turn. The theme now was the ruin of good men by bad wives, and, more particularly, the frustration of many a promising young man's high hopes by an early marriage.

'I did it myself,' said the hay-maker with bitterness. 'I married at
5 eighteen, like the fool that I was; and this is the consequence o't.'
He pointed at himself and family. The young woman, his wife, who seemed accustomed to such remarks, acted as if she did not hear them.

The auctioneer selling the horses in the field outside could be heard saying, 'Now this is the last lot – now who'll take the last lot? Shall I say
10 two guineas? 'Tis a promising brood-mare, a trifle over five years old.'

The hay-maker continued. 'For my part, I don't see why men who have got wives and don't want 'em shouldn't get rid of 'em as these gipsy fellows do their horses. Why, I'd sell mine this minute if anyone would buy her!' The fuddled young husband stared around for a few
15 seconds, then said harshly, 'Well, then, now is your chance; I am open to an offer.'

Michael Henchard, an unemployed hay-maker, has arrived with his wife, Susan, and child at a village fair and horse auction. He has had too much to drink and is becoming increasingly loud and aggressive.

Glossary

l. 10 **guinea** (n)
(old English) one pound + one
shilling = £1.05 now

l. 10 **brood-mare** (n)
female horse kept for breeding

l. 10 **a trifle** (n)
a little

l. 14 **fuddled** (adj)
befuddled, confused by drink

Comprehension check

1 What is the topic of the conversation?

2 What does Michael regret about his past?

3 Is the wife surprised by Michael's behaviour?

4 What gives him the idea of selling his wife?

Listening and speaking

Work in small groups. You are going to hear a dramatized version of what happens next in the story.

1 Before you listen, talk about what you think will happen next. Choose three ideas from the list, and compare them with the rest of the class.

– Susan becomes hysterical.
– Susan walks out, taking the child with her.
– Michael passes out in a drunken stupor.
– The auctioneer agrees to auction Susan like the horses.
– A farmer offers to buy Susan for ten guineas.
– Lots of men want to buy Susan and a fight breaks out.
– A sailor buys Susan and the child for five guineas.
– Susan is sold to someone but has to leave the child with Michael.
– Susan believes that she and the child will be better off without Michael.

2 T 3.5 Listen and tick (✓) which of the sentences in Exercise 1 are correct.

3 What are the noises that you hear?

Reading (2)
Now read the full extract and answer the questions.

Extract 2

The Man Who Sold His Wife

She turned to her husband and murmured, 'Michael, you have talked this nonsense in public places before. A joke is a joke, but you may make it
5   once too often, mind!'

'I know I've said it before, and I meant it. All I want is a buyer. Here, I am waiting to know about this offer of mine. The woman is no good to me.
10 Who'll have her?'

The woman whispered; she was imploring and anxious. 'Come, come, it is getting dark, and this nonsense won't do. If you don't come along, I shall
15 go without you. Come!' She waited and waited; yet he did not move.

'I asked this question and nobody answered to't. Will anybody buy her?'

The woman's manner changed. 'I wish somebody would,'
20 said she firmly. 'Her present owner is not to her liking!'

'Nor you to mine,' said he. 'Now stand up, Susan, and show yourself. Who's the auctioneer?'

'I be,' promptly answered a short man. 'Who'll make an offer for this lady?'
25 'Five shillings,' said someone, at which there was a laugh.

'No insults,' said the husband. 'Who'll say a guinea?' Nobody answered. 'Set it *higher*, auctioneer.'

'Two guineas!' said the auctioneer; and no one replied.

'If they don't take her for that, in ten seconds they'll
30 have to give more,' said the husband. 'Very well. Now, auctioneer, add another.'

'Three guineas. Going for three guineas!'

'I'll tell ye what. I won't sell her for less than five,' said the husband, bringing down his fist. 'I'll sell her for five guineas
35 to any man that will pay me the money and treat her well; and he shall have her for ever. Now then, five guineas and she's yours. Susan, you agree?' She bowed her head with absolute indifference.

'Five guineas,' said the auctioneer. 'Do anybody give it? The
40 last time. Yes or no?'

'Yes,' said a loud voice from the doorway.

All eyes were turned. Standing in the triangular opening which formed the door of the tent, was a sailor, who,
45 unobserved by the rest, had arrived there within the last two or three minutes. A dead silence followed.

'You say you do?' asked the husband, staring at him.

'I say so,' replied the sailor.
50 'Saying is one thing, and paying is another. Where's the money?'

The sailor hesitated a moment, looked anew at the woman, came in, unfolded five crisp pieces of paper, and threw
55 them down upon the table-cloth. They were Bank of England notes for five pounds. Upon these, he chinked down the shillings severally – one, two, three, four, five. The sight of real money in full amount had a
60 great effect upon the spectators. Their eyes became riveted upon the faces of the chief actors, and then upon the notes as they lay, weighted by the shillings, on the table. The lines of laughter left their faces, and they waited with parted lips.

'Now,' said the woman, breaking the silence, 'before you go
65 further, Michael, listen to me. If you touch that money, I and this girl go with the man. Mind, it is a joke no longer.'

'A joke? Of course it is not a joke!' shouted her husband. 'I take the money, the sailor takes you.' He took the sailor's notes and deliberately folded them, and put them with the
70 shillings in a pocket with an air of finality.

The sailor looked at the woman and smiled. 'Come along!' he said kindly. 'The little one, too. The more the merrier!' She paused for an instant. Then, dropping her eyes again and saying nothing, she took up the child and followed
75 him as he made towards the door. On reaching it, she turned, and pulling off her wedding-ring, flung it in the hay-maker's face.

'Mike,' she said, 'I've lived with thee a couple of years, and had nothing but ill-temper! Now I'll try my luck
80 elsewhere. 'Twill be better for me and Elizabeth-Jane, both. So good-bye!'

Comprehension check

1 What did you learn from the reading that you didn't learn from the listening?

2 Underline the adjectives which you think best describe Michael Henchard.
Use your dictionary to help with new words.
Give reasons for your choice.

unhappily married	immature	irresponsible
polite	sober	kind-hearted
sensible	long-suffering	self-pitying
thoughtful	insensitive	reckless
pitiable	belligerent	
disloyal	unreliable	

Which of the adjectives do you think describe Michael's wife?
Which of the adjectives describe the sailor?

3 What do the following quotations from the text mean?

'Her present owner is not to her liking.' (l. 20)
'Saying is one thing, and paying is another.' (l. 51–2)
'Upon these, he chinked down the shillings severally …' (l. 58–9)
'Their eyes became riveted upon the faces of the chief actors.' (l. 61–2)
'Come along … The little one, too. The more the merrier!' (l. 72–3)
'I'll try my luck elsewhere.' (l. 80–81)

What do you think?

What do you think happens in the rest of the novel?
- Does Michael regret his actions when he wakes up sober?
- Does he ever see his wife and child again?
- Does the sailor take them far away?
- Will Susan have better luck with the sailor?
- Does the little girl have a good and happy future?
- Which characters are happy and successful in the end?

Your teacher will give you a synopsis of the story when you have discussed your ideas.

●VOCABULARY

Suffixes and prefixes

Work in pairs. Use a dictionary to help.

1 Suffixes are often used to form different parts of speech.

respond (v) → response (n) → responsible (adj) → responsibility (n)

Prefixes are often used to change the meaning.

(**co-** = together with): **co** + respond = **co**rrespond = to exchange letters with someone

(**ir-** = not): **ir** + responsible = **ir**responsible = not responsible

2 Make new words with the base words, using the suffixes and/or negative prefixes. Sometimes you need to make small changes to the spelling.

PREFIX	BASE WORD	SUFFIX
	conscious	
	help	-able/ible
in-	kind	
	literate	-ful
un-	loyal	
	mature	-(t)ive
im-	measure	
	polite	-less
il-	popular	
	relevant	-cy
ir-	rely	
	respect	-(i)ty
dis-	sense	
	success	-ment
mis-	thought	
	understand	-ness
	use	

3 Share ideas with the whole class. How many new words did you make altogether? From which base word did you make the most new words?

4 Complete the sentences with the correct form of the word in brackets.

a What I appreciate most about my grandfather is his wisdom. His advice is always _____ and _____. (SENSE) (HELP)

b Never go to Sue with a serious problem. She's very _____ and totally _____ to other people's feelings. (MATURE) (SENSE)

c I think that boxing is a _____ sport. What is the point of trying to hit another person until they are _____? (SENSE) (CONSCIOUS)

d What I like about Tom is his jokes. They make me _____ with laughter. (HELP)

e We'd been walking along the _____ railway track for hours before we realized that the map was out-of-date and _____. (USE) (USE)

f The only thing poverty leads to is _____ and _____. (HAPPY) (LITERATE)

g My aunt isn't fond of today's children. She thinks that they are all _____ and _____. (POLITE) (RESPECT)

h The pleasure that reading brings is _____. (MEASURE)

5 What meaning do the following prefixes add?

a **self**-conscious
b **anti**-abortion   **pro**-abortion
c **non**-fiction
d **pre**-war   **post**-war
e **re**use
f **ex**-president
g **over**cook   **under**cook
h **fore**see
i **ante**natal
j **sub**marine
k **co**-author
l **bi**lingual

Find another example for each of the prefixes. Share them with the whole class.

● SPEAKING AND LISTENING

Talking about books

1 Do you often read for pleasure? What kinds of books do you like reading? When do you usually read?

2 We usually want to know some things about a book before we start reading it.
Here are some answers. Write in the questions.
Example
Who wrote it?
Thomas Hardy/Jane Austen/Saskia Lane

a _____?
In 1886/At the end of the eighteenth century/Two years ago.

b _____?
It's a romantic novel/It's a thriller/It's a biography.

c _____?
It's about a tragic marriage/It's about politics and corruption.

d _____?
A countryman called Michael Henchard and his wife, Susan/A detective called Blunket and his assistant, Sergeant Moon.

e _____?
Yes, it has. It came out quite a few years ago and starred Alan Bates.

f _____?
It ends really tragically/It's frustrating because we don't really know/They all live happily ever after.

g _____?
I thought it was great/I couldn't put it down/I didn't want it to end/It was OK but I skipped the boring bits.

h _____?
Yes, I would. It's great if you like a good love story/It's a terrific holiday read.

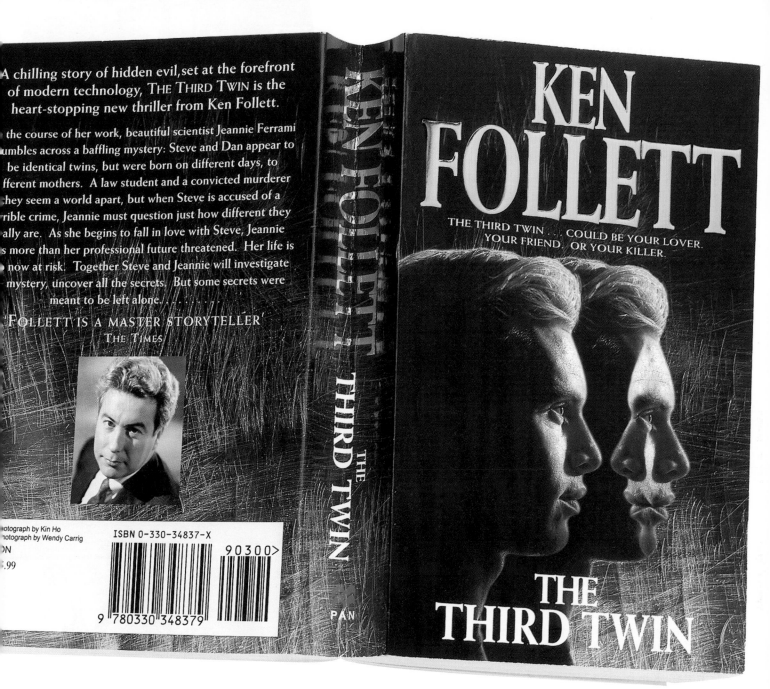

A chilling story of hidden evil, set at the forefront of modern technology, THE THIRD TWIN is the heart-stopping new thriller from Ken Follett.

the course of her work, beautiful scientist Jeannie Ferrami umbles across a baffling mystery: Steve and Dan appear to be identical twins, but were born on different days, to fferent mothers. A law student and a convicted murderer they seem a world apart, but when Steve is accused of a rible crime, Jeannie must question just how different they ally are. As she begins to fall in love with Steve, Jeannie s more than her professional future threatened. Her life is now at risk. Together Steve and Jeannie will investigate mystery, uncover all the secrets. But some secrets were meant to be left alone. . . . .

'FOLLETT IS A MASTER STORYTELLER'
THE TIMES

otograph by Kin Ho
notograph by Wendy Carrig
ON
.99

ISBN 0-330-34837-X

90300>

9 780330 348379

KEN FOLLETT

THE THIRD TWIN . . . COULD BE YOUR LOVER.
YOUR FRIEND. OR YOUR KILLER.

THE THIRD TWIN

Listening and note-taking

T 3.6 Listen to three people talking about a book they have read recently. Take notes about it under the following headings.

3 Work in pairs. Read the front and back covers of a book called *The Third Twin*.
Answer as many of the questions in Exercise 2 as you can. Which questions can't you answer?

Now ask and answer the questions with your partner about the last book you read.

	Joey	Ken	Kate
Title and author			
Type of book			
Setting			
Who and what it is about			
Personal opinion			

● WRITING AND SPEAKING

A review of a book or a film

1 When you talk or write about a book or film, which tense do you use to outline the plot and describe the characters?
Why do you think this tense is used?

2 Use the headings and prompts to help you write some notes about either a book you have read or a film you have seen which has made an impression on you. Discuss your notes with a partner.

- **Introduction to the author and book/film**
  Title?
  Type of book/film?
  When/published or made?
  Who does it star?
  Who/written or directed by?
  Is it popular/well-known?

- **Introduction to characters and outline of the plot**
  Where/When does the story take place?
  Who/main characters? What/like?
  What happens?

- **Your opinion of the book/film**
  Did you enjoy it very much? In parts? Not at all?
  Would you recommend it?

3 Write a review of your book or film. Write about 200 words in three paragraphs. Some of these expressions might help:

... was written/directed by ... in ... /... years ago
... is based on the life of a notorious bank robber/
    the author's experiences in ...
It is based on a book of the same name.
... tells the story of ... , and as the story unfolds, we
    see ...
It stars X in the title role of the Y.
It takes place in the city of Z in the 1960s.
It's set in rural England at the beginning of the
    19th century.
It is about A's relationship with her ex-husband.
In the end, B ...
What we don't learn until the end is that ...
There are several flashbacks to when he was a child ...
In my opinion, ... /I think that ... /
    I would recommend ...
What I liked best was (the way) ...
What I didn't like was ...

PostScript

Expressing interest and surprise

Work in pairs or small groups.

1 **T 3.7** Listen to the dialogue. How does the man show interest and surprise?

2 **T 3.8** Listen to a similar dialogue. What does B say? Write in her answers. Practise saying the dialogue with your partner. Pay particular attention to the stress and intonation.

A Meg's got a new boyfriend.

B _____?

A Yes. He lives in a castle.

B _____?

A Yes. She met him in Mauritius.

B _____?

These are called reply questions. They are not the same as question tags! In what ways are they different?

3 Complete the following dialogues with either an 'echo' or a reply question.

a A Sam wants to apologize.

B _____?

A Yes. He's broken your mother's Chinese vase.

B _____? Oh, no!

b A We had a terrible holiday.

B _____?

A Yes. It rained all the time.

B _____?

A Yes. And the food was disgusting!

B _____? What a drag!

c A Look! Bob's drunk.

B _____?

A Yes. He's had six glasses of whisky.

B _____?

A Yes. He doesn't like parties.

B _____? How strange!

A The poor chap can't walk straight.

B _____? How's he going to get home?

A I don't know. I never have too much to drink.

B _____?

A No. I can't stand hangovers.

d A It took me three hours to get here.

B _____?

A Yes. There was a traffic jam ten miles long.

B _____? That's awful!

A Now I've got a headache!

B _____? Poor darling. I'll get you something for it.

e A I've met the love of my life!

B _____?

A Yes. We're getting married next Saturday in Barbados.

B _____?

A Yes. We've booked a flight on Concorde.

B _____? You lucky thing!

f A I'm on a mobile phone.

B _____?

A Yes. And I've got something very important to tell you.

B _____? What is it? I can't wait!

A You'd better sit down … I'd like to marry you.

B _____? Blimey!

T 3.9 Listen and compare your answers. Practise them with a partner.

4 Your teacher will read out some sentences about himself/herself. Respond, using a reply question or an echo.

It's a deal!

Expressing quantity
Social expressions

1 Look at the contents of Jane's bag.

Make sentences with *She's got ..., There is/are ...*

Use: *a few, a couple of, lots of, several, a little, very little, not ... many, not ... much, not ... any, no, hardly any*
Don't use *some*!

2 What's in *your* bag?

LANGUAGE IN CONTEXT

Expressing quantity

1 Work in two groups.
You will read a newspaper article about the same person. The information is similar, but not the same.
Group A Read this article.
Group B Read the article your teacher gives you.
Then answer the questions.

Woman who penniless is £20m

¹ **Cherry Haines, 39**, who once worked as a market stallholder, made all of her fortune from marketing a new kind of make-up. She left England because there wasn't much employment, caught a flight to the other
⁵ side of the world, and arrived with no qualifications and very few friends.

'The flight took every penny I had. At first, I stayed with a friend. Then I had a bit of luck.' The friend gave her the name of Peter Maddox, an Australian
¹⁰ businessman. 'I rang him and told him I was the best

left England now worth

A British woman, who went to Australia with very little money four years ago, has sold her business for £20 million.

salesperson in England and that he should give me a job.'

He liked her idea for a kind of make-up that stays on the whole day, so together they formed a company to market it. At first, she wasn't earning much, but soon
15 she was getting over A$200,000 a year. 'Hard work means happiness to me,' she said.

Her brother, Roger Haines, who is spending three weeks with her in Brisbane, said, 'She left school when she was 16. She had hardly any work experience. But she
20 could sell a fridge to an Eskimo. She's amazing!'

a How much money did she have when she left England?
b When did she leave England?
c How much has she sold her business for?
d Why did she leave England?
e Did she have any qualifications?
f Did she have many friends?
g How much did she pay for her flight?
h How much did she earn at first?
i How much did she earn later?
j How long is her brother staying with her?
k What did he say about her work experience?

2 Find a partner from the other group.
Compare your answers. Notice how quantity is expressed in different ways.

very little money   just £5

3 The teacher will draw two columns on the board like the table below. Go to the board and write in the expressions from the newspaper articles.

Expressions of quantity	Actual quantity
very little money a few years all of her fortune …	just £5 four years

Which expressions of quantity mean the same?
How are they used differently?

● Grammar questions

– Why do we say … ?

*very **little** money* but *a **few** years*
*not **much** employment* but *weren't **many** jobs*

– Is this rule correct?

We mainly use *much* and *many* in questions and negative sentences.

– Who is happier, A or B?

A *I have **few** friends.*
B *I have **a few** friends.*

– *She had **hardly any** work experience.*

Does this mean she had …

| no
little
a little
a lot of | work experience? |

4 Close your books. Retell the story.

PRACTICE BANK

1 Countable or uncountable?

1 In pairs, ask and answer questions about each other beginning
How much ... ? or *How many ... ?*
Ask about:

money	pairs of jeans	coffee
times/flown on a plane		homework/a night
time/spend watching TV		sugar/in coffee

2 Are the nouns in the box below usually countable or uncountable? Write **C** or **U**. Some can be both. Think of a sentence to illustrate the difference.

Example
job C   *unemployment* U

business
C – *They opened a* **business** *together*. (= a company)
U – *We don't do much* **business** *in Russia*.
      (= the activity of making and selling)

a	money/dollar	g	coffee
b	beggar/poverty	h	time
c	traffic/lorry/van	i	gold
d	travel/journey	j	experience
e	job/work	k	apple/fruit
f	glass	l	qualification

2 Expressing quantity

1 Rephrase the sentences. Use the prompts to help you.

Example
She earns £2 an hour. *much/a lot/very little*

She doesn't earn much money.
She doesn't earn a lot of money.
She earns very little money.

a She's got two friends. *many/a lot/hardly any*
b There are six eggs in the fridge. *some/a few/enough*
c There are two eggs in the fridge. *many/enough*
d There aren't any eggs. *no/not a single/none*
e Did you spend many weeks in France? *much/a lot*
f I have four days' holiday a year. *much/hardly any*
g I've put on twenty kilos! *a huge amount/far too much*
h Ninety per cent of my friends have a car.
   nearly all/most/the majority
i Ten per cent of them smoke. *very few/hardly any*
j There isn't one of my friends who takes drugs.
   none/not one
k Ken works one hundred per cent of the time!
   all/the whole
l Yesterday I ate hardly anything at all.
   much/very little/a lot

2 Choose the correct alternative. Only one of them is right.

a I have | few / a few | cousins, but not many.

b We have | very little / a little | money, I'm afraid.

c I earn | less / fewer | money than a cleaner!

d Less / Fewer | people go to church these days.

e All people / Everyone | came to my party.

f I was burgled. | All / Everything | was stolen.

g All / Everything | I want is a cup of tea.

h He'd never had a holiday in | his all life. / his whole life.

i Everyone / All the people | was watching the Cup Final.

j A pen. Quick! | Any / Some | colour will do.

3 A class survey

You are going to conduct a survey of the shopping habits of your class. Your teacher will give you some ideas for questions. When you have done the survey, give some feedback.

All of us like shopping.

Hardly anybody buys designer clothes.

A few people spend at least £60 on trainers.

None of us can afford to shop in Harrods.

Quite a few students go shopping in the sales.

Nearly everybody looks for bargains.

LANGUAGE REVIEW

Expressing quantity

1 Look at the chart.

How much … ?	How many … ?
all	all/every
most	most
much	many
a great deal/amount of	a large number of
a lot/lots of	a lot/lots of
some	some/several
a little	a few
less	fewer
little	few
no/none	
not … any	

2 Some quantifiers can be used with a noun, without a noun, or with a noun phrase.

Some people don't like dogs.
*'Do you need any money?' 'It's all right. I've got **some**.'*
*I took **some of your money**. I hope that's OK.*

3 Different quantifiers are used in different ways.

All (of) the people *in the room stood up.*
*Have you got **everything**?* (NOT ~~Have you got all?~~)
***None of my friends** was/were at the party.*

4 *Few* and *little* are negative. *A few* and *a little* are positive.

*I have very **little** money. It's a shame.*
*Fortunately I have **a few** very good friends.*

📖 **Grammar Reference: page 149.**

● READING AND NOTE-TAKING
Three thousand years of world trade

Pre-reading task

Work in small groups.

1 Look at the pictures. Where are these places? What's happening?

2 All of the items in the box have been imported and exported over the centuries. Use a dictionary to check any new words.

flint tools	metalware	copper
gold	silver	tin	slaves
fodder	glassware	textiles
grain	figs	olive oil	wine
honey	corn	spices	pottery
drugs	silk	leatherwork
armour	tomatoes	potatoes
cocoa	beans	sugar	tobacco
coffee	soft drinks	cars
clothes	tea

3 Discuss the questions, referring to the imports and exports in the box.

– Which items are no longer traded in the modern world?
– Which items are luxuries and which are necessities?
– Which are raw materials and which are manufactured goods?

Read the article about the history of world trade. Then answer the questions.

Three thousand years of world trade

In the beginning

For thousands and thousands of years, people produced most of what they needed for themselves. They grew or
5 **hunted for their own food, and made their own simple tools. But little by little they learned that they could have more varied goods by trading.**

Little is known about the beginnings
10 **of trade. Perhaps it was English flint, used to make primitive tools, and much traded in Europe thousands of years before Christ. Or was it the Egyptians, as early as 3000 BC,**
15 **travelling down the African coast as far as the Zambezi River in search of gold, silver, and slaves?**

The Ancient World – BC

The earliest trade we *do* know
20 something about is the caravan trade across the deserts of Asia around 2500 BC, to and from cities in **Mesopotamia**, **Egypt**, and **Arabia**. These caravans had to carry fodder for the animals and food
25 for the drivers and merchants. Not much space was left for the cargo. As a result, the goods carried were light but valuable, things such as gold and precious stones – that is, luxuries and
30 not necessities.

After this, trade by sea started to become more common. The **Phoenicians** on the coast of Syria are thought to have been the first to develop commerce by sea
35 around 1000 BC, trading from ports in Syria to Crete, Cyprus, Rhodes, and other Greek islands, and also to North Africa. The Phoenicians were manufacturers. They exported metal-
40 ware, glassware, and textiles. These were traded for raw materials, especially tin, copper, and silver. This trade also was mainly in luxuries for the ships were small.

45 The Phoenicians lived at the same time as the **Greeks** and the **Romans**. Athens was the first big commercial city in Europe, and it was the first community to import and export necessities (not
50 just luxuries) in large quantities. Grain was imported for the increasing population from the shores of the Black Sea, and exports included figs, olive oil, wine, honey, pottery, metalware,
55 and textiles. Greek armies marched into Persia, Central Asia, and India, and brought back luxury goods such as spices, drugs, and silk.

The Ancient World – AD

60 The **Roman Empire** (27 BC–476 AD) was the next big trading community. The city of Rome itself produced little, but it imported a lot. It was the political capital and financial centre of 65 the Empire.

Increasing quantities of luxuries were imported from the east and from North Africa, but these were not *bought* by the Romans. They were the tax paid to 70 Rome by the various peoples that it had conquered. Imports included tin, slaves, cloth, and jewels. The Romans also traded with China, and brought back silkworms to start a silk industry 75 in Europe.

In the fifth century AD, **Byzantium** (later called **Constantinople**, and now **Istanbul**) became the political capital of the Roman Empire, and remained the 80 world's commercial capital until the 12th century. Its importance was founded on manufacturing – textiles, leatherwork, armour, pottery, and artistic metal work. The Byzantine coin, known as the 85 *bezant*, became the first single currency of European business.

The Middle Ages

In the 12th and 13th centuries, **Venice** and **Genoa** became the world's leading 90 trade centres. In 1271, the Venetian, Marco Polo, went by land and sea to China and helped establish trading links. Venice was well placed to be the main European commercial centre. It 95 had, of course, the sea, and it was by sea that luxuries such as spices and silks arrived from the East. These were then re-exported in fleets of ships to ports in Spain, England, and Flanders. 100 During the late Middle Ages, **Bruges** became the leading trade centre in northern Europe. Other goods went overland, across the Alps to French and German cities.

105 The Modern World

The modern world began as the 'Age of Discoveries'. The great voyages of Spanish and Portuguese explorers, such as Christopher Columbus (1492), 110 Vasco da Gama (1498), and Ferdinand Magellan (1519), opened up new trade routes to the Americas, Africa, and India. This was the beginning of ocean travel.

Britain and other countries of northern 115 Europe formed big companies, and each was given a certain part of the world to explore and exploit. The new companies penetrated into distant lands, and brought back their products, 120 many of which were new and unknown: tomatoes, potatoes, cocoa, green beans, and corn. By the 17th century, the Dutch dominated the world's trade, with the French and the English as their close 125 rivals. All three nations opened up the tropical lands of the East and West Indies, and imported sugar, tobacco, tea, and coffee into Europe.

During the 19th century, the industrial 130 revolution led to greater production, and the pattern of world trade started to become what it is today.

Today

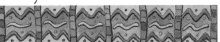

Today, mass advertising persuades 135 people of many different nationalities to use the same products. Millions of people around the world drink the same soft drinks, drive the same cars, wear the same clothes, and eat the 140 same hamburgers.

In previous centuries, trade was more local, and people's tastes varied from one country to another. Imports used to bring diversity. It is ironic that 145 today's vast international markets have resulted in a world with more homogeneous tastes.

Comprehension check

1 Why did people first start trading?
2 How much do we know about the early traders?
3 Why were luxuries, not necessities, the earliest goods to be traded?
4 What were the Phoenicians the first to do?
   What did they import?
5 Athens had two 'firsts'. What were they?
   Why was grain imported by the Greeks?
6 Did Rome manufacture a lot? Why didn't the Romans pay for their imported goods?
7 Why was the *bezant* important?
8 What did the big companies of northern Europe do?
9 Name the key trade centres in the following periods:

   > 1000 BC
   > 8th century AD
   > 13th century AD
   > 17th century AD

   Why did they become important?
10 What did imports use to bring to people's lives?
   What is ironic about the international markets today?

Discussion

1 Do you agree that people's tastes today are more homogeneous? Why?
   Which products do you know of that are found in most parts of the world today?

2 What does your country export and import? What are the reasons for this?

Note-taking and report writing

1 Read the text again. Make notes under these headings.

	Dates	Places	People	Goods
In the beginning				
The Ancient World – BC				
The Ancient World – AD				
The Middle Ages				
The Modern World				

2 Discuss your notes with a partner. Find the places on the map.

3 Use your own knowledge and an encyclopaedia to write notes about trade in your own country, past and present. Talk together in small groups about the results of your research.

4 Write a brief report from your notes.

● VOCABULARY AND PRONUNCIATION

1 export: /ˈekspɔːt/ or /ɪkˈspɔːt/?

1 Look at these words. Where is the stress when the word is used as a noun? And when it's a verb?

a export   d increase   g refund   j transport
b import   e progress   h produce   k insult
c decrease   f record   i permit   l protest

2 Ask another student to practise the words. Give instructions like this.

(c as a noun!) ('decrease)   (g as a verb!) (re'fund)

3 Fill the gaps with one of the words in its correct form.

a Scotland _____ a lot of its food from other countries.
   Its _____ include oil, beef, and whisky.

b I'm very pleased with my English. I'm making a lot of _____ .

c Ministers are worried. There has been an _____ in the number of unemployed.

d But the number of crimes has _____, so that's good news.

e How dare you call me a liar and a cheat! What an _____!

f There was a démonstration yesterday. People were _____ about blood sports.

g People usually buy CDs these days. Not many people buy _____ any more.

h Don't touch the video! I'm _____ a film.

i Britain _____ about 75% of its own oil.

   T 4.1 Listen and check your answers.

2 refuse: /ˈrefjuːs/ or /rɪˈfjuːz/?

1 These words have different meanings according to the stress. Check the meaning and the pronunciation in your dictionary.

a refuse   d desert   g invalid
b present   e content   h contract
c minute   f object

2 Ask another student to practise the words.

(g as a noun!)   ('invalid)

3 Answer the questions using the words.

a What does a dustman do?
b What's a UFO?
c What's the Sahara?
d What do you get lots of on your birthday?
e What are pages 2 to 5 of this book?
f Write another word for each of these:

> happy   a written agreement
> out-of-date (passport)   very small
> to complain or protest about something
> to say you won't do something

   T 4.2 Listen and check your answers.

3 row: /raʊ/ or /rəʊ/?

1 These words have different meanings according to the pronunciation. Check the meaning and the pronunciation in your dictionary.

   row   tear   used   live   lead
   wind   use

2 Practise saying the following sentences.

a This programme is coming to you /laɪv/ from Mongolia.
b Mind that nail! You'll /teə/ your shirt. Oh!
c Listen to that /wɪnd/ howling outside.
d The /juːs/ of mobile phones is strictly forbidden in this library.
e Listen to the neighbours! They're having a terrible /raʊ/.
f Where do these stairs /liːd/?
g I hate mornings! I'm not /juːst/ to getting up so early.

   T 4.3 Listen and check your answers.

3 In pairs, write a sentence to illustrate the other meaning of the words.

● SPEAKING

A business maze

Work in small groups.

You have reached one of life's crossroads! You've been made redundant, and some big decisions about your future have to be made.

Read the problem on the card and talk together until you all agree on what to do next.
Your teacher will give you your next card with more information and more decisions.
Carry on talking until you get out of the maze.
You might succeed, or you might fail!

> **1** You were working as a chef in a large restaurant. You have been made redundant as the restaurant is being converted into a cinema. You have received £10,000 redundancy money. You have a family to support, and cannot survive for long without an income. You want to start a restaurant in your local town as you believe there is a need for one. It is going to require more than your £10,000, so what are you going to do?
>
> > Approach the bank for the extra funding to get your plans underway. **go to 8**
>
> > Go into business with a partner. A friend of yours was also made redundant and received the same amount of money. Why not do it together? **go to 22**

Post-maze activity

1 Appoint a spokesperson from each group.
Tell the rest of the class about the decisions that your group took.
In retrospect, did you make any wrong decisions?

2 Activities such as these are used for management training exercises. Why, do you think?

● LISTENING

'An English restaurant in France? You must be joking!'

T 4.4 You will hear an interview with Tom and Sue Higgins, an English couple who opened an English restaurant in Lyon, France, over ten years ago.

1 Listen to the interviewer's introduction. Answer the questions.

a Why might it not be wise to open an English restaurant in Lyon?
b What do the French think of English food?
c What is the name of Tom and Sue's restaurant?
d What are the interviewer's two questions?

2 What other questions about Tom and Sue and their restaurant would you like answered in the interview? Add to the list below.

Why did they decide to do it in Lyon?
Where did they get the money from?
Are they doing well?

Write your questions on the board.

3 Listen to the rest of the interview. Answer your questions. Discuss your answers first in pairs, and then with the whole class.

Discussion

What sort of businesses might succeed in *your* town?
Do any of you want to start a business?

PostScript

Social expressions

1 Match a line in **A** with a line in **B**.

a ☐   b ☐   c ☐   d ☐   e ☐   f ☐   g ☐   h ☐

A	B
a Could I use your phone for a moment?	1 **Let me see.** Yes, I can make the morning.
b What film would you like to see tonight?	2 Has it? **Let me have a look.** I'll try and fix it.
c Everyone says you're mad. Did you know that?	3 **Hang on a sec.** Where are you going?
d I'll give you £6,000 for your car. That's my final offer.	4 **I don't care** what other people think. That's their problem, not mine.
e When he told me he'd smashed my car, I was furious!	5 **I don't mind.** Whatever you want.
f Oh, no! The photocopier's jammed again!	6 **By all means.** Help yourself.
g Can we meet next Thursday?	7 **I bet** you were. I'd have hit him.
h Bye! I'm off now!	8 **It's a deal!** It's yours!

T 4.5   Listen and check your answers.
Make sure you understand the expressions in bold.

2 Do the same again.

a ☐   b ☐   c ☐   d ☐   e ☐   f ☐   g ☐   h ☐

A	B
a I'm really sorry, but I can't go out to the cinema with you this week.	1 **How come?** Can't you afford it?
b I walked out of my job. I just couldn't take it any more.	2 Hey! **I was kidding.** It was just a joke.
c What if I forget everything in the exam? What if my pen runs out?	3 **I can't be bothered.** I've left five messages for him, and he's never replied.
d Have you applied for that job?	4 **For goodness' sake** stop worrying! You'll be fine. Just don't panic!
e Are you going to phone Andy again?	5 **Never mind.** Let's try again next week.
f I don't know what to do. Do I tell her the truth, or do I say nothing?	6 **I see what you mean.** You're in a very difficult position.
g We aren't having a holiday this year.	7 No, **there's no point.** I'm not qualified for it. **I wouldn't stand a chance.**
h Why did you tell everyone that I'm in love with Mike? It's not true!	8 **I don't blame you.** I'd have done the same thing myself.

T 4.6   Listen and check your answers.

3 Work in pairs. Think of other ideas that will prompt some of the expressions in **B**.

4 Read some of your prompts to another pair. They must respond.

Whatever will be, will be

Future forms
Telephone conversations

1 Match a line of dialogue to a cartoon.

a I'll see you tomorrow. Bye!
b The train to Dover leaves at ten past ten.
c We're having a party next Saturday. Can you come?
d Tomorrow's weather will be warm and sunny.
e Where shall we go on holiday this year?
f I'm going to lead an honest life from now on.
g In a hundred years' time, we'll all be driving solar-powered cars.
h The builders say they'll have finished by the end of the month.

2 <u>Underline</u> the future forms.

LANGUAGE IN CONTEXT

Future forms

1 **T 5.1** Look at the pictures and listen to some people talking about the future. Try to guess who says what. Put a number 1–8 next to the names.

2 Work in pairs. Answer the questions.

a Where's Ellen going next July? Why?
b Who'll be visiting Joan? What will they do?
c What does Alex say about school? What's he going to do when he grows up?
d Why are Tony and Marie excited?
e Where's Penny going tomorrow? How's she getting to school? What time does the train leave?
f What does Amy hope she'll be doing in the next few years?
g What is Simon going to do if he gets good results in his A-levels? And if not?
h What's Mike doing tomorrow?

3 Here are the answers to some of the questions in the interviews. Write the questions.

a A ginger cake.
b In her own flat.
c Newcastle University. (*Which … ?*)
d For a year or two.
e With his son and some friends.
f Arsenal and Manchester United. (*Who … ?*)
g In four weeks' time. (*… due?*)
h 9.30.

● **Grammar questions**

– Do these sentences from the interviews refer to the present or the future?

I'm waiting for my exam results.
We're all moving to Hawaii.

The train leaves at 9.30.
We move every couple of years.

– What's the difference between these sentences?

What do you do in the evenings?
What are you doing this evening?

Give me your bags. I'll help you to carry them.
Sorry I can't come out tonight. I'm going to help Jack fix his car.

We'll have supper at 8.00.
We'll be having supper at 8.00.

I'll write the report tonight.
I'll have written the report by tonight.

PRACTICE BANK

1 Choosing future forms

Use each expression once to fill the gaps in the pairs of sentences.

a *get/'ll get*
'I've got a headache.'   'Stay there. I _____ you an aspirin.'

I'm a newspaper junkie. I _____ five newspapers a day.

b *'ll see/'m going to see*
I can't do my homework tonight. I _____ a movie.

'What are you going to give me for my birthday?' 'I don't know yet. I _____.'

c *are you going to do/will you do*
So you're going to America for a year! What _____ when you get there?

I'm sure you'll pass your exams, but what _____ if you fail them?

d *'ll come/'m coming*
I _____ with you if you like.

I _____ with you whether you like it or not.

e *are you doing/are you going to do*
What _____ about that leaking tap? You said you'd fix it ages ago!

What _____ this weekend?

f *'s raining/'s going to rain*
It _____ tomorrow, so now's the time to cut the grass.

Oh, no! It _____! That means we can't play tennis.

g *'m getting/'m going to get*
I _____ a new car on Monday.

I _____ a new car some time. This one's so unreliable.

h *'ll crash/'s going to crash*
Look out! He _____!

Don't lend Peter your car. He's a lousy driver. He _____ it.

i *is starting/starts*
My TV programme _____ in thirty minutes.

My husband _____ a new job next week.

2 We'll be flying at 35,000 feet ...

> 1 The Future Continuous can express a future action that will take place in the normal course of events. The focus is *not* on a decision, or an arrangement or willingness.
>
> *When the President goes to China next month, he'**ll be taking** his family with him.*
>
> 2 The Present Simple is often used with a future meaning in subordinate clauses.
>
> *I'll phone you when I **get** home from work.*
>
> 3 The Present Perfect is used to express the idea of completion.
>
> *As soon as I'**ve read** the book, I'll give it back to you.*

Put the verb in brackets in the correct tense: the Present Simple, the Present Perfect, the Future Simple, or the Future Continuous. Sometimes more than one tense is possible.
In the text, there are several examples of the Future Continuous, because the captain wants to reassure the passengers. Everything that will happen during the flight is normal and under control!

This is your captain speaking...

On this afternoon's flight, we will be flying at 35,000 feet.

I think we'll fly at 25,000 feet today. No, I've changed my mind, we did that yesterday. What about 50,000 feet? Maybe that's a bit high. I know, we'll fly at 35,000 feet.

Good morning, ladies and gentlemen. Welcome on board this British Airways flight to Rome. In a very short time, just as soon as we (a)_____ (receive) permission, we (b)_____ (take off). When we (c)_____ (reach) our cruising speed of 550 miles an hour, we (d)_____ (fly) at 35,000 feet. Our flight time today is two and a half hours, so we (e)_____ (be) in Rome in time for lunch!

The cabin crew (f)_____ (serve) refreshments during the flight, so just sit back and relax. We hope you (g)_____ (enjoy) the flight. If you (h)_____ (need) any assistance, just press the button and a flight attendant (i)_____ (come) to help you.

(Later on during the flight)

If you (j)_____ (look) out of the right-hand side of the plane, you (k)_____ (see) Mont Blanc.

In a few moments' time, the crew (l)_____ (come) round with duty-free goods. We (m)_____ also _____ (give out) immigration forms. When you (n)_____ (fill) them in, please place them in your passport. They (o)_____ (collect) as you (p)_____ (go) through passport control.

In twenty minutes' time we (q)_____ (land). Please put your seats into the upright position.

You are requested to remain seated until the plane (r)_____ (come) to a complete standstill. Before you (s)_____ (leave) the plane, please look around to make sure you (t)_____ (not leave) any of your possessions behind you.

We hope you (u)_____ (fly) again soon with British Airways.

T 5.2 Listen and check your answers.

3 Discussing grammar

1 Complete the sentences with the verb in the Future Simple, Future Continuous, or Future Perfect. Use ONLY these tenses.

make

a 'Don't be late tonight.' 'OK. I _____ a big effort to be on time.'

b You'll know where the party is. We _____ so much noise that you'll hear us from the other end of the street.

c Ask me again tonight what I want for my birthday. I _____ up my mind by then.

have

a Come round about 8.00 tonight. We eat at 7.00, so I _____ supper by then. We can go straight out.

b 'What would Jennie like to drink?' 'She _____ a glass of wine, I think.'

c We need Harry's advice on this matter. I _____ a meeting with him some time over the next few days, so I'll ask him.

see

a When I've been to Mustique and Barbados, I _____ all the islands of the Caribbean.

b I'm looking forward to meeting you again. You _____ how much my English has improved.

c My cousin has temporarily moved into the flat downstairs, so I _____ a lot of him for the next few months.

2 Complete the questions with the most natural future form. Sometimes there are several possibilities.

a What time _____ (your plane arrive)?

b Which hotel _____ (you stay) in?

c What _____ (do) while you're on holiday?

d How long _____ (you be) away for?

e What _____ (you do) if you don't like the hotel?

4 *I hope so/I don't think so*

1 T5.3 Listen to the dialogues and fill in the gaps.

a Do you think you'll ever be rich?

I _____ so.

I _____ one day.

It's possible, but I _____ it.

I'm sure I _____ .

I'm sure I _____ .

b Are you going out tonight?

Yes, I am.

I think _____ , but I'm not sure.

I _____ be.

c Do you think the world's climate will change dramatically in the next fifty years?

I _____ think so.

I hope _____ .

Who _____ ? Maybe.

2 Work in pairs. Ask and answer similar *yes/no* questions about future possibilities in *your* life. Here are some suggestions.

a fly on Concorde/go to the Caribbean/see the Northern Lights/marry someone famous/speak perfect English/have grandchildren

b go to the cinema soon/go swimming/meet friends

c we discover life on Mars/there be world peace/there be another world war/people live longer/a cure for cancer

LANGUAGE REVIEW

Future forms

There are several future forms in English.

1 *Will* expresses a prediction seen as a future fact.

One day I'll die.

Will also expresses intention or willingness.

Give me a ring, and we'll go out for a drink.
Will you **marry** me?

2 *Shall* is used in questions to ask for instruction, to offer, and to make suggestions.

*What time **shall** we come round?*
***Shall** I make some tea?*

3 *Going to* expresses an intention thought about before the moment of speaking.

*We're **going to get** married next spring.*

Going to also expresses a prediction when it is based on present evidence. We can *see* the future from the present.

*Look at those clouds! It's **going to rain** soon.*

4 The Present Continuous expresses personal arrangements.

*I'm **meeting** Pam for lunch tomorrow.*

5 The Present Simple expresses future events that are based on a timetable or calendar, and events that are seen to be unalterable.

*Next term **starts** on 12 April.*
*We **leave** for Paris at dawn tomorrow.*

6 The Future Continuous expresses an activity that will be in progress at a specific time in the future.

*This time tomorrow **I'll be flying** to Spain.*

7 The Future Perfect expresses an action that will be completed *before* a specific time in the future.

*Don't phone after 11.00 because **I'll have gone** to bed by then.*

📖 **Grammar Reference: page 150.**

● READING AND SPEAKING

I'll marry you, but only if ...

Pre-reading task

Discuss the following questions in groups.

1 When is St Valentine's Day? What happens? Have you ever done anything romantic on this day?

2 In a wedding ceremony in your country, what are the wedding vows that a man and woman traditionally exchange? What do they promise to do? What is the divorce rate in your country?

3 Have the marriages of any rich and famous people been in the news recently? Who?
Many film stars now have *prenuptial agreements*. What are these? Why do people have them?

"I'll marry you but only on a few conditions..."

'Nothing for us is spontaneous,' says Clifford. 'Everything we do, we plan.'

When Clifford met Annie, they found one thing in common. They both love lists. So together they have written the ultimate list, a list of rules for their marriage. 5 This prenuptial agreement itemizes every detail of their lives together, from shopping to sex. *Timothy Laurence* met them in Florida in the apartment that they share.

The living room is neat and tidy, with a dining table already laid for a meal that has yet to be cooked. All the ingredients 10 for the meal are in the kitchen, prepared, weighed, and waiting in a line. It is his turn to cook. Annie is chatting over a cup of coffee by the pristine kitchen bar when her fiancé pours himself a cup and joins her. He touches her arm. She tenses, looks at him anxiously, and asks, 'Oh, sorry. Did I say 15 something wrong?'

'No, no. I was just showing affection,' Clifford explains ponderously.

'Oh, I see,' says Annie.

His hand returns to her arm, and this time she relaxes. It is 20 a significant moment, because spontaneity is not at the heart of this relationship. Love, for Clifford and Annie, means following a book of rules.

A signed, legal document

They have become curiously famous since details of their 25 prenuptial contract were publicized. They wanted a legal contract, signed and witnessed by lawyers. Their agreement is intended to regulate the chaotic heart, and smooth the path of true love before the journey of marriage has begun. **'We will have healthy sex 3 to 5 times per week'**, it declares, 30 and continues through every aspect of married life, from the wedding itself, to a trip to the supermarket: **'We will spend $400 a month'**, to who is boss when it comes to the big decisions. They are getting married in six months' time. **'The ceremony will last twenty minutes. The reception will be** 35 **held in a restaurant on Miami beach. We will invite a total of twenty guests each, who will be served two drinks, one of which may be alcoholic.'**

List of rules

So what are some of the other rules that will lead to 40 married bliss?

- Once we are married, we will each receive an allowance of $70 per week to cover haircuts, eating out, gifts for friends, and spending money.
- We won't raise our voices at each other. If we get angry, we 45 will count to 10 and take a deep breath.
- We will not use tobacco products.
- We will go to bed and turn out the lights by 11.30 pm.
- Family leadership and decision-making will be Clifford's responsibility. Annie will make decisions in emergencies 50 and when Clifford is not available.
- We will buy unleaded fuel, and we won't let the fuel gauge get lower than half a tank.

If any of these rules are broken, a fine will have to be paid out of personal savings. 55

Everyone wants to know whether they are the saviours of modern marriage, or the butchers of romance. 'Did we put anything in the contract about love?' asks Annie, a little uncertainly. 'I think so,' says Clifford. Ah, yes, they did: '**We will provide unconditional love and fulfil each other's basic needs.**' Oh, good. So that's all right then.

Their prenuptial contract is a response to uncertainty, and a plan for emotional and financial security for the future. At 39, Clifford has been through two divorces and has two sons. Annie, 31, was married briefly and disastrously in her early twenties. As Clifford likes to point out, the divorce rate for first-time marriages is now 54 per cent. 'Nobody plans to fail,' he says, 'but a lot of people fail to plan. I'm going to write a book about our experience of a fully planned and programmed marriage. I just know that it will be a bestseller.'

When Clifford met Annie

Clifford and Annie met at a dance, and started a cautious romance. He took her out to a movie and dinner, and gave her roses with a card signed *with affection* that she still keeps in her handbag. They started their own small marketing business, and in the running of the business discovered that they were both 'goal setters'. One day, not having anything else to talk about, they decided to create the perfect budget.

'We were really excited that we could agree on something so vital and fundamental to any enterprise, whether it's a business or a marriage,' says Clifford.

With so much romance in the air, their relationship deepened, and as the weeks passed, they began to make lists of increasingly personal concerns. From the start, they agreed that the big marriage breakers were money, behaviour, sex, and children. 'Nothing is going to make this marriage go wrong,' says Clifford. 'Everything has already been planned.'

'**In five years, we will have moved from our present address, and we will be living in a beach house overlooking the ocean.**'

When Annie met Clifford

Annie sees their arrangements slightly differently. For her, the prenuptial contract was a way of getting to know Clifford – a kind of courtship, 'just probing and asking questions. If we don't like and respect each other, this union won't last.' She liked what she found, including a mutual fondness for lists. 'I'd made a list of what I wanted in a man, what I liked, and what was unacceptable. I had prayed to God to find a man who was my father, only 30 years younger.'

She is very keen to have children, but Clifford admits to 'having problems' with the prospect of more kids, more college fees. Their contract states: '**We will not start a family for the first two years of our marriage.**' 'So I'll be pregnant in three years,' Annie says, and then pauses. 'No, sooner than that. I'll be pregnant in 30 months …'

Such is the wild intensity of passion in the heat of Florida.

Comprehension check

Read the text more carefully and answer the questions.

1 Find some things that Annie and Clifford have in common, and some things that they *don't* have in common.

2 Annie and Clifford say that marriages fail because of arguments about money, behaviour, sex, and children. Which of their rules refer to these four things?

3 Are the following statements true (✓) or false (✗)? Correct the false ones with the right information and discuss your answers.

a Clifford does all the cooking.
b He prepares everything very carefully.
c Their apartment looks messy but comfortable.
d Annie misunderstands why Clifford touches her.
e They want the contract to ensure an uncomplicated divorce if they split up.
f There will be no alcohol at their wedding.
g If any of the rules are broken, they will divorce immediately.
h Clifford has no doubts that both his book and his marriage will be successful.
i On their first date, Clifford took Annie out to a dance.
j Annie had no idea what her perfect man would be like until she met Clifford.

Language work

1 Find a word in the text with the same or similar meaning to the following.

lines 9–23	talking extremely clean boringly and seriously
lines 39–55	perfect happiness money paid as a punishment
lines 71–81	a plan of how money will be spent
lines 90–105	time before marriage when a couple get to know each other

2 What do you know about …
… Annie and Clifford's wedding?
… Clifford's book?
… where they're planning to live?
… when they're planning to have children?

What do you think?

1 Are Annie and Clifford 'the saviours of modern marriage, or the butchers of romance'?
Is it possible to 'regulate the chaotic heart and smooth the path of true love'?

2 Do you think the best couples …
… are of a similar age and background?
… have a similar character and interests?

3 Who makes the decisions in your house?

● VOCABULARY

Word pairs

> ⚠ Look at the sentence from the reading text.
>
> *The living room is **neat and tidy**.*
>
> In English there are many pairs of words joined by a conjunction, usually *and* but not always. The order of the words is fixed.
>
> *I still see Jane **now and again**.*
> *She ran **up and down** the road.*
> *Marry me or leave me. It's **all or nothing**.*
> *The traffic was so bad on the way to the airport that it was **touch and go** as to whether we would catch the plane.*

1 Complete the sentences using a word or group of words from the box.

> compromise/be flexible   generally speaking
> exact details   put up with it   things
> be patient and find out later   the wrong way round
> advantages and disadvantages

a In any relationship you have to be prepared to _____. You can't have your own way all the time.

b I didn't buy much at the shops. Just a few _____ for the kids.

c You've got your T-shirt on _____. The words should be at the front.

d It's difficult to explain the _____ of the rules of cricket. It's so complicated.

e 'What have you bought me for Christmas?'
'You'll have to _____.'

f 'Oh, no! The Burtons are coming for supper! I hate their kids!'
'I'm sorry, but you'll just have to _____. It's only for an hour or so.'

g It was a very tempting job offer. I weighed up the _____, but I decided in the end that I wouldn't take it.

h Britain has its faults, of course, but _____ it's a pleasant place to live.

2 Do Exercise 1 again, using one of these pairs of words. Put a letter a–h in the correct box.

☐ wait and see   ☐ ins and outs
☐ back to front   ☐ odds and ends
☐ give and take   ☐ grin and bear it
☐ by and large   ☐ pros and cons

3 Match a word in **A** with a word in **B** and a word in **C**. Look for synonyms and antonyms. Careful! There are more words in **C** than you need!

A	B	C
now		tired war bigger
more		here quiet
safe	and	police later before
peace	or	surely then
sooner	but	steadily ill order
slowly		end earlier
sick		quickly less
law		sound healthy

4 Write similar sentences to those in Exercise 1, leaving gaps where the pairs of words should go. Give them to other students for them to complete.

WRITING

Formal and informal letters

1 Look at the organization of a formal letter in English. Is it the same as in your language? Think about …

… the position and content of the two addresses and the date.

… the beginnings and endings of letters.

2 Choose the words that are more formal or appropriate in the letter. What makes a letter more or less formal?

3 The letter below is a formal *informal* letter to an English news, then ask if he/she coul nights. Explain why. Think a open and close the letter, and to write the address on the envelope. Your teacher will give you an address.

Reservations Manager
Carlton Hotel
78, Park Lane
Bristol
BH12 3GR

June 16

Dear **Jack/Sir or Madam**

I am writing/This is just a note to confirm a reservation that **was made/I asked you for** this morning by telephone. The reservation, for **a couple of/two** nights, is for **me/myself**, David Cook.

I want/would like a room with a bathroom, from 12–14 July inclusive. **I will be attending/'m going to pop into** the Trade Fair that **is being held/ is going on** in Bristol that week.

Is it all right/Would it be possible for me to have a room at the back of the hotel? **I think/am afraid** that the room **I was given/you gave me** last year was **rather/really** noisy.

Thank you/Thanks for sending me the brochure **about/regarding** your conference facilities, which I **got/received** this morning. They look **most interesting/great. Unfortunately/I'm sorry I can't give you/am unable to provide you with** any definite dates **at the moment/now, as/because** we have yet to **finalize/sort out** the details of our sales conference. **But/However, I will contact you/'ll drop you a line** as soon as **I can/possible.**

I look/'m looking forward to meeting you on 12 July.

Best wishes/Yours faithfully

David Cook

117 Fulham Palace Road London SW 11
Phone 0171 437 8955
Fax number 0171 437 6900

● LISTENING AND SPEAKING

The reunion

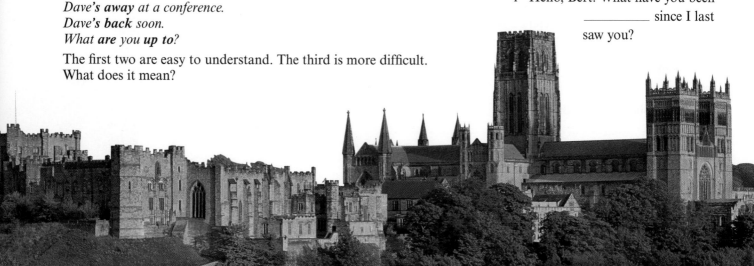

Three friends, Alan, Sarah, and James, were all at university together in Durham, a town in the north of England. Now, ten years later, they are planning a reunion.

1 Divide into two groups.

T 5.4 Group A You will hear Alan phoning Sarah.

T 5.5 Group B You will hear Sarah phoning James.

Your teacher will give you a map of Durham with some gaps. As you listen, complete what you can of the map and the chart below. The following names are mentioned.

Elvet Bridge	The Kwai Lam Restaurant	Leeds	Sunderland
Hallgarth Street	the Midlands	Fairbrother's jewellers	
St Bede's College	The County	The Three Tuns	The Lotus Garden

	Alan	Sarah	James
Travelling from?			
How?			
Leaving at what time?			
Arriving in Durham at?			
Staying where?			
Going to which restaurant?			
Where is it?			
Where are they going to meet? What time?			

2 Check your answers with people in your group.

3 Find a partner from the other group. Swap information to complete the chart and the map. What might go wrong with their arrangements? Or will everything work out all right? What's going to happen?

Language work: *Hot Verbs (2): to be*

1 Look at these sentences from Alan's conversation with Sarah.

*Dave's **away** at a conference.*
*Dave's **back** soon.*
*What **are** you **up to**?*

The first two are easy to understand. The third is more difficult. What does it mean?

2 There are many expressions with the verb *to be* + adverb or preposition. Complete the sentences with words from the box.

on	for	into	out	down
up to	out of	around	off	
up with	up	over		

a You're in a terrible mood. What's _____ you?

b Ugh! This milk's _____! Just smell it.

c She's a bit of a hippy. She's _____ meditation, yoga, everything alternative.

d The tide's _____. Let's walk across to the island!

e About ten per cent of the population is _____ work.

f I'm all _____ wealthy people paying higher taxes. I think it's a great idea.

g 'Where's Pete?' 'I'm not sure. Give him a shout. He's _____ somewhere.'

h Come on, kids! Aren't you _____ yet? It's seven o'clock. Get out of bed!

i I had a sore throat and swollen glands, so I went to the doctor's. Now I'm _____ antibiotics.

j Everyone's disappointed because this year's profits are _____ on last year's by ten per cent.

k 'What was the score in the match?' 'Ssh! It's not _____ yet.'

l Hello, Bert! What have you been _____ since I last saw you?

PostScript

Beginning a telephone conversation

1 Beginning a phone conversation can be difficult! What's the difference between these two calls?

> Hello. The Regent Hotel. Kathy speaking. How can I help you?

> Hello. I was wondering …

> Hello. 267899.

> Hello, Pat. It's me, Dave.

> Dave! Hi! How are you?

> Not bad. How's everything with you?

> Oh, you know, we've all got the flu, and Mike's snowed under. What are you up to?

> This and that …

2 Here is the beginning of a telephone conversation between two people who *don't* know each other. Put it in the right order.

1 Hello. TVS Computer Services. Darren speaking. How can I help you?

☐ Certainly. Who's calling, please?

☐ Good morning. Could I speak to your customer services department, please?

☐ (*Pause*) OK. You're through now. Go ahead.

☐ One moment, Mr Jones. I'm trying to connect you.

☐ Thank you.

☐ Yes, please.

☐ This is Keith Jones.

☐ I'm afraid the line's busy at the moment. Will you hold?

10 Hello. Is that customer services? I was wondering if you could tell me …

T 5.6 Listen and check your answers.

Ending a telephone conversation

1 Here is the end of a telephone conversation between two work colleagues, Andy and Barry. Put it in the right order.

1 A So, Barry. It was good to talk to you. Thanks very much for phoning.

☐ A I certainly will. And you'll send me a copy of the report?

☐ A That's great, Barry. Have a good weekend!

☐ B My pleasure. By the way, how's your golf these days? Still playing?

☐ B Same to you, too! Bye, Andy.

☐ B OK. I don't want to keep you. So, you'll give me a ring when you're back, right?

☐ A No, not much. I just don't seem to find the time these days. Anyway, Barry …

☐ B It'll be in the post tonight.

☐ A It's true. Right, Barry. I must fly. I'm late for a meeting.

☐ B What a shame! You used to enjoy it so much.

11 A Bye, Barry.

T 5.7 Listen and check your answers.

2 Who's trying to end the conversation? Who wants to chat? How does Andy try to signal that he wants to end the conversation? How do they confirm their arrangements?

Practice

When we are speaking to someone we know, we usually have *small talk* first. Why? What can small talk be about?

Work in pairs. Your teacher will give you a role card for a phone conversation. Decide if you think small talk is called for, and if so, what you can talk about. When you are ready, sit back to back and have your conversation.

People, places, and things

Relative clauses
Participles and infinitives
English signs

Test your grammar

1 What is the difference between these sentences?

a My son, who lives in New York, is an engineer.
My son who lives in Manchester is a psychologist.

b Politicians who tell lies are to be despised.
Politicians, who tell lies, are to be despised.

c I had a cocktail, which was very unusual.
I had a cocktail that was very unusual.

d I've met the man I want to marry.
I've met the man that I want to marry.

e I don't know where to park the car.
I don't know where I parked the car.

2 Correct the mistakes in these sentences.

a I was fascinating to read what happened at the end of the story.
The film was horrified. There was so much blood in it.

b When I arrived at the party, there were people who dancing and chatting.
Most of the people injure in the accident were able to go home.

c My grandfather, whose 75, still goes swimming every day.
We have a dog which name is Groucho.

LANGUAGE IN CONTEXT

Relative clauses, participles, and infinitives

1 Read the text about Bill Gates, his company, *Microsoft*, and his house in Seattle. There are gaps in the text. Fill the gaps with a clause below. Write a number 1–16.

1 discussing the plots and swapping opinions
2 why *Microsoft* has been so successful
3 he fancied
4 of which he owns 39% of the shares
5 whose software is used
6 estimated at £18 billion
7 overlooking Lake Washington
8 he can't afford
9 leaving his wife behind
10 what to do
11 that he's packed with high-tech gadgetry
12 that can be run by clicking on icons
13 encoded with their personal preferences
14 who is now a very successful businesswoman
15 that allows him
16 which put him among the top ten students

The man who could buy anything

Bill Gates is the richest private citizen in the world. There is nothing (a) … . Every morning, when his alarm clock goes off, the software tycoon is $20 million richer than when he went to bed. His wealth is based on his company, *Microsoft*, (b) … . He has a personal fortune (c) … , which is more than the annual economic output of over a hundred countries.

He is not shy about spending it. He has built a mansion (d) … (e) … and TV monitors, some taking up an entire wall. Visitors are given a smart card (f) … , so that, as they wander from room to room, their favourite pictures will appear on the screens, and the music they like will play. The card is programmed so that only the most intimate friends can open all the doors.

This cold-blooded approach to human relationships also seems to be true of his love life. When he went out with an ex-girlfriend, Ann Winblad, (g) … , the couple conducted much of their relationship by going on virtual dates. Each would drive alone to the same movie at the same time in different towns, and then talk about it afterwards on their mobiles, (h) … . When finally he got married, he and his wife, Melinda, signed a prenuptial agreement (i) … to go on an annual holiday with his ex-lover, Ann, (j) … .

Gates has been called 'King of the Nerds', but this simply isn't fair. In the ninth grade at school, he got A's in all the subjects he took, (k) … in the nation. Gates went on to Harvard University, where he managed to be in the same class as the girls (l) … by inserting a piece of software into the college computer. But he never finished college. When he left, he knew exactly (m) … . He started up his own computer company.

The reason (n) … is because Gates saw that his fortune lay in software, not hardware. He became a billionaire at 31, and since then *Microsoft* has created Windows, which is a system (o) … with a mouse.

Now the multi-billionaire, (p) … in two-thirds of the world's computers, is developing the HPC, or hand-held personal computer. It is his intention that there should be a computer in the pocket of everybody in the whole world.

2 Answer the questions.

a How wealthy is Bill Gates?
b How much does he earn a day?
c What is special about his house?
d What is unusual about his relationships with women?
e What did he do to the computer at Harvard?
f What is the secret of his success?
g What is Windows?

● Grammar questions

– When do we use the relative pronouns *who*, *that*, *whose*, and *which*?
– Find examples in the text of when English uses no relative pronoun.
– In which of the sentences below is the meaning of the participle *active*? In which is it *passive*?

*He went out, **leaving** his books on the table.*
*She tidied up the mess **left** by the guests.*

PRACTICE BANK

1 Pronunciation and punctuation

1 **T 6.1** You will hear six sentences. The first three contain examples of defining relative clauses (D), and the second three have examples of non-defining relative clauses (ND).
What is the difference in pronunciation? *Why* is the pronunciation different? How are pauses expressed in writing?

2 **T 6.2** Listen to some more sentences. Write D or ND. Practise saying them.

a _____   c _____   e _____   g _____
b _____   d _____   f _____   h _____

2 Relative clauses

1 If a noun is already clearly defined, and we know *which* noun is being referred to, it is more likely to be followed by a non-defining relative clause.

My youngest daughter Kate, who you know … (ND)
The Channel Tunnel, which opened in 1995, is now … (ND)
*Police are looking for **a man** who was seen running away …* (D)

Decide if the gaps in the sentences are more likely to be filled with a defining or a non-defining relative clause.

a The apple tree at the end of our garden _____ needs to be chopped down.

b People _____ live longer.

c She married a man _____ .

d Let me introduce you to Peter James _____ .

e Did I show you the photographs _____ ?

f We saw *West Side Story* last night _____ .

g Jane's the sort of person _____ .

h I'm looking for a book _____ .

i The Great Barrier Reef _____ is the largest coral reef in the world.

j My great aunt Freda _____ is coming to lunch.

k I was speaking to someone _____ .

l Our house in the country _____ is much used by all the family.

2 Here are the sentences which contain the information missing from Exercise 1. Put them in the correct sentence. Rewrite them as relative clauses, and insert commas and a relative pronoun where necessary. Leave out the relative pronoun if possible.

> He works in our Paris office.
> You went to school with this person.
> It has information about tropical fish in it.
> They do regular exercise.
> My grandfather planted it seventy years ago.
> We bought it as a weekend retreat.
> It is one of the best musicals I've ever seen.
> She met him on holiday in Turkey.
> I was telling you about her last night.
> You can always go to her with a problem.
> It is situated off the north-east coast of Australia.
> I took them in Barbados last month.

3 *-ed* or *-ing* participles

1 T 6.3 Listen to the dialogues. For each dialogue, say how the woman feels and why. Use the adjectives in the box and the nouns a–j.

Example
weather

It's raining again!

Oh, no. That's awful.

She's depressed. The weather is depressing.

> exciting/excited   disappointing/disappointed
> depressed/depressing   fascinating/fascinated
> relaxing/relaxed   annoying/annoyed   tiring/tired
> amusing/amused   frightening/frightened
> embarrassing/embarrassed   boring/bored

a gossip   f job
b exam results   g story
c holiday   h documentary
d ghost   i behaviour
e journey   j situation

2 In each pair of sentences, the same verb is used twice, once as a present participle (*-ing*) and once as a past participle (*-ed*).
Decide what the missing verb is, then write it in the correct form.

a I hurt my leg _____ football.
Bridge is a card game _____ by four people.

b On my camera, there is a sticker which says _____ in Japan.
I have a job in a café _____ sandwiches.

c I've spent the whole morning _____ an essay.
On the wall, there was some graffiti _____ in big black letters.

d Goods _____ in the sales cannot be exchanged.
I've spent all my money _____ Christmas presents.

e The police caught the burglar _____ into a house.
Careful! There's a lot of _____ glass on the floor.

f Books _____ out of the library must be returned within three weeks.
There were Japanese tourists everywhere, _____ photographs and buying souvenirs.

4 Describing

1 Add the words and phrases from the box below to this short sentence to make one long sentence.

The man walked along the road.

middle-aged	that led from the station to his home	slowly
exhausted after a hard day's work	and carrying a briefcase	
wearing a crumpled suit	pausing only to look up at the night sky	

2 Work in pairs. Your teacher will give you another short sentence. Try to make it as long as possible!

3 Find a picture in a magazine. Describe it to a partner, without showing it. Can your partner draw it?

5 *I didn't know what to do*

Complete the sentences using a question word and an infinitive.

a Shall I wear a suit? Or just a jacket? Do I need a tie?
I don't know _____ .

b We could go to Marco's restaurant. Or an Indian. Or a Chinese.
I can't decide _____ .

c The photocopier needs paper, but I can't put it in.
Could someone show me _____ ?

d Shall I phone the police or not? I'm not sure _____ or not.

e Do I turn left for the station? Or right? Or go straight on?
Can you tell me _____ ?

f Do I write this exercise? Or copy it? Or learn it by heart?
I don't understand _____ .

Relative clauses

1 Defining relative clauses tell us exactly *which* person or thing is being talked about.

The girl *who just walked in* is going out with my brother.
Bill Gates has built a house *that cost over £50 million*.

2 We can leave out the pronoun if it is the object of the clause.

The girl *you were talking to* is going out with my brother.
The house *Bill Gates has built* overlooks a lake.

3 Non-defining relative clauses give us *extra* information about a person or thing. They are more common in formal, written English.

Peter, come and meet Alison Jones, *who's just joined the staff*.
He spent ten years writing his autobiography, *which came out last year*.

Participles

1 Participles can be used as adjectives before a noun.

a *fascinating* story
a *boring* film
a *broken* heart
developed countries

2 Participles can come after a noun.

Who's that girl *wearing a red suit*?
I cleared up the mess *made by my friends*.

Infinitive clauses

The infinitive can be used after question words. It expresses ideas such as obligation and possibility.

I don't know *what to say*.
(= what I should say)
Tell me *how to get* to the station.
(= how I can get)
Have you decided *where to go*?

📖 Grammar Reference: page 152.

I've never seen anything like it!

Pre-reading task

1 Look at the photos, the captions, and the titles of the articles. Find some strange facts about …

  … Professor Mangle-Wurzle
  … Antarctica
  … the black box

2 Find other words for:
mad strange

Reading

1 Decide which article you want to read in detail.
What questions do you want answered when you read the article?

Where does he live?
How many people live in Antarctica?
Why is it called 'the black box'?

2 Now read the article.

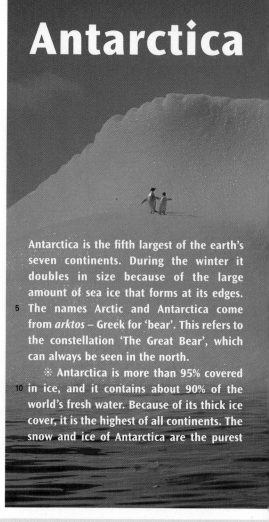

Antarctica

Antarctica is the fifth largest of the earth's seven continents. During the winter it doubles in size because of the large amount of sea ice that forms at its edges.
5 The names Arctic and Antarctica come from *arktos* – Greek for 'bear'. This refers to the constellation 'The Great Bear', which can always be seen in the north.
  ✳ Antarctica is more than 95% covered
10 in ice, and it contains about 90% of the world's fresh water. Because of its thick ice cover, it is the highest of all continents. The snow and ice of Antarctica are the purest

KING OF THE ECCENTRICS

Could it be that being completely crazy is not only good fun but good for your health?

Dr David Weeks, an American psychologist who works at the Royal Edinburgh Hospital, is extremely well qualified to comment on eccentricity.
5 **He is the author of a five-year study of 'The Great British Eccentric'.**

One of his most striking findings was the good health that eccentrics enjoy. 'Almost all of them visit the
10 doctor only once every eight or nine years.' They are also a happy lot. 'They are very curious about everything. This gives them a goal in life, which is a recipe for happiness.'
15 Of all the eccentrics he has come across, Dr Weeks believes that Professor Jake Jonathon Zebedee

Mangle-Wurzle is the most remarkable.
'He displays all the usual characteristics
20 – he's obstinate, non-conformist, and creative – but he's more extreme than my other cases.'

The professor lives on the outskirts of Huddersfield in his very own
25 kingdom of Wurzle-land. He rarely ventures out of his kingdom except to perform eccentric feats, such as his famous drive from Leeds to Huddersfield, in reverse.
30 He is something of a celebrity, giving free guided tours to people from all over the world. He rejects all religious belief and he preaches daily, trying to convert his kingdom to

35 atheism. The only problem with this plan is that all his followers are sheep.

The professor has just divorced his third wife and claims he is delighted. 'It's the best Christmas gift I've ever
40 had.' This development might have been predicted by Dr Weeks' research. His study shows that there are more marriages, separations, and divorces among eccentrics than in the general
45 population. 'They admit that they are people who are difficult to work with and live with. They often feel that they are ahead of their time, and that it is the rest of the world that is completely
50 insane, not themselves.'

THE COLDEST, HIGHEST, DRIEST, WEIRDEST PLACE ON EARTH

in the world. The general isolation from the remainder of the world has allowed it to avoid the industrial pollution that is common to the other continents.

❋ Antarctica is the coldest continent. The lowest temperature ever recorded anywhere on earth, −88.3°C, was in 1960, at the Soviet Union's Vostok Station.

❋ Antarctica can be classified as a true desert, as the equivalent of just 7cm of water falls annually. It hasn't rained at the South Pole since the end of the Pleistocene era, 1,000,000 years ago. The interior has almost continuous daylight during the summer and continuous darkness during the winter.

❋ It has only two species of flowering plants, and virtually no flying insects. The surrounding ocean, however, abounds in living creatures. Large numbers of whales feed on the rich marine life. Seals and birds live and breed, but the most prominent inhabitant of the Antarctic is the penguin, of which there are over twelve million.

❋ Today, around a thousand people call Antarctica home for several years at a time. Braving winds that freeze the flesh, the constant threat of snowblindness, and the intense, unremitting cold, they are there for the extraordinary scientific treasures that await discovery. The ice retains ancient atmospheric samples and meteorites; the skies offer a direct line to space. This is the one place still untouched by man, that is a barometer for the potentially ruinous impact our species is having on the planet.

The Orange Black Box
The mysterious machine that records crashes

There's a story that is retold whenever a plane crash hits the headlines; if only the aircraft were made of the same material as the black box, then everybody would survive.

The legendary invincibility of the famous box is familiar to most of us. Yet for such a well-known object, it's remarkably mysterious. How many of us know that the 'black' box is in fact painted fluorescent orange?

'It was originally called a black box in the days when anything to do with electronics was new and strange,' explains Pete Cook, from a flight recorder manufacturer. 'They're painted orange nowadays to make them more easily visible in the event of a crash.'

There are two kinds of black box; the flight data recorder (FDR) and the cockpit voice recorder (CVR). Both are normally stored at the rear of an aircraft, where the fuselage meets the upper tail fin – the part of planes that has the best survival record. The same principle applies to human passengers – you're safer at the back.

Despite their reputation, neither box is in fact indestructible. However, they can withstand a temperature of 1,100°C for 30 minutes and 250°C for 10 hours. They must also be able to survive an impact force of 3,500g – that's 3,500 times the force of gravity.

To take this kind of strain, flight recorders are encased in two thicknesses of titanium. Memory chips hold the flight data.

While FDRs make an electronic record of the plane's mechanical performance, CVRs record the communication between the crew. 'After a crash in water, they send out a sonar 'ping' so that they can be found,' says Cook. 'But they are still only recovered in 80 per cent of accidents.'

Comprehension check

1 Did you find the answers to your questions?

2 Here is a list of questions that relate to the three articles. Put a tick (✓) next to the questions that go with your article, then answer them.

a What is the story that is told again and again?
b What is the origin of its name?
c How is he typical of his kind?
d Why is there so little pollution?
e How does he spend his days?
f Where are they stored? Why?
g How does he feel after his third divorce?
h Is it impossible to destroy them?
i Is there much plant and animal life?
j What living creatures are there in the seas around?
k How are they made?
l Why are they happy people?
m Why is the area special from a scientific point of view?
n What do these people think of the rest of the world?
o Are they always found after a crash?

3 Find people who read the other stories. Tell them about what you read. Together, answer all the questions.

What do you think?

Which article do you find most interesting? Which facts do you find most remarkable?

VOCABULARY

Synonyms

English has the largest vocabulary of all languages. This is partly because there are so many synonyms.

Great *fantastic* **brilliant** *wonderful* nice *Marvellous*

1 Find words in the text 'King of the Eccentrics' with the same or similar meaning to these words.

a writer
b inquisitive
c an aim, an ambition
d unusual/surprising
e stubborn
f faith
g confess
h mad

2 Match a word in **A** with a synonym in **B**.

A	B
boring terrified nasty handy annoying 'd prefer noise miserable clever argue hate dangerous mend sure	irritating fix row talented convinced dull risky 'd rather unhappy unpleasant scared stiff sound can't stand useful

3 We often use synonyms to avoid repeating words. Complete the sentences with a word from Exercises 1 and 2. Notice that sometimes the word class changes, for example, from adjective to noun.

Example
'He's completely mad, you know.'
'Oh, yes. Insanity runs in the family.'

a 'Isn't this lesson dull?'
'Yep. It's so _____ I'm falling asleep.'

b 'Peter's always late for everything. I find it so irritating.'
'Mmm. It _____ me, too.'

c 'Weren't you terrified when the dog attacked you?'
'I was absolutely _____.'

d 'Very unusual weather for the time of year.'
'Yes, it's _____ warm, isn't it?'

e 'We live just five minutes from the shops, which is _____.'
'Yes, it must be very useful.'

f 'I've lost faith in this government.'
'Me, too. I don't _____ a word they say.'

g 'There's a very _____ smell in this room.'
'Yes. There's something very unpleasant.'

h 'Isn't mountain climbing dangerous?'
'Well, I like to take a few _____.'

i 'What's that noise?'
'It _____ like our neighbours are having a party.'

j 'Jane and Harry are one of those couples who are always rowing.'
'I know. Their _____ last for days.'

4 **T 6.4** You will hear some lines of dialogue. Reply, using a synonym in your answer.

LISTENING AND SPEAKING

Advertisements

Pre-listening task

1 What's your favourite advertisement at the moment?
Is it on the TV or the radio?
What's the advert for? What's the story?

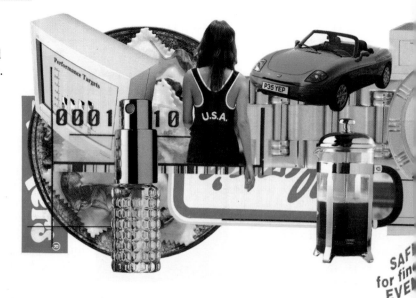

2 Find an advertisement from a newspaper or magazine that appeals to you, and bring it to class.
Talk about what the advert is for, and why you like it.

Listening

T 6.5 You will hear seven radio advertisements. Before you listen, there are two things you need to know.

– In order to watch television in Britain, people need to buy an annual licence. It costs about £80.
– In a quiz, if a contestant says, 'Pass', it means *I don't know the answer*.

Listen and answer the questions.

Which advert … ?

… is selling soap powder?
… is trying to recruit personnel?
… is for a new car?
… is selling computer hardware?
… is giving a recipe?
… is threatening punishment?
… is about shaving?

Comprehension check

1 Complete the chart.

	What's the advert for?	Name of product	Characters in the advert	Setting/place
a				
b				
c				
d				
e				
f				
g				

2 What is the selling point for each advert?

3 Answer the questions about each advert.

a What does John need?
How can you get more information about it?

b What is strange about the language in the advert for soup?
What are the ingredients?

c How does the woman try to make the robot go away?

d Describe Sarah's play shirt.
What do you think Sarah wants to bring into the house?

e What doesn't the minister want to talk about?

f How can the daughter afford a new car?
Why does the father compare her to the mother?

g What is an infantry soldier paid to do?
What should you do if you're interested?

Group work

Devise a radio or television advert. Choose a product or service of your own, or one of the following.

– a BMW sports car
– *Dazzle* washing-up liquid
– *Bonzo* dog food
– *Blue Mountain* coffee
– a restaurant in town
– a bank for students

My favourite part of town

1 What's your favourite town or city? Why do you like it? Which parts of it do you particularly like?

2 Read the description of a part of London. Match the pictures to the description.

SOHO

MY FAVOURITE PART OF TOWN

One of my favourite parts of London is Soho, which is right in the centre, and includes Piccadilly Circus, Shaftesbury Avenue, and Leicester Square. One of the main reasons I like it is that it is always lively and colourful, with people dashing around going about their business, which is mainly honest but not always. The place is a bit of a mess, and the buildings aren't the most beautiful in London, but the streets are always interesting, with surprises around every corner. The name is derived from a hunting call, 'So-ho', that huntsmen were heard to cry as they chased deer in royal parklands. It has been a cosmopolitan area since the first immigrants, who were French Huguenots, arrived in the 1680s. More French arrived escaping the revolution during the late 18th century, followed by Germans, Russians, Poles, Greeks, and Italians. Soho is packed with continental food shops and restaurants. More recently there have been a lot of Chinese from Hong Kong. Gerrard Street, which is pedestrianized, is the centre of London's Chinatown. It has restaurants, dim sum houses, Chinese supermarkets, and in February, there are the New Year celebrations. Many famous people have lived in Soho, including Mozart, Karl Marx, and the poet T. S. Eliot. It has a reputation for attracting artists, writers, poets, and people in the media. Shaftesbury Avenue is in the heart of London's theatre land, and there are endless clubs, pubs, and cafés. There are also street markets, advertising agencies, clothes shops, music publishers, and recording studios, which makes it an exciting place to live and work. Piccadilly Circus is like a magnet for young people from all over the world. They like to sit on the steps under the statue of Eros, celebrating the freedom and friendship of youth. It is said that if you wait long enough at Piccadilly Circus, you'll meet everyone you've ever known!

3 Divide the text into four or five paragraphs. What is the purpose of each paragraph?

4 The description is part fact and part opinion. Find examples of both.

5 Underline examples of relative clauses and participles.

6 Write a description of your favourite part of a town. Write about 300 words. Divide the paragraphs into ...
   – general impressions,
   – personal impressions
   – history
   – a description of some particular aspects
   – a conclusion

PostScript

English signs

Where would you see these signs? What do they mean?

1 Best before end: *(see cap)*

2 *Self Service Please Take a Tray*

3 NO VACANCIES

4 *UNDER NEW MANAGEMENT*

5 **Express** till
Ten items or fewer

6 PUBLIC CONVENIENCES
100yds ➡

7 P.Y.O. STRAWBERRIES

8 *DO NOT* exceed the stated dose

9 **Queue this side**

10 *Watch out! Pickpockets about!*

11 **CAUTION CATTLE CROSSING**

12 Closing down **sale** *Everything must go*

13 *SPECIAL* CUT and BLOW DRY £15

14 *TODAY'S SPECIALS ARE ON THE BOARD*

15 *Please give up this seat for the elderly and infirm, or for people with small children*

16 POSITION CLOSED

17 P Mon–Sat 8am–6pm **2 hours** No return within the hour

18 **TRESPASSERS WILL BE PROSECUTED**

19 **DIVERSION AHEAD**

20 *Gone to lunch. Back at 2 o'clock*

1 Grandma's reply

1 Read Grandma's letter to Sean. Put the verb in brackets into the correct form.

22 St Bede's Terrace,
Newcastle-upon-Tyne.
Tuesday

My dear Sean,

How lovely (a)_____ (get) your letter! Mummy is right! I will really enjoy (b)_____ (help) you with your schoolwork, and I will try very hard (c)_____ (remember) what it was like when I was a little girl all those years ago.

When the war started, I was just five and I'll never forget (d)_____ (watch) my grandfather dig a big black hole in the back garden. This was our air raid shelter. At first I was really scared of (e)_____ (go) into it. Every time the siren went off, I started (f)_____ (tremble) and I was sick, actually sick with fear. I refused (g)_____ (leave) my bed. I didn't find it easy (h)_____ (sleep) in that shelter. But soon, (i)_____ (get) used to (j)_____ (live) in the cities was so dangerous that the government decided (k)_____ (send) all the children away to the countryside. I think I was lucky because I was able (l)_____ (go away) to my aunt's. Some children were forced (m)_____ (stay) with total strangers. My aunt lived in a small town, called Alston, high in the hills, not too far from Newcastle. And guess what, Sean, she had a sweet shop! Mrs Crozier's Sweet Shop. But, oh dear me, at first I was so unhappy, I couldn't stop (n)_____ (cry) because I couldn't help (o)_____ (worry) about my mother back home. My aunt let me (p)_____ (have) as many sweets as I wanted, but I was too miserable (q)_____ (eat) many. Silly me! Most children didn't have the chance of (r)_____ (get) lots of sweets because sweets were rationed. That meant that you couldn't buy all you wanted. You were only allowed (s)_____ (buy) a small amount. Lots of other things were rationed, too. It was almost impossible (t)_____ (get) butter, cream, meat, fruit, vegetables, and petrol. We did without a lot of things during the war. Can you believe that just after it ended, someone gave me a banana and I didn't know what (u)_____ (do) with it?

Sean, I hope this is useful. I'm longing (v)_____ (see) you all. Give my love to Mummy, Daddy and Liam. Don't worry, he'll be much more fun soon.

Lots of love and kisses,

Grandma xxx

2 **T 7.2** Listen and check your answers.

2 Discussing grammar

Match a line on the left with a line on the right.

a They stopped playing football | because they were tired of working.
They stopped to play football | because it got dark.

b I simply don't remember giving | you any money yesterday.
Please remember to give | my best wishes to your parents.

c Try counting | from 1 to 10 in Arabic. I bet you can't!
Try to count | sheep if you can't get to sleep.

d We prefer staying at the Ritz | whenever we're in London.
We'd prefer to stay at the Ritz | next time we're in London.

e He seems to drink too much. | He's fallen asleep.
He seems to be drinking too much. | He's rarely sober.
He seems to have drunk too much. | He's swaying.

f I like going | home now, please.
I like to go | to the cinema.
I'd like to go | to the dentist twice a year.

3 *We'd love to!*

1 Sometimes the whole infinitive need not be repeated if it is understood.

Example
A Can you and Mary come to lunch next Sunday?
B Oh yes, we'd *love to* .

Write a reply to **A**, using the verb in brackets.

a A Are we going to have a break?

B No, _____ (not have time).

b A Can I smoke in here?

B No, _____ (not allow).

c A I can't help you do your homework this evening. Sorry.

B Oh, but _____ (promise).

d A Why did you do Exercise 2?

B Because you _____ (tell).

e A You said you'd phone me last night.

B I'm really sorry, _____ (mean), but I forgot.

f A Have you finished marking the homework yet?

B Sorry, _____ (not have a chance).

2 **T 7.3** Listen and check your answers. Practise the conversations with a partner. Pay particular attention to the stress and intonation.

LANGUAGE REVIEW

Verb patterns

-ing form

The *-ing* form of the verb can be used …

1 … after certain verbs.
I *love hearing* stories about when you were little.
He *can't stand playing* with his brother.

2 … after prepositions.
I'm good *at cooking*.
After leaving school, I went to university.

3 … as the subject of a sentence.
Living in the cities was so dangerous.
Smoking is bad for your health.

Infinitives

Infinitives are used …

1 … after certain verbs.
What are you *planning to do*?
We *can't afford to go* out very often.

2 … after certain adjectives.
I find it *difficult to make* new friends.

-ing or infinitive?

With some verbs there is no change in meaning.

It *started raining/to rain*.

With some verbs there is a change in meaning.

I tried *to put* out the fire. (This was my objective.)
I tried *pouring* water on it. (This was my method.)

📖 **Grammar Reference: page 153.**

READING AND SPEAKING

Pre-reading task

Use your dictionary to help with new words.

1 Which of the following household items do you think were in use fifty years ago?
Which do you have in your home?

personal computer	fridge
camcorder	electric razor
radio	washing machine
video recorder	deep freeze
tin opener	microwave oven
CD player	food processor
tumble drier	music system
iron	cassette recorder
vacuum cleaner	dishwasher
word processor	jacuzzi
television	mobile phone

2 Imagine life in your family fifty years ago. How did your parents and grandparents live? How was their daily life different from today?

3 If you lived then, what would you miss about your life today? What wouldn't you miss? Write two lists. Compare your ideas with your partner and the rest of the class.

Reading

You are going to read about the Jones family. Read the text quickly, then discuss these questions.

1 Identify the people in the main picture. How do you know who's who?

2 What was the experiment that they agreed to do?

3 Which of the items in the box above are mentioned in the article? <u>Underline</u> those which are.

The family who turned back the clock

THE JONES FAMILY HAVE NINE TV SETS, SIX COMPUTERS, THREE CARS, AND EVERY DOMESTIC APPLIANCE.
What would their life be like without them?
Melanie Adams reports

When Malcolm Jones woke up last Monday, he heard the birds singing. Not remarkable, you might think, especially given that he lives near a
5 forest. But birdsong in the Jones household is usually drowned by a tidal wave of electronic music crashing around the house as soon as his four children wake up.
10 This is a family who have chosen to fill their home with every conceivable gadget. They have nine television sets, including one in each bedroom and in the kitchen. All the children have
15 their own personal computers and CD players. Of course, there are all the usual appliances we all take for granted, such as the washing machine, tumble drier, dishwasher, deep freeze, microwave oven,
20 and video recorder, but they also have an electric trouser press, two power showers, an Olympic-sized spa bath and jacuzzi, three cars, and a music system which plays throughout the whole house.

25 ### The experiment

What happens if all the props of modern living are removed?
To help us find out, we asked the Joneses to turn back the clock fifty
30 years and to switch off all their labour-saving gadgets and push-button entertainment for three days. We also wanted them to stop using their cars. The family, comprising Malcolm, 48,
35 Carol, 43, and their four children Emma, 17, Richard, 14, Tamsin, 9, and Tom, 7, were not enthusiastic, but everyone, except for Emma, agreed to try. (She

couldn't stand the thought of being
40 without the telephone and her car, which she had only just learnt to drive, so she refused point-blank to join in.) The other three children were not allowed to use their computers or watch TV. They
45 were banned from opening the freezer to get out fish fingers and oven chips. Malcolm was forbidden to use his electric razor and mobile phone, but allowed to use his car for work. Carol
50 was encouraged to go everywhere on foot or by bicycle (women rarely drove 50 years ago), told to ignore the washing machine and dishwasher, and she was discouraged from using the telephone.

The much-dreaded three days got under way!

Old-fashioned meals, games, and entertainment were planned for the
60 evenings. After eating together at the kitchen table, they sat playing cards, putting off doing the washing-up because they all hated doing that.

Carol was surprised at how long
65 everything took. 'By the time I had washed up the breakfast things and got back from walking the children to school, it was nearly lunchtime. Getting to the shops, which normally takes five minutes
70 in the car, took at least an hour, so it was impossible just to pop out for a loaf of bread. It was strange having to wait until the washing dried in the garden before getting the ironing done, instead
75 of simply using the drier.'

Although Carol found it quite difficult to get used to the length of time it took to do things, she enjoyed having a slower, more relaxed pace of life. Also, the lack of
80 electronic entertainment, particularly the TV, had a dramatic effect on the children. They got on much better together and seemed to enjoy each other's company more, although they clearly believed that
85 they were suffering. Tamsin even spent some time gazing at the blank TV screen in her bedroom.

'All sorts of things that we had put off doing got done,' said Carol. 'Bikes got
90 mended, rooms tidied, bookshelves sorted, hamsters cleaned out. Tamsin and Tom started to play games together and even read stories to each other.'

95 What Malcolm liked most was the peace. 'I usually start the day by watching the business news on TV from bed. Then I press the music button while I shower and get dressed. I didn't miss any of this,
100 I just enjoyed hearing the birds singing and chatting to Carol. I think the whole experience did the children a lot of good. If it were my decision now, I'd throw all the televisions away.'

105 The children vigorously denied that any good had been done to them. Richard spoke for them all when he said, 'It was awful. I missed my music, I missed the computer games, and I missed the TV. We
110 had to read *books* instead!'

Carol's feelings were the most ambiguous. 'I enjoyed doing more things together as a family. But as the housewife, I didn't like my day being
115 so full of household chores. When you've got a dishwasher, you stack it as you go through the day and turn it on at night. But you can't leave dirty dishes in the sink all day, so you've got to keep
120 doing the washing-up. Also, without a phone and a car, I felt really isolated.'

All of this just goes to show that, fascinating as the experiment was, you cannot turn the clock back. This
125 is doubtless a big relief to the Jones children!

Comprehension check

Work in groups. Read the article again and answer the questions.

1 What is the first thing the children usually do when they wake up in the morning?

2 What does this family own which is more than the average family owns?

3 What were some of the rules of the experiment for each member of the family?

4 Who refused to join in the experiment? Why?
Who enjoyed the experiment most? Why? Who enjoyed it least? Why? Who had mixed feelings? Why?

5 Choose one member of the Jones family and imagine you are him/her. Describe your typical day to the others in your group.

'Well, the first thing I usually do when I wake up is …'

Now describe a day for the same person during the experiment.

'During the experiment, when I woke up I wasn't allowed to … , so …'

6 **T 7.4** Which member of the family is most likely to have said the following? Why?

a There's no way I'm going to give up using my car!

b It's a beautiful morning, isn't it dear?

c No, I haven't ironed your white shirt yet! I haven't had the time.

d Come on! Stop gazing at that blank screen. Let's have a game of Scrabble.

e Well, I'm not doing it! I did it last night. Anyway, I want to mend the puncture on my bike.

f Damn! I forgot to buy sugar!

g If it were up to me, I'd throw the lot out!

h Personally, I think life was much harder fifty years ago.

i Never again! That was the longest three days of my life!

Practise saying their comments with appropriate stress and intonation.

Language work

1 Put the following phrases from the text into your own words.

a ... birdsong ... is usually drowned by a tidal wave of electronic music crashing around the house ... (l. 5–8)

b ... fill their home with every conceivable gadget. (l. 11–12)

c ... the usual appliances we all take for granted ... (l. 16–17)

d ... the props of modern living ... (l. 26–7)

e ... labour-saving gadgets and push-button entertainment ... (l. 31–2)

f ... she refused point-blank ... (l. 42)

g The much-dreaded three days ... (l. 56)

h ... the lack of ... the TV, had a dramatic effect on the children. (l. 79–81)

i The children vigorously denied that any good had been done to them. (l. 105–6)

j This is doubtless a big relief to the Jones children! (l. 124–6)

2 Go through the text and <u>underline</u> all the verb patterns with -ing forms and infinitives.

● VOCABULARY AND LISTENING

Hot Verbs (3): get

1 The verb *get* is very common in spoken English. It has many different uses. Here are some examples from the text about the Jones family.

a You**'ve got** a dishwasher.

b I **got back** from walking the children to school.

c She found it difficult to **get used to** the length of time things took.

d You**'ve got to** keep doing the washing-up.

e All sorts of things **got done**.

f They **got on** much better **together**.

Replace the words in bold with one of the expressions below in the correct tense.

> have to   become accustomed to
> be done (passive)   return   have/own
> have a (better) relationship

2 Write answers to the following questions about yourself.

a Have you got a pet/a CD player?

b What have you got to do when you get home tonight?

c How do you get to school?

d What time do you usually get to school?

e How many TV channels can you get?

f When did you last get angry? Why?

g How do you get on with your parents?

h How often do you get your hair cut?

i In what ways is your English getting better?

Compare your answers with a partner. Work together to rewrite the questions without using *get*.

Phrasal verbs with *get*

Get can combine with particles to make phrasal verbs.

1 Complete each group of sentences with one of the particles from the box below. (Careful, only six of the particles are used.)

> at   away   into   off   on   out   over   round   through   up

a You always get | of doing the washing-up. It's not fair.
   How did our secret get | ? Everyone knows now!
   I got a great book | of the library. You can borrow it.

b You're always getting | me! Leave me alone!
   The detective got | the truth through careful questioning.
   I can't get | the sugar. It's right at the back.

c It took me ages to get | the operation.
   He couldn't get his point | to me at first so he explained it again.
   I can't get | how much your children have grown.

d Sam is always getting | to something naughty!
   We got | to page 56 in the last lesson.
   I had to get | at 5 a.m. to catch the plane.

e I couldn't get | to Joe. I don't think his phone's working.
   We got | a huge amount of money in Paris.
   I failed, but Sue got | the exam with flying colours.

f She couldn't get her ring | her finger because it was so swollen.
   Oliver finally got | with Claire at Stuart's party.
   Ben stole a car but he got | lightly because he was only sixteen.

2 There are four more particles in the box. All of them combine with *get*. Choose one of them, and research the meanings in your dictionary. Tell the rest of the class what you find out.

Listening

Fast Car—a song by Tracy Chapman

1 T 7.5 Here are some lines from a song called *Fast Car* by Tracy Chapman. Listen and complete the gaps. They all contain expressions with *get*.

> You _____ a fast car.
> Maybe together we can
>
> But me myself _____.
> I've got a plan to _____
> You and I can both _____
> You see my old man _____
> I said somebody _____
> We _____ a decision
> I know things will _____
> You'll find work and I'll
>
> _____
> And I _____ that pays all our bills
> I _____ and I ain't going nowhere

2 Listen again and read the tapescript on page 137 to check your answers.

● WRITING AND DISCUSSION

Contrasting ideas

1 How often do you watch television? Which are your most and least favourite programmes?
One half of the class make a list of all the *good* points about TV. The other half make a list of only the *bad* points. Compare your ideas.

2 Join the ideas in **A** and **C** with the correct linking words in **B**. Change the punctuation where necessary.

A	B	C
I always watch the news on TV	even though / whereas	John always watches sport. / it's usually depressing.
He writes all personal letters by hand	although / despite	he has a computer. / having a computer.
It took only an hour to get to the airport	However, / in spite of	the traffic. / they still missed the plane.
Some couples argue all the time	Nevertheless, / whereas	others never do. / their marriages still work.
Kathy rarely uses her mobile phone	However, / even though	Kevin uses his all the time. / she has one.

Look again at the lists of good and bad points about TV. Join some of them with some of the words in **B**.

3 Complete the following statements in a suitable way.

a His idea is brilliant in theory. However, it …
b My brothers love playing computer games, whereas I …
c On the one hand, cars are really convenient to get you from A to B, but on …
d I'm going to drive into London, even though …
e Foreign travel is very exciting, but at the same time it …
f The critics slammed Ed Newhart's latest film. Nevertheless, …
g Their daughter is often sullen and moody, despite always …

4 Which modern inventions would you find it most difficult to live without? Discuss your ideas with a partner.

Choose *one* invention which you feel is very necessary to your life (it could be anything from the Internet to an electric toothbrush) and answer the following questions about it.

– What invention have you chosen and why?
– What are its advantages? Compare these with any disadvantages.
– Why is it important to you? Give your personal opinion.
– Write some final concluding comments.

First make notes, then expand the notes into an essay of about 200–300 words.

PostScript

Soundbites

1 Where would you hear the following? Who is speaking to who?

OK, folks. Don't go away now. We'll be back in a few minutes just after the break.

With respect to my Right Honourable friend, I have to say that I find his statement to be inconsistent with the truth.

It's not fair! Everyone else is allowed to go.

Ooh! Hear, hear!

I don't care about everyone else. You're not, and that's all there is to it.

Things aren't what they used to be.

You can say that again. It was different in our day, wasn't it?

Open wide and say 'Ah'. Oh, dear.

Ish it bad newsh?

Will passengers in rows A to K please board now?

A big Mac with regular fries and a strawberry milkshake.

Eat here or take away?

I can't find my gym kit.

Think. Where did you last have it?

Mummy! I need a wee-wee!

News is coming in of a major hold-up on the A45 Colchester bypass. Drivers are advised to avoid this area if at all possible.

Has Kelly Jones' latest album been released yet?

Well, I'm just going to put my feet up and have a nap, if that's all right with you.

Could you develop this for me?

Normal six by four?

Yeah, that's fine.

When do you want them by?

Let passengers off first. Move right down inside the car.

This time tomorrow's all right.

2 **T 7.6** Listen to the dialogues. Do the background noises help you to identify the situations?

Thanks for having me!

'scuse fingers!

8 Famous for fifteen minutes

Modal auxiliary verbs
Exaggeration and understatement

1 All modal verbs can be used to express degrees of probability.
Which of these sentences express probability? Put a ✔. Which don't? Put a ✘.

Example
She *must* be very rich. ✔ (probability)
You *must* do your homework. ✘

a We *might* go to Hawaii for our honeymoon.
b You *mustn't* smoke in this part of the restaurant.
c He *can't* be coming. It's already after ten o'clock.
d She *could* speak three languages fluently by the time she was five.

e He *could* be working in the library.
f The weather forecast says it *may* snow tomorrow.
g Good morning. *May* I speak to Mr Jones?
h *Will* you help me do my homework?
i That *will* be Ken on the phone. He promised to ring.
j You *should* see a doctor as soon as possible.
k It's eight o'clock. They *should* be arriving soon.
l They *must* have won the lottery.
m You *should* have told her the truth.

2 What concepts do the other sentences express?

Example
You *must* do your homework. (obligation)

LANGUAGE IN CONTEXT

Modal verbs of probability

1 Read the newspaper headlines. What do you think has happened to the man and the woman? Read the ideas below. Which do you agree with?

A
'Excuse me ... I've just jumped off the Empire State Building!'

He must be *Superman*!
He can't be serious. He must be joking.
He might be a bungee-jumper.
He could have come down by parachute.
He might have been trying to commit suicide.
He may be acting in a film.
He must have injured himself.
His story will be in all the newspapers.
He may become famous.

B
40 YEARS IN BED – WITH FLU

She probably doesn't have flu. (can't)
_____

It's likely that she has had a more serious illness. (must)
_____

Perhaps she is just very lazy. (might)
_____

It's not possible that the doctor told her to stay in bed for so long. (couldn't)
_____

Surely someone has been looking after her. (must)
_____

She will probably find it very difficult to walk again. (may)
_____

2 Rewrite the ideas in **B** using the modal verb in brackets.

3 Read the complete newspaper stories. Which of the ideas in **A** and **B** were correct? Answer these questions.

a Why did Jason jump off the Empire State Building? Why has Mrs Teppit spent forty years in bed?

b Who are the other people in the stories? What did they do?

'Excuse me ... I've just jumped off the Empire State Building!'

On Christmas Eve, Bob Stichman was working in his office on the 85th floor of the Empire State Building in New York, when he heard a knock at the window. He looked up and saw a man standing on the window ledge asking to come in. 'I thought I was dreaming. You don't meet a lot of guys coming in through the window of the 85th floor!' The guy was Jason Hosen, a young, unsuccessful artist, who was so broke and alone that he had decided to kill himself. He had taken the elevator to the 86th floor and then hurled himself towards the tiny cars 1,000 feet below on Fifth Avenue. However, strong winds had blown him onto the window ledge of the 85th floor, which is where he met Bob Stichman. His story appeared on TV, and hundreds of people have offered to have him stay for Christmas.

40 YEARS IN BED — WITH FLU

Doctor Mark Pemberton, who has just taken over a medical practice in rural Suffolk, visited a 74-year-old widow, Mrs Ada Teppit at her home in the village of Nacton. Mrs Teppit has been bedridden for 40 years. The doctor examined her but couldn't find anything wrong. He questioned her daughter, Norma, aged 54, and to his amazement discovered that 40 years ago the village doctor had ordered Mrs Teppit to bed because she had influenza and told her not to get up until he returned. He never returned so she never got up. She has never married nor had any job other than taking care of her mother. Mrs Teppit's muscles have wasted, and she has put on a lot of weight. She may never walk again. Her daughter has been looking after her.

Way The N...

Other uses of modal verbs

1 All of the comments below were made by people in the two newspaper stories. Who do you think is speaking to who?

'Excuse me. *May* I come in?'

'You *must* stay in bed until I return.'

'I've *had to* look after her since I was 14.'

'I *couldn't* believe my eyes.'

'You *should have been* examined years ago.'

'She *won't* get up.'

'I *can't* find anything wrong with you at all.'

'I *ought to* call the police.'

'*Can* I get up soon?'

'You *should* try to lose weight.'

'She told me that I *couldn't* get married and that I *had to* look after her.'

'*Will* you spend Christmas with us?'

'You'll *have to* have physiotherapy.'

'You *mustn't* do anything like this again.'

'You *don't have to* do everything for her.'

2 What concepts do the verbs in italics express? Permission? Obligation/advice? Ability? Willingness/refusal?

● Grammar questions

– Which of these statements express the greatest degree of certainty? Which express less certainty? Which expresses the least?

*That **'ll**/**won't** be the postman.*
*That **must**/**can't** be the postman.*
*That **should** be the postman.*
*That **could**/**couldn't** be the postman.*
*That **may** be the postman.*
*That **might** be the postman.*

– All the above statements could be in answer to the question
*Who **is** that at the door?*
Change each one to answer the question
*Who **was** that at the door?*

– What is the past of these sentences?
He can see someone at the window.
She must call the doctor.
He has to tell the police.
She won't get out of bed.
You should call the police.
We needn't hurry. (Careful!)

PRACTICE BANK

1 Discussing grammar

1 Which of the words in the right hand column can fit into the sentences on the left? Sometimes several will fit. Discuss the possibilities with a partner.

a _____ I ask you a question about this exercise?

b _____ you help me with this exercise, please?

c He'll _____ hurry if he wants to get here in time.

d I _____ be able to come round and see you tonight.

e Sally _____ read when she was only three.

f I _____ be seeing Theo later this evening, but I'm not sure.

g You _____ be feeling very excited about your trip to Florida.

h They _____ have finished dinner by now.

i You _____ pass the exam easily. You've worked really hard.

j She always _____ leave work early on Fridays.

k That _____ be the taxi.

must

can

may

might

could

should

will/'ll

have/has to

2 Underline the correct answer.

a I'm sorry I'm late, I *had to go/should have gone* to the post office.

b You *mustn't/don't have to* go to France to learn French, but it helps.

c You *mustn't/don't have to* drive if you've been drinking.

d I'm sorry. I *may not/cannot* be able to come to your party on Saturday.

e You lucky thing! How *could you/were you able to* get Madonna's autograph?

f I just waited outside the stage door and asked her if I *could/was able to* have it.

g The car *wouldn't/couldn't* start this morning, so I was late for work.

h I *wouldn't/couldn't* start the car this morning, so I was late for work.

i Do this exercise for homework. You *shouldn't/mustn't* have any problems with it.

j We *needn't have paid/didn't need to pay* to get into the museum. It was free.

2 Listening and speaking

1 **T8.1** Listen to and read one side of a telephone conversation, then answer the questions below.

- Hello. Kingsbridge 810344. Rod speaking.
- Oh, hi Miranda. Why all the excitement?
- Yes, I can. I remember you doing it in the coffee bar. It was the one in the *Daily Express*, wasn't it? Didn't you have to name loads of capital cities?
- You can't have! I don't believe it. What's the prize?
- You must be kidding! That's brilliant. For how long?
- Well, you should be able to do quite a lot in three days. And the Waldorf Astoria! I'm impressed! Isn't that on Park Avenue?
- I thought so. Not that I've been there of course.
- And *what* could possibly be even better than that?
- Wow! That's fantastic. That's something I've always wanted to do. D'you know it only takes three and a half hours, so you arrive before you've left … if you see what I mean.
- You can't be serious? You know I'd love to! But why me? Surely you should be taking Richard.
- Oh, sorry! I didn't know. I really am sorry. When did this happen?…

Work in pairs. What deductions can you make about:
- the relationship between Miranda and Rod?
- the reason she is so excited?
- what she was doing in the coffee bar?
- where she is going?
- how she is travelling?
- the thing that Rod has always wanted to do?
- the relationship between Miranda and Richard?
- the future relationship between Miranda and Rod?

What do you think Miranda's exact words were in the conversation?

2 **T8.2** Listen to the full conversation between Miranda and Rod. Were your deductions correct?

3 Go through the complete tapescript on page 138 and underline all the modal verbs.

3 Stress and intonation

Work in pairs. Take it in turns to be A or B.

1 Student B should respond to A's remarks using the words in brackets. Make changes where necessary and continue the conversations further.

Example
A I've never seen Tina eat meat.
B *I know. She must be a vegetarian.* (must, vegetarian)
A *But I've seen her eat fish.*

a A Oh no! I've lost my passport.
  B (could, leave, in the taxi)

b A It's an early start for us tomorrow.
  B (What time, have?)

c A The traffic's not moving. We'll never get to the concert.
  B (Don't worry, should, time)

d A I've brought you some flowers. I hope you like tulips.
  B (How kind, needn't)

e A All the teachers are going on strike!
  B (Brilliant, don't have, come, tomorrow)

2 **T8.3** Listen to the sample answers, paying particular attention to the stress and intonation. Are they the same as your replies?

LANGUAGE REVIEW

Modal auxiliary verbs

The main modal verbs are *must, can, could, may, might, should, ought to, will,* and *would.* All of these can be used to express degrees of certainty or probability. They also have other uses.

1 Degrees of certainty about the present

Certainty	She **will**	
	She **must**	
	She **could**	**be** at home.
Possibility	She **may**	**have** a high salary in that job.
	She **might**	**be earning** a lot of money. (continuous infinitive)
	She **should**	
Certainty	She **can't**	
	She **won't**	

2 Degrees of certainty about the past

Certainty	She **will**	
	She **must**	
		have been at home. (perfect infinitive)
	She **could**	
Possibility	She **may**	**have had** a high salary in that job.
	She **might**	
		have been earning a lot of money.
	She **should**	
Certainty	She **can't**	
	She **won't**	

3 Other uses of modal auxiliary verbs

Modal verbs also express concepts such as obligation (mild or strong), permission, ability, and willingness.

There are other verbs which express similar meanings. These are *have to, need to,* and *be able to.*

📖 **Grammar Reference: page 155.**

● READING AND SPEAKING

Get me Jane Austen's fax number!

Pre-reading task

1 What do you know about these people? Why are they famous? Were they famous in their lifetimes? Which of them do you think were rich as well as famous? Were their lives happy?

Jane Austen   **Marilyn Monroe**   Anne Frank

Mozart   *Shakespeare*   ANDY WARHOL

Eva Perón   Van Gogh

2 Look at the pictures of the two women. What do you think is the connection between them?

Reading

You are going to read about the English writer, Jane Austen (1775–1817). Since the age of cinema and television her novels have become more and more popular. Why do you think this is?

1   The following sentences have been removed from the text. Read them.
What do you learn about the life and work of Jane Austen?

a   The family often had to entertain themselves at home.

b   Jane Austen herself couldn't possibly have imagined this kind of worldwide fame.

c   Jane must have felt particularly miserable at this time because she found it difficult to continue with her writing.

d   Just as in most romantic novels, you may say, …

e   By this time she was 27, and by the standards of the day, 'on the shelf'.

f   They shouldn't have been written with the sole aim of commercial success.

g   … which may have been started as early as 1793, …

2   Read the text. Where do the sentences go?

Jane Austen
– The hottest writer in
HOLLYWOOD

When the BBC screened its latest adaptation of Jane Austen's novel *Pride and Prejudice*, it was watched by a record 18 million British viewers. The series was then 5 sold to 18 countries round the world, from America to Australia, from Iceland to Israel. There are Jane Austen fans in all corners of the globe, and even special Jane Austen 10 discussion groups on the Internet.

(1) … In her lifetime she never once travelled abroad, indeed she hardly ever left the south of England. When she died a spinster, in 1817, only four of her 15 six novels had been published, all anonymously, and she had earned a grand total of £648.65 from her books. Now, nearly 200 years later, sales of her novels rival modern bestsellers such as 20 John le Carré, reaching 35,000 a week. There have been film and television productions of not only *Pride and Prejudice*, but also *Emma*, *Persuasion*, and the Oscar-winning *Sense and* 25 *Sensibility*. Her house in Chawton in Hampshire is visited by 200 people a day.

The secret of her success

What makes her worldwide success so surprising is the narrowness of 30 **the world her stories portray,** 'three or four families in a country village,' as Jane Austen herself said. However, according to Nigel Nicolson, author of *The World of Jane Austen*, 35 the explanation for her enduring success is very simple: 'Her novels are love stories, always ending in a wedding. **They show a wonderful understanding of the little moves** 40 **that young people made then, and still do make, towards and away from each other**. They are also very funny.' Or, as the author P D James wrote, 'All the books have the same 45 basic plot – searching for and finding the right mate.' (2) … but the difference is that these were written by a genius.

The life and loves of Jane Austen

She was born in 1775, the seventh of eight children. Her father was the Reverend George Austen. They were 55 not well off, and lived in a rambling rectory in the village of Steventon in the Hampshire hills. (3) … By the time she was 12, Jane was writing stories about heroines imprisoned in 60 haunted castles, being rescued by glamorous heroes.

In Jane's own life there were three romantic attachments. The first was a handsome Irish law student called 65 Tom Lefroy, who she met in 1795, but who had to return to Ireland a year

later. The second, in 1801, was a young man called Samuel Blackall, who she fell in love with when on holiday in Devon, but who tragically died suddenly, soon after. The third was a large young man called Harris Bigg-Wither, whose proposal she briefly accepted in 1802, but 'he had nothing to recommend him but his size', so she changed her mind.

(4) … She knew only too well that marriage was important for someone in her position, for the only work suitable for a penniless clergyman's daughter was school teaching or being a governess. Jane wrote to her niece: 'Single women have a dreadful propensity for being poor – which is one very strong argument in favour of matrimony.' Thus in her novels, it is not just love, but also money which makes the institution of marriage so important.

In 1801 the family had moved to Bath, where she was very unhappy. To make matters worse, in 1805 her father died, leaving his widow, Jane and her only sister Cassandra, also unmarried, even poorer than before. For four years they had to move from house to house, often staying with relatives. (5) … Finally in 1809 her brother Edward allowed them to live in a house on his estate in Chawton, only a few miles from Steventon where she had grown up. Here she was much happier, despite being the poor relation, dependent on charity. She not only revised her earlier novels but was able to write new ones, using her experiences to satirize and make fun of the social inequalities she saw around her. At last in 1811, *Sense and Sensibility*, (6) … was the first of her novels to be published.

In 1816, Jane Austen fell ill with a disease of the kidneys. She died on July 18, 1817, in the arms of her sister, Cassandra. She was only 41.

Jane Austen, Hollywood star

The influence of cinema and television has led to worldwide fame for this quiet-living spinster with a sense of fun. People see the movie and then read the book. Not everyone is pleased by this. Winifred Wilson, member of the Jane Austen Society, says, 'These screen adaptations should have kept closer to the text. **They are too heavy on romance and too light on satire.** (7) …' However, the actress Emma Thompson, who adapted *Sense and Sensibility* for the cinema, won't accept this. She says her screenplay is full of satire, and deals with the relationship between love and money. She went to Jane Austen's grave in Winchester Cathedral to say thank you for the Hollywood Oscar she won for the film. As she said at the Oscar ceremony in Los Angeles, 'I do hope Jane knows how big she is in Uruguay.'

Comprehension check

Work in small groups and discuss the answers.

1 What significance do the following names have in relation to Jane Austen?

Steventon – *the village where Jane was born.*

Chawton	Cassandra
The BBC	Nigel Nicolson
The Internet	P D James
Iceland	John le Carré
Bath	Tom Lefroy
Devon	Winifred Wilson
Uruguay	Emma Thompson
Winchester Cathedral	*Emma*
Edward	Oscar

2 What do these numbers in the text refer to?

41	18 (x3)	four (x3)	648.65	200 (x2)	eight	12
1802	1805	1811				

3 Explain the lines in the text in bold in your own words.

What do you think?

– Do you think Jane Austen had a happy life, or do you feel sorry for her?
– Do you think she would have enjoyed the fame she has today?
– In what ways have the lives of women changed since Jane Austen's time?

VOCABULARY AND PRONUNCIATION

Making sentences stronger

1 Adverbs and adjectives that go together

1 Look at the adjectives in the box. Find some with similar meanings. Which adjectives go with which of the adverbs on the left? Why?

very **absolutely**	good bad big starving valuable silly disgusting fabulous funny interesting incredible pleased exhausted delighted clever priceless dirty beautiful hilarious tired ridiculous awful freezing hungry brilliant frightened fascinating terrified surprising huge right filthy fantastic gorgeous cold

2 The adverb *quite* differs in meaning in these two sentences.

> You're **quite right**.
> The film is **quite good**.

In which sentence does *quite* mean *a bit*? In which does it mean *absolutely*?
Give some more examples with the adjectives in the box. What is the rule?

3 **T 8.4** Listen to the short dialogues and complete the gaps.

A That film was _____ _____, wasn't it?

B _____? It was _____ _____!

A You must have been _____ _____ when you passed your exam.

B _____? I was _____ _____!

Make similar short dialogues using adjectives from the box. You could talk about films, books, the weather, holidays, sports, people you know, yourself. Pay particular attention to practising the stress and intonation.

2 Adverbs and verbs that go together

1 Certain intensifying adverbs and verbs often go together. Sometimes there is a logical link. Which verbs in **A** can go with the adverbs in **B**?

A	B
agree	badly
advise	convincingly
behave	distinctly
believe	fully
consider	seriously
forget	sincerely
lie	strongly
recommend	totally
remember	tragically
die	
understand	

2 Underline the correct adverb.

a I *totally/fully* forgot my grandmother's birthday.
b He lied so *convincingly/sincerely* that I *totally/strongly* believed him.
c They *strongly/seriously* advised us to book the tickets in advance.
d I *distinctly/fully* remember packing the sun cream.
e Mozart *tragically/seriously* died when he was still quite young.
f I can't *distinctly/fully* understand what you mean.
g I *absolutely/strongly* adore chocolate ice-cream.
h She is *sincerely/seriously* considering giving up her job.

3 The Oscar ceremony

1 Replace each word underlined with a stronger adjective or adverb.

'I am quite pleased to receive this award. I am very grateful to all those nice people who voted for me. 'Kisses and Dreams' was an interesting movie to work on from start to finish. And I thank all those clever and talented people involved in the making of this very good film. Nobody could have really known that it would be such a big success, especially those who told us at the start that the plot was boring and silly. They have now been proved very wrong. My particular thanks go to Marius Aherne my good director; Julietta Brioche my beautiful co-star; Roger Sims for writing such a funny and exciting story. I really adore you all.'

2 **T 8.5** Listen to the sample answer and compare your choice of adjectives and adverbs.

LISTENING AND WRITING

The greatest superstar of all!

Pre-listening task

1 Look at the posters advertising some musicals. Have you heard of any of them? Who wrote them?

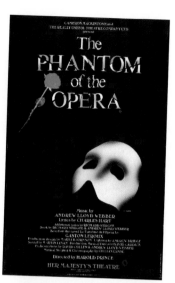

2 **T 8.6** Listen to some song extracts. Do you know which of the musicals above they are from?

3 What is the meaning of the words underlined?

a *It wasn't just a successful show, it was a smash hit.*

b *I wasn't just interested, I was absolutely intrigued.*

c *They didn't just criticize it, they hammered it!*

d *You're not allowed to talk about it. It's a taboo subject.*

Listening

Work in pairs or small groups.

Part one   *The writer*

You will hear an interview with Tim Rice, who wrote the lyrics for *Jesus Christ Superstar*. It was first performed in the 1970s, but has been performed many times since. Andrew Lloyd Webber composed the music.

1 Discuss the following before you listen.

a What are some of the main events in the life of Jesus Christ? Who were some of the main characters in his life?

b Why do you think Tim Rice and Andrew Lloyd Webber chose to write a musical about Jesus Christ?

c Name some famous people that you would call 'superstars'. Why do you think Rice and Lloyd Webber called Jesus Christ a 'superstar'?

d Why do you think some people protested about the musical?

2 **T 8.7**   Listen to the first part. What does Tim Rice say about the questions in 1 above?

3 Are these sentences true or false? Correct the false ones.

a There haven't been many versions of the story of Jesus.

b At first they wanted to write about Judas Iscariot.

c They always knew it would be a success.

d The record was an immediate success in America.

e He saw a baby being christened with the name Jesus Christ Superstar.

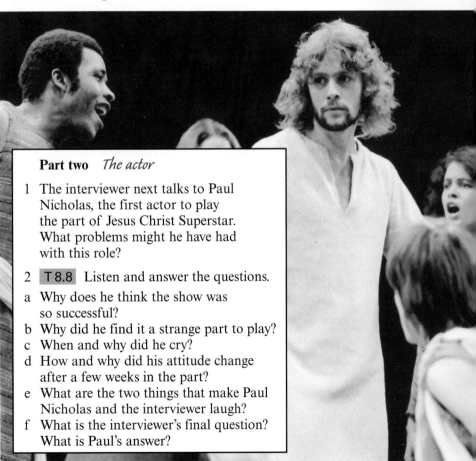

Part two   *The actor*

1 The interviewer next talks to Paul Nicholas, the first actor to play the part of Jesus Christ Superstar. What problems might he have had with this role?

2 **T 8.8**   Listen and answer the questions.

a Why does he think the show was so successful?

b Why did he find it a strange part to play?

c When and why did he cry?

d How and why did his attitude change after a few weeks in the part?

e What are the two things that make Paul Nicholas and the interviewer laugh?

f What is the interviewer's final question? What is Paul's answer?

Writing

A letter from a fan

1 Work in groups. Discuss the following questions. Which famous people do you admire? What do they do? Have you ever belonged to a fan club? Have you ever written a fan letter to anyone who you admire?

2 Read the fan letter written to an actor called Zubin Varla, who played the role of Judas Iscariot in *Jesus Christ Superstar*. What is the aim of each paragraph? Discuss possible endings for each one.

77 Buttermere Rd
High Wycombe
Bucks
March 1st

Dear Zubin

Last weekend my sister and I saw you (for a second time) in your show Jesus Christ Superstar. It was a magical evening and I felt that I just had to write and tell you...

Your voice is truly spectacular, really strong and powerful. I think Judas is an extremely difficult part because everybody knows he is a traitor, and they hate him. But you portrayed him in such a way, and with such passion, that I think we began to understand his confused feelings. The other members of the cast...

I hope you don't mind me writing to you. I expect you get loads of fan letters. I was wondering if you had a fan club of any sort that I could write to. It would be great to find out more about you. I am sixteen and hope to be in a musical when I am older. I go to dance and drama school four times a week. We put on shows every summer, and my teacher says...

Thank you again for a wonderful evening. If you have time, I would be very grateful if...

Good luck in your future career.
Love
Joanna Jackson

PS We're coming to see the show again next week. It would be great if...

3 Write a fan letter to someone who you admire.

PostScript

Exaggeration and understatement

1 Which nationalities have the reputation for being passionate, spontaneous, and temperamental?
Which nationalities are more controlled and reserved?

2 Which of these declarations of love are exaggerated?
Which are understated?

I quite like you, you know. D'you think you might get to like me?

My whole being yearns and burns for you.

You're a dear old thing, and I'm really rather fond of you.

I worship the ground you walk on.

My heart aches to be near you.

3 Match a line in **A** with a line in **B**. Use your dictionary to look up new words.

a ☐   b ☐   c ☐   d ☐   e ☐   f ☐   g ☐   h ☐   i ☐   j ☐   k ☐   l ☐   m ☐

A	B
a I'm starving. I could eat a horse.	1 Yes, it was a nice little break, but all good things must come to an end.
b I'm absolutely dying for a drink.	2 You're not kidding. He's as thick as two short planks.
c His family are pretty well off, aren't they?	3 Yes, my throat's a bit dry, I must say.
d You must have hit the roof when she told you she'd crashed your car.	4 What! He was totally smashed out of his brain!
e I think Tony was a bit tipsy last night.	5 What? That little thing wouldn't hurt a fly!
f I can't stand the sight of him.	6 I know. It *is* a bit wet, but we mustn't grumble, must we?
g He isn't very bright, is he?	7 I'll say. We had to fight our way through millions of people to get to the drinks.
h Look at the weather! It's vile again.	8 OK. I feel a bit out of breath, too.
i What a fantastic holiday!	9 Well, yes, I was a bit upset.
j I'm knackered. Can we stop for a rest?	10 I suppose it did take rather a long time to get here.
k He invited quite a few friends to his party.	11 You can say that again. They're absolutely loaded!
l Well, that journey was absolute hell!	12 I must admit, I'm not too keen on him, either.
m They've got this huge great dog called Wizzer. I'm terrified of it.	13 Yes, I'm a little peckish, too.

Which lines are examples of exaggeration? Which are understatements?

4 **T 8.9** Listen and check your answers. In pairs, practise the dialogues.

Nothing but the truth

9

Questions and negatives
Being polite

Test your grammar

1 Make the sentences negative. Sometimes there is more than one possibility.

a I agree with you.
b I think you're right.
c I told her to go home.
d We had lunch at 12.00.
e I've already done my homework.
f You must get a visa.
g The postman has always got something for me.
h (Who wants an ice-cream?) Me.

2 Write the missing questions.

a '_____ you _____?'

   'Jazz, and rock 'n' roll.'

b '_____ you _____ cinema?'

   'About once a fortnight.'

c '_____ she _____?'

   'She's quite tall, with red hair. She's very nice.'

d '_____?'

   'Christopher Columbus.'

e 'I had a long chat with Helen yesterday.'

   '_____ talk _____?'

   'Oh, this and that.'

LANGUAGE IN CONTEXT

Questions and negatives

1 Think of some lies that these people might tell.

> a young boy to his mother   a car salesman   a politician
> a student to the teacher   an estate agent

2 The people in the cartoons are all lying. Why are they lying? What's the truth?

> Saturday night? Oh, I'm sorry. I'm baby-sitting then, so I can't come. Thanks anyway Mark. 1

> I tripped over the cat as I was coming in last night. 2

> I'm just going round to Laura's to watch telly. I'll be back about 11.00. 4

> I'm having a great time at college. I've made lots of friends, and I go out every evening. My room-mate is OK, but he snores. 5

> I'm in bed. I've got a temperature of 101, and I can't move.

T 9.1 Listen to the truth. Did you guess why they were lying?

3 Match a question to a cartoon. Put a number 1–7 next to each question. Answer the questions.

a ☐ Who wants to speak to me?
b ☐ How is he *really*?
c ☐ I wonder why she doesn't like him.
d ☐ Who's she going out with?
e ☐ What happened last night?
f ☐ What did she buy it for?
g ☐ What's his room-mate like?

● Grammar questions

In the questions in Exercise 3, find …

… questions without an auxiliary verb.
… an indirect question.
… questions with a preposition at the end.
… a question that asks for a general description of someone.
… a question that asks about someone's health.
… another way of asking *Why?*

I really like your new dress. It suits you.

3

I'm afraid Miss Jones is out of the office at the moment. Can I take a message?

7

PRACTICE BANK

1 General knowledge quiz

1 Work in pairs.
Your teacher will give you a quiz.
You don't have the same information.
Ask and answer questions.

Example

Student A	**Student B**
Christopher Columbus discovered America in … (When?)	Christopher Columbus discovered America in 1492.
Pablo Picasso, the Spanish artist, painted *Guernica* in … (When?)	… (Who?) painted the picture *Guernica* in 1937.

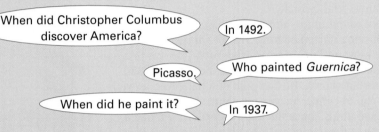

When did Christopher Columbus discover America? — In 1492.

Who painted *Guernica*? — Picasso.

When did he paint it? — In 1937.

2 Make some comments about the answers in the quiz. Some of your sentences might be indirect questions.

Examples
I didn't know | *who wrote 'Dracula'.*
I already knew |
I wonder what the Centennial Exposition in Paris was all about.
I didn't know that Einstein campaigned for nuclear disarmament.

2 Short questions

1 We can answer a statement by asking for more information. These questions can be very short.

Examples
'I went out for a meal last night.' **'Who with?'**
'Tell me a story.' **'What about?'**

Write short questions with a preposition to answer these statements.

a She gave away all her money.
b Can I have a word with you, please?
c I danced all night.
d I need £5,000 urgently.
e Peter's writing a book.
f I got a lovely present today.
g I bought a birthday card today.
h Sh! I'm thinking!
i Do you think you could give me a lift?
j Can you clean the sink, please?

2 Make the short questions into longer ones. Sometimes you need to change the sentences.

Example
Who did you go out for a meal with?
What do you want me to tell you a story about?

T 9.2 Listen and check your answers.

3 Vegetarians don't eat meat

1 **T9.3** Read and listen to this story. There are lots of contradictions in it. Find them.

Example
He's a vegetarian, so he doesn't eat meat. Why was he eating a hot dog?

My mate Stuart is a funny bloke. He's an insomniac, he's dyslexic, and he's an atheist.

He's single, unemployed, and lives all alone in a small basement flat without even a pet for company. Also he's vegetarian and teetotal, and he doesn't touch caffeine. He's pretty anti-social, actually.

I went round to see him last Sunday. As I walked up the drive, his dog started barking. His wife answered the door, and we went upstairs to their living room. He was in a bad mood because he had overslept that morning and had been late for church. He had a bit of a hangover, as well. Over a cup of coffee, he told me about the wild party that they'd had at his house the night before. They'd had a barbecue in the garden with hamburgers and hot dogs. One of his favourite pastimes is crosswords, and he spends all his lunch break at work doing them.

'So how are you, Stuart?' I asked him the other day.

'KO, mate, KO. How about you?'

Anyway, as I said, Stuart's an insomniac, dyslexic, atheist. So the joke is that he lies awake all night wondering about the existence of dog. Get it?

2 Make a negative sentence about these people. Use your dictionary.

> agnostics   vegans
> claustrophobics
> agoraphobics   workaholics
> animal rights campaigners
> traditionalists

4 Who is it?

Describe someone in the room, using only negative sentences. Can the others guess who it is?

> She can't cook.

> She didn't pass the test last week.

> She never arrives on time.

5 Negative questions and pronunciation

1 **T9.4** Read and listen to these questions.

a Do you like seafood?
   Yes, I do.

b Don't you like tea or coffee?
   No, I don't.

c Have you ever been to Russia?
   No, I haven't.

d Haven't you done your homework yet?
   Yes, I have.

e Can you type?
   No, I can't.

f Can't you swim?
   Yes, of course I can!

Which questions express the attitude of the speaker? How does the speaker feel in these questions? In questions d and f, does *Yes* mean *Yes, you are right. I haven't/I can't*? Or does it mean *You are wrong. I **have** done it/I **can** do it*?

2 **T9.5** Listen to the intonation and the contracted forms of the negative questions. Practise saying the questions.

> Don't you ... Can't they ... Aren't you ...
> Hasn't she ever ... Isn't that ... Haven't I ...
> Hasn't the postman ... Weren't you ...
> Didn't you ...

3 In pairs, ask and answer negative questions. Ask about these things. Remember! The person who asks the questions must sound surprised.

have got a dictionary/boyfriend/girlfriend/ computer at home

like pizza/learning English/parties

have ever been to a disco/abroad

come to school yesterday/have anything to eat yesterday

can cook/dance/play the piano

LANGUAGE REVIEW

Questions

Notice these question forms.

1 *How* + adjective/adverb

How | **big** is your car?
| **often** do you come here?

2 *What/which* + noun

What films have you seen recently?
Which newspaper do you read?

3 Prepositions usually go at the end of questions.

*Who did she go out **with**?*
*What did you say that **for**?*

4 There is no inversion (and no *do/does/did*) in subject questions.

Who broke the window?
What happens if I press this button?

5 There is no inversion (and no *do/does/did*) in indirect questions.

*I don't know when the party **starts**.*
*Could you tell me where the station **is**?*

Negatives

Notice how the negative is formed in these sentences.

She | **hasn't** got | any money.
| **doesn't** have |

*She told me **not to lose** her book.*
*I **don't think** it's a good idea.*
*We **never** go **anywhere** interesting.*
*'Who broke the window?' '**Not** me.'*

Negative questions

Negative questions usually express the speaker's surprise about a negative situation.

Haven't you **had** breakfast yet? It's 10 o'clock.
Can't you swim? I thought everyone could swim.
You haven't eaten a thing. **Didn't** you **like** it?

📖 **Grammar Reference: page 157.**

● READING

Mysteries of the universe

Pre-reading task

As you go through your day, do you ever ask yourself any of these questions?

- Why are we here?
- Why are people different?
- When I lose things, where do they go?
- Is the person sitting next to me a time traveller?
- Why did the dinosaurs disappear?
- Is there life on another planet?
- How did the world begin, and how will it end?
- What do animals think about?
- Will we ever find a cure for all disease?

Look at the ten paragraph headings in the reading text on pages 92-3. Which of these topics will be discussed?

Reading

1 Read the texts and answer the questions.

a Why is it most likely that there is life on another planet?
  Will alien life forms look like us?

b What do comets consist of?

c Why is it hard to find a cure for colds?

d What three things came into existence with the Big Bang?
  What happened *before* it?

e Why could genetics explain left-handedness? What is the reason against this explanation?

f What do our body and brain do while we're asleep?

g When do we yawn?
  What happens when we yawn?

h According to the laws of physics, is it possible to travel in time?
  What are scientists worried about?

i What are the two possibilities for the future of the universe?

j What explanations are given for the disappearance of socks?

2 Here are the last sentences from some of the texts. Which text do they belong to?

a Meanwhile, the only thing to do is to rest in bed for a few days.

b But people sharing the same experience, such as students in a boring lecture, may start to imitate each other without realizing it.

c And if this is the case, then they've always been with us!

d However, the wisdom of this training is questionable.

e This suggests that we need dreams as a sort of escape from reality.

f It's a long shot, but imagine the implications if they find what they're looking for!

g If there was a beginning, does that mean there will be an end?

3 What do these numbers refer to in the texts?

50	zero	1.4 billion billion	1929
a few billion		9 to 12 billion	
10 per cent	a third		
billions of years from now		decades	

Mysteries

Here is a list of the top ten mysteries of the universe. What is the answer to these puzzles that have plagued human beings for thousands of years? The answer is 'Nobody knows'.

1 Are we alone in the universe?

Probably not. Just the size of the universe makes it unlikely. Alien life forms might not be too far away, either. This year American astronomers discovered a planet capable of sustaining life just 50 light-years away.

But alien life almost certainly won't be like us. Biochemists have calculated that the chances of the chemical combinations necessary to produce life are minute. The possibility that alien life forms will resemble us is zero. NASA is planning a huge deep-space telescope to search for signs of alien life.

2 Where do the oceans come from?

While the world's seas and oceans have been home to life for over three billion years, the origin of the 1.4 billion billion tonnes of water that they collectively contain remains a mystery. It seems to have condensed out of the early earth's atmosphere, but how it got there in the first place isn't known.

One possible theory is that it was dropped on our planet by comets. These gigantic chunks of frozen vapour and dust are rich in water. According to some scientists, satellite pictures have shown that tiny comets continue to hit the earth, topping up our oceans all the time.

3 WILL THERE EVER BE A CURE FOR THE COMMON COLD?

Perhaps, but not yet. The big challenge facing scientists trying to rid mankind of this misery is finding a drug that can combat the huge and ever-changing variety of cold viruses. Researchers are looking for features that all such viruses share. Whichever drug company comes up with something is guaranteed to make a fortune.

4 How old is the universe?

The date of the Big Bang has caused astronomers trouble since they discovered that the universe was expanding in 1929. At the time, measurements of the rate of expansion suggested an age of a few billion years. Latest figures, using the Hubble Space Telescope, suggest nine to twelve billion years.

But what happened before the Big Bang? No one knows. According to current theories of the birth of the universe, not only matter but also space and time came into being with the Big Bang. If correct, these theories imply that there was no 'before' the Big Bang. However, this proposition raises many fundamental questions.

of the universe

5 Why are some people left-handed?

About 10 per cent of the population is left-handed, and it seems to run in families. The cause, therefore, seems obvious: genetics. However, identical twins, who have identical genetic blueprints, aren't necessarily both left-handed or right-handed. This would appear to disprove the theory that being left-handed is inherited.

Even at birth most babies tend to move one arm, usually the right, more than the other. Some scientists believe that the use of left hand or right hand is a result of the baby's environment. Most children can be trained to use and to prefer the right hand for any activity.

6 WHY DO WE SLEEP?

On average we spend a third of our lives sleeping, but no one really knows why. The most popular theory is that sleeping gives the body and brain a chance to recover from the stresses of the day. But beyond this vague statement, we don't know what this recuperation consists of. Warm-blooded species, including humans, birds, and mammals, seem to need more sleep than cold-blooded creatures such as fish and reptiles, so there is a possibility that we sleep in order to save energy. Sleep deprivation produces hallucinations.

7 WHY IS YAWNING INFECTIOUS?

This is a tough one. No one even knows what purpose yawning serves at all. But we do know that fatigue, boredom, and anxiety can trigger off a yawn.

Like crying and laughing, yawning is a variant of normal breathing. Yawning is a reflex action, not under conscious control. The mouth opens wide and you take a longer, deeper breath than usual. Yawning momentarily raises the heart rate, forcing more blood to the brain. One theory is that yawning makes you more alert by making you breathe in more.

Yawning isn't infectious in the clinical sense of the word.

8 Does nature allow time travel?

Amazingly, there is nothing in the known laws of physics to prevent us from zooming off into the past or future. Exactly how one would build a time-machine is anyone's guess, but many scientists have a bigger worry – paradoxes such as killing your mother before she gave birth to you. Maybe Nature has a clever way of getting round these. Or maybe there's an as yet undiscovered barrier to time travel. But just think! If at any time in the future time travel becomes possible, then time travellers are with us now!

9 HOW WILL THE UNIVERSE END?

This depends on how much matter exists in the cosmos. If it exceeds the so-called critical density, gravity will bring the current cosmic expansion to a halt and trigger a contraction or implosion billions of years from now. Alternatively, the universe may expand for ever. After decades of research, astronomers still don't know precisely how much matter exists in the universe, and so cannot predict accurately how the universe will end. The consensus, however, is that the cosmos will expand for ever.

10 Where do all the odd socks go to?

Open any sock drawer and you'll find odd socks. Theories about what happens to them range from disappearing down black holes in the universe to being eaten by washing machines. Another explanation is that in every house there lurks a place where all the missing things live …

What do you think?

Which mysteries do you find the most interesting? What mysteries would you like answered?

Why do I never have enough money?
What will life be like in 2050?
Why is my bus never on time?

VOCABULARY

Making connections in texts

1 Antonyms and synonyms often
  occur in texts. Which are
  the antonyms and synonyms in
  these sentences?

*If there was a beginning, does that
mean there will be an end?
… gravity will bring the current
cosmic expansion to a halt and
trigger a contraction …
… astronomers still don't know
precisely how much matter exists in
the universe, and so cannot
predict accurately …*

2 Write in antonyms for these words.

Word	Antonym
huge	
happiness	
guilty	
criticize	
reward	
cruelty	
dangerous	
succeed	
genuine	
improve	
admit	
permanent	
profit	
brave	
attack	
crazy	

3 What's the opposite of … ?

a tough question	fair hair
tough meat	a fair decision
rich food	a sweet apple
a rich person	sweet wine
a strong man	a hard exam
a strong taste	a hard mattress
clear instructions	a free man
a clear sky	a free seat

4 There can be near antonyms in a text.
  *Peter said he **understood** the lecture, but it **didn't make any sense** to me at all.*
  The word class can change, for example from adjective to noun.
  *At first they thought the picture was **genuine**, but then it was found to be
  a **fake**.*

5 Complete the sentences with words from the box. Put the words in the
  correct form.

> improve safe casualty mystery solve succeed criticize fail
> survive good fun encourage a disaster get worse danger

a He's a very _____ businessman, but he has always _____ to
  find happiness.

b I thought the party would be _____, but it was _____ from start
  to finish. I didn't know anyone and I didn't speak to anyone.

c I'm pleased to say that there have been many _____ in your behaviour
  this term, but unfortunately your work _____.

d 'Were there many _____ in the accident?' 'No, it was a miracle.
  Everyone _____.'

e I tried to fix my computer, but the instructions were a total _____ to
  me. Fortunately, my son _____ the problem in five seconds.

f Bungee jumping sounds _____, but it's _____ enough if
  you're careful.

g Our teacher is strict, but fair. He can be very _____ if we make silly
  mistakes, but he does give us lots of _____ if we've tried hard.

6 What is the effect of using antonyms in these sentences?

*'Jenny's **thick**, isn't she?' 'Well, she isn't very **bright**, it's true.'
'What **lousy** weather!' 'No, it's not very **nice**, is it?'*

In pairs, write similar dialogues. How could you describe the following both
honestly and tactfully?

> a terrible dinner party   an awful holiday   an unsuccessful meeting
> an uncomfortable hotel   a terrible football match   a difficult exam

● LISTENING AND SPEAKING

Saying 'I won't'

Pre-listening task

1 When did you last go to a wedding? Whose was it? Where was it? What happened?

2 What do you need to do if you plan to get married? What preparations are necessary for the actual wedding day? Write a list and then compare it with a partner's.

3 Look at the photos of Elizabeth, George, and Nicole. They each have a story about a wedding. The cartoons tell part of their story. What can you see? Discuss what you think has happened.

Elizabeth

George

Nicole

Listening

1 **T 9.6** Read and listen to the introduction to a radio programme.

> This is Radio 4. This week in File on Life **Saying 'I won't'** or **What stopped the wedding?**
>
> The photographer may be booked, the cake may be iced, and the dress may fit perfectly, but suddenly it's all off. What stops the wedding and forces one half of the happy couple into saying 'I won't'? Listen to the stories of Elizabeth, George, and Nicole.

2 Look at the cartoons below. What do you think stopped the weddings of Elizabeth, George, and Nicole?

3 Listen to the rest of the programme. Are your ideas correct? What exactly do the cartoons above and below illustrate?

Comprehension check

Answer the questions about each of the stories.

1 Who was he/she going to get married to?

2 Why didn't he/she get married?

3 Who called off the wedding in each case?

4 Which other people are mentioned? What part do they play in the stories?

5 Who said these lines? What are they referring to?

a *He was like my brother.*

b *... he thrust a piece of paper in my hand and ran.*

c *... it was a really smashing day.*

d *Come on, it's just nerves.*

e *... she couldn't fill the forms in, she had a panic attack.*

f *It was such a relief, it was like a cork coming out of a bottle, it all just poured out.*

g *All I can remember is dancing non-stop.*

h *... I just can't do it, I can't face it.*

i *We had so much in common.*

6 Imagine you are these people.
Elizabeth's mother (story 1)
Vicky (story 2)
A wedding guest (story 3)

Retell each story from that person's point of view.

The song

1 **T 9.7** Listen to the whole song. Can you remember any of the words?

2 Turn to page 140. Read the words and listen to the song.

WRITING

Joining sentences

1 Sentences can be joined using conjunctions. Conjunctions introduce clauses such as time, reason, result, purpose, condition, and contrast.

Time	Reason	Result	Purpose	Condition	Contrast
when(ever)	because	so ... that	so that	if	but
while	as	such ... that	in case	unless	although
as (soon as)	since			as long as	even though
until	so				
after					
since					

Your teacher will give you an exercise on conjunctions.

2 Some adverbs express the speaker's attitude to what is being said.

What a terrible journey! **Anyway**, *you're here now, so come on in!*
Anyway means I want to change the subject.
Actually, *my name's Peter, not Tom.*
I'm going out tonight, **actually**. *Sorry I can't help.*

Actually is used to make what you're saying softer, especially if you're correcting someone, disagreeing, or complaining.

3 Here is a witness's account of a crime. Choose the best expressions to join the sentences.

It happened at about 6.00 yesterday evening, (a) *while/after* I was coming home from work. (b) *Because/Whenever* I can, I walk to work (c) *if not/except* when it's raining, (d) *because/so that* I like the exercise. (e) *In fact/Anyway*, I was coming down Station Road, and (f) *just as/since* I was walking past number 38, I heard a noise. It was (g) *so/such* a loud noise that I stopped. It sounded (h) *as/as if* a chest of drawers had been knocked over. I know that a lot of old people live alone on this street, so (i) *naturally/surely* I was a little concerned. (j) *Firstly/At first*, I didn't know what to do. I went up to the front door and listened (k) *for see/to see* if I could hear anything. (l) *Of course/In fact*, the front door was ajar, (m) *so/then* I pushed the door and went in. It was (n) *so/such* dark that I couldn't see anything, (o) *but/although* my eyes soon got used to it.

I went into the dining room, and there on the floor was the body of an old man. He had been attacked. (p) *Even though/As soon as* I saw him, I was scared (q) *in case/unless* the burglar was (r) *still/always* in the house. I knelt down to feel his pulse.

(s) *However/Although* he had been badly beaten up, he was still alive, (t) *fortunately/obviously*. I went to look for a damp cloth (u) *because/so that* I could bathe his wounds, then found his phone and dialled 999. I stayed with him (v) *until/unless* the ambulance arrived, and (w) *when/by the time* the police came, he had woken up and was talking about the attack. (x) *Apparently/Actually*, he had been working in his garden when a man had jumped on him. He didn't see him, and he didn't hear him, (y) *as well/either*.

The old man is now in hospital, and (z) *as soon as/as long as* he takes things easy, he should make a complete recovery.

PostScript

Being polite

1 What are 'white lies'? What would you say in these situations?

- You're having a meal with your host family. You've forced yourself to eat something you really don't like, when your host says, 'You must have some more!'
- A friend has just had a baby who you think looks like any other new-born baby. 'Isn't he absolutely gorgeous?' she coos. What do you say?

2 **T 9.8** Listen to the pairs of dialogues. One is more polite than the other. Say which one is more polite, and why.
In pairs, look at the tapescripts and practise the dialogues.

3 Make these requests more polite. Use the expressions below.

Give me a lift.	What's the time?
Lend me your pen.	Where is there a phone?
Help me find my glasses.	When do we have lunch?

Could you … ?	*Do you think you could … ?*
Would you mind … ?	*Do you know … ?*
I wonder if you could … ?	*Do you happen to know … ?*

4 **T 9.9** Listen to the requests and invitations, and refuse them politely. Use one of these expressions.

That's very kind of you, but …	I'd love to, but …
I'm terribly sorry. I'm afraid I …	
Believe me, I would if I could, but …	

T 9.10 Listen and compare your answers.

5 **T 9.11** You are going to a dinner party in London. Your name is Pat. Listen to the conversation, and when you hear a *Ping!* you must speak! You have brought some flowers for your hosts.

4 Write a description of a crime or accident through the eyes of a witness. Write about 350 words.

10 Things ain't what they used to be!

Expressing habit
Time expressions

Test your grammar

1 Read the sentences and <u>underline</u> those words which express habit and frequency.

a I very rarely go to church.
b My Aunt Dora used to go to church regularly.
c I usually watch my son's football matches.
d My father used to watch me playing football.
e I have to take this medicine regularly.
f We occasionally visit my uncle in Scotland.
g We used to stay with my grandparents in the country.
h We'd go skating on the village pond.

i She hardly ever writes home but she often phones.
j She'll frequently e-mail us.
k My computer's *always* breaking down.

Which of the sentences express present habit? Which express past habit?

2 How often do you think the actions in Exercise 1 happen or happened? Use the time expressions in the boxes.

Examples
My children go to the dentist <u>regularly</u>.
We <u>used to</u> walk in the park.

They go to the dentist twice a year.
We used to walk/walked in the park every Sunday.

once	a day		day
twice	a week		year
three times	a fortnight	every	weekend
	a month		Christmas
	a year		Sunday

LANGUAGE IN CONTEXT

Past and present habit

1 Look at the photograph and read about a lady called Rosemary Sage. Discuss with a partner which words could complete the gaps.

LIVING HISTORY

Rosemary Sage is 100 years old. She lives in the village of Hambledon, Surrey. Many people (a) _____ daily from Hambledon to work in London. Rosemary has only been to London once in her life, when she went to the zoo sixty years ago! Her daily routine goes back to a time before there were any commuters in the village. It never varies. At the start of each day she (b) _____ wood for the fire, on which she (c) _____ a large kettle of water. Then she (d) _____ some of the water to her wash-house in the garden and she (e) _____ . Next she (f) _____ a cup of tea. She has no means of heating or cooking apart from the open fire. Her home is like a working museum, and her clear memory is a precious source of knowledge of old country ways. She (g) _____ stories of when she was young. In those days the Lord and Lady of the Manor (h) _____ all

2 The words below are the actual words which appeared in the original newspaper article. Put them into the correct gaps in the text.

> gathers and chops   commute
> 'll boil   would freeze over
> used to own   'll get washed
> 'll make herself   'll carry
> 'm used to   'd go skating
> 's always telling   'd spend
> rented   get used to

T 10.1 Listen and check your answers.

3 Discuss the ways in which your ideas for filling the gaps differed from the actual words and verb forms used.

the cottages and they (i) _____ them to the villagers for 2s 9d (14p) a week. Every winter the village pond (j) _____ and she (k) _____ with her six brothers and sisters. Every summer they (l) _____ one day at the seaside. Other than that and her one trip to London, she has hardly ever left the village. She is perfectly content with her life. She has no bath, no fridge, and no telephone. 'I could never (m) _____ such 'modern' appliances at my age,' she says. 'I (n) _____ the old ways. I'm far too old to change.'

● Grammar questions

– In which of the following sentences can *used to* be used? In which can *would* be used? In which can neither be used? Why?

> *We lived in London when I was a child.*
> *We went to the park every Sunday.*
> *We went to the zoo last Sunday.*

– Which of the pairs of sentences below express the speaker's attitude? What *is* the attitude?

a	*Our cat plays*	
	Our cat'll play	*with a ball of string for hours.*
b	*Our cat is **always** playing*	
	*Our cat **will** play*	*on the kitchen table.*

Put the sentences into the past.

PRACTICE BANK

1 Discussing grammar

Work in pairs. Discuss which sentence in **B** *best* continues the sentence in **A**.

	A	B
a	My grandfather smokes a pipe. He'll sit and smoke it every evening after dinner. He *will* smoke it at the dinner table.	My mother gets really annoyed at this. He always enjoys doing this. It's a habit he's had for over fifty years.
b	We once went skiing in Colorado. We used to go to skiing in Colorado.	We'd fly to Denver and then we'd drive up into the Rockies. We flew to Denver and then we drove up into the Rockies.
c	John usually does the cooking, John used to do the cooking, John's used to doing the cooking, John's getting used to doing the cooking,	because he's been doing it for so many years. but he isn't tonight. but he doesn't any more. but it's taking a long time.
d	It rained on my wedding day. It *would* rain on my wedding day.	Everybody got very wet. This is so typical of the kind of thing that happens to me.
e	He always brings Mel to our parties, He's *always* bringing Mel to our parties,	which is just fine by us. and nobody can stand her! It drives us crazy!

2 Listening and speaking

1 You are going to hear Kathy talking about her first friend, Gillian. Read some information about Gillian and look up any new words in your dictionary. Do you think they are still friends?

My First Friend

a *She used to live up the road in a big white house.*
b *We used to go to the same school but we never used to see much of each other at school.*
c *Her dad used to have a really good job.*
d *We fought a lot.*
e *We both used to love going to the cinema.*
f *We learned all of the words of the songs.*
g *We'd have these huge rows.*
h *I thought she was spoilt rotten.*
i *She always got four flavours and an ice lolly.*
j *She never shared a thing. She was always bursting into tears.*
k *She once fell off her bike and broke her front teeth.*
l *I used to go on holiday to Blackpool with her and her Auntie Ethel.*

2 **T 10.2** Listen very carefully to all that Kathy says. There are some small differences in each of the sentences. Change them to *exactly* what you hear. Careful! One of the sentences is *not* on the tape. Mark it with a ✗.

3 Go through the sentences a–l with a partner and for each one try to remember some of the extra information you heard. Listen again to check.

4 Prepare a short talk about *either* one of your first friends *or* one of your first teachers. Give it to the rest of the class and answer any questions they may have.

3 Short answers and pronunciation

1 Complete the answers. Use *usually*, *used to*, or a form of *be/get used to*, in the positive and the negative. Add any other necessary words.

Examples
'Do you translate every word when you read?'
'No, but I *used to*.'

'You didn't like your new teacher, did you?'
'No, but we soon *got used to* her.'

a How often do you get homework?
Well, we _____ twice a week.

b Do you read many books in English?
Well, yes, I do now, but I _____ .

c Do you find it easy to use your monolingual dictionary?
I didn't at first, but I soon _____ .

d Do you look up every word that you can't understand?
Well, I don't now, but I _____ when I was a beginner.

e How can you understand English when it is spoken so quickly?
Well, I suppose I _____ .

f Did you do much pronunciation practice when you were first learning English?
Oh, yes we did. We _____ every lesson.

g How do you find using the telephone in English?
It's not easy, but I think that gradually I _____ .

2 **T 10.3** Listen and check your answers. Practise the questions and answers with a partner. Go through them again and change the answers so that they are true about you.

LANGUAGE REVIEW

Verbs forms expressing habit

Present habit

1 The Present Simple is the most common tense for expressing present habit. It is often used with adverbs of frequency.
*He **usually** travels by train.*

2 *Will* expresses characteristic behaviour. This is how you expect someone or something to behave. It is usually contracted, and not stressed.
*She**'ll spend** hours just staring out of the window.*
*In Canada it**'ll snow** for days without stopping.*

3 The Present Continuous can be used to express an annoying habit with adverbs of frequency such as *always*, *continually*, and *constantly*.
*I**'m always losing** my car keys.*

4 *Will*, when decontracted and stressed, can also express annoying behaviour.
*She **WILL** put on the radio whenever I'm trying to work!*

Past habit

1 *Would* is the past form of *will* above.
*She**'d spend** hours just staring out of the window.*
*She **WOULD** put on the radio whenever I was trying to work!*

2 *Used to* expresses past states and actions.
Used is a verb.
*He **used to be** rich.* (= a state)
*He **used to do** his homework while watching TV.* (= an action)

Would can be used to express a past action, but not a past state.
*He**'d do** his homework while watching TV.*
NOT ~~He'd be~~ …

Be/get used to + noun/-ing

Here, *used* is an adjective. It means *familiar with or accustomed to as a result of experience.*

*I was brought up on a farm, so I**'m used to** hard work.*
*I lived in the country for twenty years, but I**'m slowly getting used to** living in a city.*

📖 **Grammar Reference: page 157.**

● VOCABULARY

Money, money, money!

1 All the words in columns **A** and **B** have something to do with money. Match a word in **A** with its *closest opposite* in **B**. Use your dictionary to check new words.

A	B
generous	waste
spendthrift	second-hand
luxury	well off
brand new	loss
hard up	stingy
deposit (v)	expenditure
save	overdrawn
in the black	penny-pincher
debt	withdraw
tight-fisted	extravagant
income	priceless
worthless	millionaire
beggar	necessity
profit	loan

2 Complete the following sentences, including words from **A** or **B**.

a Tom couldn't afford a brand new car …

b Do you see that vase? We thought it was worthless. I paid only 50p for it in a jumble sale, but …

c I think that nowadays a car is a necessity, but my grandmother says …

d My two daughters are so different. One regularly saves her pocket money, the other …

e Susie's always getting into debt and then she has to go to her father …

f I was so sure my account was in the black, but I've just got an angry letter …

g You'd never believe that he used to be a millionaire, now …

h Ted's so tight-fisted. He's worn the same suit every day for work for 15 years, but his wife …

i Anna's always complaining about being hard up, but compared to me …

j Mr Micawber's advice to his young friend, David Copperfield, in the year 1850:

'Annual _____ £20, annual _____ £19 and six shillings, result happiness.

Annual _____ £20, annual _____ £20 and six pence, result misery.'

3 Would you be happy or miserable if you:
- fell on hard times?
- lived on a shoestring?
- lived in the lap of luxury?
- were living rough?
- couldn't make ends meet?
- were rolling in money?
- had to penny-pinch?
- were made of money?
- were down and out?
- had to tighten your belt?
- had a business that was doing a roaring trade?
- lost a quid and found a fiver?

● READING AND SPEAKING

MONEY MAKES THE WORLD GO ROUND

Work in pairs or small groups.

Pre-reading task

You are going to read about four very different people, and the role that money plays in their lives. Discuss these questions.

1 The texts are about an aristocrat, a divorced mum, a taxman, and a miser. Which of them do you think is wealthy? Who is poor? What attitude do you think each has to money? How do their lifestyles differ?

2 The following words were said by one of the four people. Who said what? There are two statements for each person. Check any new words in your dictionary.

a 'Money's been tight since I split up from my husband four years ago.'

b 'In my job it's possible to become a bit of a social leper.'

c 'I don't believe one should spend what one hasn't got.'

d 'I'll organize an office collection for earthquake victims, but I won't give anything myself.'

e 'I'd baulk at buying a couple of packets of crisps as well.'

f 'Sometimes I'll go wild and buy something just to cheer myself up, but I always regret it.'

g 'We always do our own repairs to the house, or we'll put a bucket out to catch the leaks if we can't.'

h 'People think I've got a fortune stashed away somewhere.'

Reading

1 Read all *four* texts quickly and find out who said what. Were there any surprises? Which of the four is the richest? Who is the poorest?

2 Choose *two* of the texts and read them more carefully. Answer the questions.

a What is his/her job? How much does he/she earn?
b Does he/she get on well with his wife/her husband?
c What does he/she say about clothes and food?
d What else does he/she spend money on?
e Does he/she give any money to charities or good causes?
f In what ways does he/she try to save money?
g Does he/she have any extravagances?
h What do you learn about his/her friends and/or family?

Speaking

1 Find someone who chose different texts from you. Go through the questions together and compare the information.

2 Which people do these words describe? Why?

> thrifty   skinflint   well off   hard up
> privileged   underprivileged

3 Discuss how money (or the lack of it!) affects your life.

PEOPLE AND THEIR MONEY

Who's rich and who's poor these days? Gina Brooks tracks down four people from very different walks of life.

THE ARISTOCRAT

LADY CHRYSSIE COBBOLD, 58, lives in Knebworth House, Hertfordshire, the family home of her husband David, 60, a financier. They have four grown-up children.

'Knebworth House is run as a business but it doesn't make enough money to pay us. I have no regular salary. I never really spend money because I don't have it and I'm not bothered about clothes. I spend about £2,000 a year on them. There have been moments when we thought we might have to sell the house, but now I think there'll be enough money for the next generation to keep the house, but they won't inherit much more than that.

Money is the only thing my husband and I row about. I'm always worrying about money. I don't believe one should spend what one hasn't got. My husband likes having parties, going to restaurants, having guests for the weekend. In summer we'll have up to 16 people at weekends. They're usually quite good and they'll bring a bottle of wine, but they still have to be fed.

We always do our own repairs to the house or we'll put a bucket out to catch the leaks if we can't. I'll go to any lengths to save money. I'll put up wallpaper, do all the painting, make curtains and upholstery. As a child I used to get only 5p a week pocket money and I'd do anything to get more money. I'd even pick bunches of flowers from our garden and sell them to the local funeral parlour.

If you have a big house, people think you must be well off, but it just isn't true.'

THE DIVORCED MUM

ANGIE CROSS, 27, has four children, aged from 5 to 10. She lives in Frinton-on-Sea in Essex. She gets £585 a month state benefit and also works as a part-time barmaid for £21 a week.

'Money's been tight since I split up from my husband four years ago. The kids always come first, but special occasions for them are rare. They're lucky if we go to McDonald's once a month. All their school uniforms are second-hand. When I was a kid I used to get lots of treats. I'd go riding and I used to have piano lessons. I feel dreadful not being able to give my kids the things I had. Every month I work out exactly what has to be paid and what can wait. I have to be very careful with money, and that doesn't come easily because by nature I'm very extravagant. My biggest extravagance now is a packet of ten cigarettes.

My monthly food bill comes to about £350, and towards the end of the month we have beans on toast three nights out of seven. I usually make the kids a packed lunch for school, but occasionally I don't have enough food to make one, so I tell the kids to have a school dinner and say they've forgotten their dinner money. It's not really telling lies because I'll always pay as soon as I can.

I get very depressed and I frequently sit down and cry. Sometimes I'll go wild and buy something just to cheer myself up, but I always regret it. I once spent £30 on some clothes but I felt really guilty. What I want more than anything else is a holiday and new shoes for the kids. Who knows? I might win the lottery!'

THE TAXMAN

BOB WILDEN, 24, is a tax inspector. He earns £23,558 per annum. His wife, Denise, 20, earns £7,500 as a part-time secretary. They live in Maidenhead, Berkshire. They have no children.

'I'm mean in some ways, generous in others. I'll be first at the bar to buy a round of drinks, but I'd baulk at buying a couple of packets of crisps as well. I'll go hungry rather than stop for a snack at a motorway service station. We always buy food in bulk so it's cheaper. We frequently cook in bulk, too, and put it in the freezer. Denise and I never row about money. We both indulge ourselves now and then. She'll spend £40 at the hairdresser's and I won't penny-pinch on the kind of malt whisky I get. I never spend much on clothes though, probably about £95 at the most. I don't need to look smart to be a taxman.

Denise generally gives £20 a month to animal charities, but she won't donate to beggars wearing £100 trainers. I'll give the real down-and-outs a quid sometimes. My widowed mum is a pensioner and lives alone, so I always make sure that she has enough to eat.

I have four credit cards, but one is never used. A bill for £700 arrived this morning for one of them. It frightened us to death. Occasionally we have to get loans to clear our credit card debts. In my job it's possible to become a bit of a social leper. Some friends are always boasting to me about how they dodge paying tax. I don't like that. I don't like paying tax either, but I'd never dodge it.'

THE MISER

MALCOLM STACEY, 38, is a part-time BBC journalist and author of two books about money. He earns £50,000 per annum. He lives in York with his wife Jo, 32. They have two young children.

'I never buy luxuries and I never buy a round of drinks. When colleagues go out to the pub, I'll stay in the office and say I'm expecting a phone call. I'll never invite people to dinner, but I never feel guilty about accepting their invitations. I know they invite me to have someone interesting to talk to. The meanest thing I've ever done was to go to a wedding without a present. I just took some wrapping paper and a tag saying 'Love from Malcolm' and put it onto the table with the other presents. I got a thank-you letter from the bride. She obviously thought she'd mislaid the present.

People don't believe I can be so stingy. I'll organize an office collection for earthquake victims but I won't give anything myself. I've put a wishing well in the front garden. I would never ask passers-by to throw money in, but I collect it when they do. I hardly ever use my car; we grow our own vegetables and we recycle everything. We never buy new clothes, we get them second-hand from charity shops for about £2 a garment. We can live on £5 a week.

I've always been mean. When I was a child I would never buy flowers for Mum, but I'd give her a bouquet from her own garden. My wife gets embarrassed by my meanness, but we never row about money. People think I've got a fortune stashed away somewhere. I don't care what they think.'

Language work

Hot Verbs (4): come and go

There are many common expressions with the verbs *come* and *go*. These examples come from the texts.

I'll go to any lengths ...
The kids always come first ...
My monthly food bill comes to about £350 ...
Sometimes I'll go wild ...

Decide which verb fits these sentences.

a Mini-skirts *came/went* into fashion in the 1960s.
b Ugh! The milk's *come/gone* sour!
c I don't feel old, but I'm beginning to *go/come* grey.
d This sweater won't *go/come* in my suitcase. I'll have to carry it.
e Jane and I have *come/gone* to an agreement. I'll shop if she cooks.
f 'It's my dream to meet someone famous.' 'I hope your dream *goes/comes* true.'
g Most of my money *comes/goes* on bills.
h With coffees and VAT, your bill *goes/comes* to £90.
i How did your interview *go/come*?
j Britain *came/went* second in the 100 metres.
k I think I must be *going/coming* mad.
l The time has *come/gone* to make a decision.
m My brother's business *came/went* bankrupt.
n That tie *goes/comes* really well with your jacket.
o Everything will *come/go* right in the end.

● LISTENING

HOMELESSNESS

Pre-listening task

Discuss the questions as a class.

1 Where do people live when they have no home? How do they live?
2 Who are they? How could they have ended up homeless?
3 Do you think politicians are interested in the problem? Why/why not?

Part 1 Listening

T 10.4 Listen to a radio interview with Oliver McGechy, who runs a home for alcoholics and homeless people in Guildford, a wealthy town near London. Answer the questions.

a Why is Oliver particularly suited to running a home for alcoholics and homeless people?
b What is the average lifespan for homeless people in Europe? How is this moving back to Victorian days?
c What is just 'the tip of the iceberg'?
d What is Oliver referring to when he says … ?
'… they've probably lost all of the network which has supported them within society.'
'… they're into a downward spiral …'
'… there's little political gain in supporting homeless people.'
e Who are the people who become homeless?
f What question does Oliver ask the interviewer?

Part 2 Listening and reading

The second person to be interviewed is Chris Caine, aged 33, who is staying in the home that Oliver runs.

1 Chris is a Londoner and speaks with quite a strong London accent. Read the exact transcript of the first part of what he says. Try to work out what he is saying. What differences do you notice from standard English?

I Chris, can you tell us why it was that you ended up homeless?
CC Well, I 'ad a house wiv a woman that I … er took on, wiv 'er kids and I 'ad a job'n all, workin' at the Royal Mail Post Office … erm I dunno about … what … er two, two years it was into the relationship and all of a sudden, like, she just wanted out, so … er I tried to patch fings up which really didn't work, yer know, so I ended up going back to the woods, well, yer know where I was before …
I Back to the woods?
CC Yeah.
I How d'you mean? Literally to the woods?
CC Yeah. I used to live out in the woods.

2 Your teacher will give you a copy of the complete interview with Chris. Listen and read at the same time. Answer the questions.

a How did Chris become homeless?
b What does the interviewer express surprise about?
c Why does Chris feel more at ease living in the woods than in the town?
d Why did he leave the woods? What did he use to do there?
e What jobs has he had?
f What does he miss most about not having a home? Does he enjoy being alone?
g What hurts Chris most of all?
h Where do homeless people sleep?
i Which takes Chris the longest to get used to, being on the road or living with the rest of society?

Part 3 Listening

Listen to the conclusion of the programme. What does Chris say about drink? Do you think that Chris has a good chance of getting a job and a home again?

Discussion

These were the opening words of the interviewer.

'Why is it that, even in the richest countries in the world, there are so many homeless people?'

Which rich countries do you know of where homelessness is a problem? Is there a problem of homelessness in your country? If so, do you know any reasons for it? How do you feel about homeless people? Do you try to help if you can? Why/Why not?

Writing about a period in history

1 Choose a time in the history of your country that interests you and do some research into the kind of lives people used to lead then. Try to find out information about the following topics:

   Homes and Food   Health
   Pastimes   Education

2 Which period did you choose? Why? Discuss your findings as a class.

3 Read the text about Britain in the time of the Tudors. Check new words in your dictionary. Write in the correct paragraph headings from Exercise 1.

LIFE IN TUDOR BRITAIN

The Tudors ruled Britain from 1485 to 1603. Henry VIII and Elizabeth I were both Tudor monarchs.

∍ 1 _____

Tudor towns were very small and overcrowded. The cobbled streets were narrow, filthy, and very unhealthy. Few people lived to be older than 40, and children often died before they were five. Open sewers carried the filth to the nearest river, rats and flies thrived, spreading diseases such as typhus and plague.

∍ 2 _____

The rich lived in mansions in the countryside. These were very big with up to 150 servants. They had a great many chimneys because so many fires were needed to keep the vast rooms warm, and to cook the food for their huge feasts, which consisted of up to ten courses. They would regularly eat venison, blackbirds, and larks but rarely had potatoes because although explorers such as Sir Walter Raleigh had brought them to Britain, they were not, as yet, grown very frequently by British farmers. Honey was normally used to sweeten food; sugar was only rarely available, but when they did have it, they put it on all their food, including meat! The poor never had sugar or potatoes and seldom ate meat. They would occasionally catch rabbits and fish but most of the time they ate bread and vegetables such as cabbage and turnips.

∍ 3 _____

Poorer children never went to school. Children from better-off families had tutors to teach them reading and French. However, boys were often sent to schools which belonged to the monasteries and there they would learn mainly Latin in classes of up to 60 boys. The school day went from dawn until dusk, and the schoolmasters would frequently beat their pupils.

∍ 4 _____

The rich used to go hunting to kill deer and wild boar for their feasts. They also enjoyed fencing and jousting contests. The poor watched bear fighting and also played a kind of football where they jumped on each other, often breaking their necks and backs. There were some theatres and people enjoyed watching plays, particularly those of a young playwright called William Shakespeare.

PostScript

Time expressions

1 Use your dictionary and check that you understand the meaning of the words underlined in **A**.

A	B
a I've been <u>brushing up</u> my German	in the olden days.
b I <u>came across</u> this old newspaper <u>cutting</u>	all day long.
c We <u>made it</u> to the airport	by Friday at the latest.
d Despite the <u>blizzard</u> our plane took off	some time soon.
e I have to <u>put up with</u> this <u>poky</u> office	many years ago.
f They've promised to fax us the <u>trade figures</u>	lately.
g I'll get <u>in touch</u> with James	Take your time!
h He <u>moans</u> about the weather	It's a waste of time.
i We used to go <u>rambling</u> in the hills	in record time.
j He'll sit in his chair, <u>muttering</u> to himself	for hours upon end.
k Men would often wear <u>tights</u>	the other day.
l You should never <u>gobble</u> your food!	by the end of the week.
m Please <u>drop in</u> to see us again	at the end of the week.
n Don't look up every word.	before long.
	just in time.
	on time.
	for the time being.

2 How many natural-sounding sentences can you make using a line in **A** with time expressions in **B**? Work alone, then check your ideas with a partner.

3 Write your own sentences to illustrate the meaning of each of the expressions in **B**. Then work in small groups and compare your sentences.

4 Compare Tudor Britain with the period you have researched. Are there any similarities? Write a similar piece about your period using the four headings.

If only things were different!

Hypothesizing
Moans and groans

1 Read about Tom's Monday morning blues in column **A**.

'I've got those Monday morning blues!'

A		B
a It's Monday morning.		
b I've overslept.		it had.
c My alarm didn't go off.		there was.
d I drank too much last night.		I could.
e I feel sick.	**I wish**	it wasn't.
f There isn't any coffee.		I had.
g My flatmate *will* play his		I hadn't.
music very loudly.		I didn't.
h I haven't ironed my shirt.		he wouldn't.
i I can't go back to bed.		

2 Join a regret in **A** with a wish in **B**. One line in **B** is used twice.

3 Complete the sentences about Tom's Monday morning blues.

If it _____ Sunday morning, Tom _____ stay in bed till lunchtime.

If his alarm _____ gone off, he _____ have overslept.

If he _____ had too much to drink last night, he _____ feel sick now.

LANGUAGE IN CONTEXT

Past and present wishes

1 Work in pairs. Look at the pictures. Each one illustrates someone's wish. Can you guess what the wish is?

2 **T 11.1** Listen to the people expressing wishes. Which wish goes with which picture? Put a letter a–h next to a picture.

3 Complete their wishes.

a I wish I lived _____ .

b If only I _____ such a quick-tempered person.

If I _____ at George the other day, we _____ friends.

c I wish _____ faster.

I wish _____ longer holidays.

d If only animals _____ .

e If only I _____ my car on the double yellow line _____ that ticket.

f I wish _____ to my grandmother more.

g I _____ languages.

But if I hadn't studied politics, I _____ Andy.

h I _____ that huge slice of chocolate cake.

4 What are the facts behind each of the wishes and regrets?

Example
He lives in a cold climate, probably in England.

● **Grammar questions**

– Which of these sentences are about the present? Which are about the past?

a *I wish I **lived** in a warmer climate.*

b *I wish I **had taken** that job in New York.*

c *If I **lived** in a warmer climate I **wouldn't get** so many colds.*

d *If **I'd taken** that job in New York, **I'd have met** the President.*

e *I'd rather he**'d given** me a gold watch.*

– All of the sentences express unreality. Which tense is used to express unreality about the present? Which tense expresses unreality about the past?

– Decontract the verb forms in the last two sentences.

PRACTICE BANK

1 Reading and roleplay

1 **T 11.2** Read and listen to the texts about Leanne and Holly. They are both thirty years old, but their lives are very different. Underline like this:

_____ the sentences which express the reality of their lives.

- - - - - - - - - - - - - - - the sentences which express unreality or hypothesis.

Whose life's perfect anyway?

LEANNE KELLY housewife

'Colin and I got married when we were both sixteen. Of course, now I wish we'd waited and I wish I'd had more time to enjoy myself as a teenager, 'cos by the time we were seventeen we had the twins. Now we've got six children, which wouldn't be so bad if Colin wasn't unemployed and if we lived somewhere bigger. This flat has only two tiny bedrooms and it's on the tenth floor. If only there was a park nearby, where the kids could play. I'd rather we had a house with a garden, though. I try to be optimistic but the future's pretty bleak, really.'

HOLLY HARPER magazine editor

'Of course, I know that I'm very lucky. I have a hugely successful career and a beautiful apartment overlooking Central Park. But now I wish I hadn't had to focus so single-mindedly on my work. I know my marriage wouldn't have been such a disaster if I hadn't. I was devastated when Greg and I split up. My mom keeps saying, 'Holly, you're not getting any younger. It's time you started dating again.' I must admit, when I look out of my window at the kids playing in the park, I kinda wish that I lived out of town and had some kids of my own.'

2 Use these words to form conditional sentences.

a Leanne's life/better/if/Colin/a job.
b If/not/married so early/she/time/enjoy her teenage years.
c If/not/married so early/have six children now.
d If Holly/not work hard in the past/she/not have a successful career now.
e If she/spend less time at work/her marriage/not break up.
f If she/not work in New York/she/live in the country.

3 Imagine you are journalists who are going to interview Leanne or Holly for a magazine article. Work together to think of questions you could ask.

4 Work in pairs. One of you is the journalist, the other is Leanne or Holly. Begin the interview like this:
Hello, Leanne/Holly, it's very good of you to agree to be interviewed. Can I begin by asking you how old you are?

2 Wishes to facts

Read the hypotheses and complete the reality.
Add a sentence.

Example
I wish I lived in the countryside but *I don't. I live in the town.*

a I wish I spoke English fluently, but …
b If only I didn't get so nervous before exams, but …
c You should have worked harder for your exams, but …
d I'd rather you didn't borrow my things without asking, but …
e I wish my brother wouldn't keep interrupting me when I'm working, but …
f If you'd told me you loved me, we would never have split up, but …
g If my father hadn't gone to work in Malaysia, he wouldn't have met my mother, and I'd never have been born, but …
h It's time those children were in bed, but …

3 Facts to wishes

1 Read the reality and add some wishes. Express them in as many ways as you can.

Example
We went to Blackpool for our holiday and it rained the whole time.
I wish we hadn't gone to Blackpool. If only we'd gone to Spain! We shouldn't have gone to Blackpool. If we'd gone to Spain the weather would have been hot and sunny. I'd rather we'd gone to Spain.

a We didn't have any pets when I was a child because we lived in a flat.
b I have fine, mousey-brown hair and I'm short-sighted.
c My parents really wanted me to become a doctor, not a teacher.
d They think that my youngest brother's a layabout. He won't even look for a job.
e I come from a huge family. I've got seven brothers and one sister.
f I can't remember my grandmother because she died when I was only three.
g I didn't start learning a foreign language until I was fifteen.
h I didn't get the job I applied for in Barcelona because I can't speak Spanish.

2 What do you wish was different about your family? Your work? Your school? You?

4 *Would* or *had*?

T 11.3 Listen to the sentences. They all contain 'd. Say if 'd = *would* or *had*.

Examples
I wish he'd listen. = *would*
If he'd listened, I'd have understood. = *had* and *would*

LANGUAGE REVIEW

Hypothesis

Tenses can be used to express both fact and non-fact (hypothesis). Tenses which express fact refer to *real* time.

*I **have** a boring job. I **don't earn** much money.* (Present fact)
*I **didn't work** hard. I **failed** all my exams.* (Past fact)

Tenses that express non-fact do *not* refer to real time. The verb moves *one tense back* to show unreality.

*I wish I **had** a good job. If only I **earned** more money. I wish I'd (= had) **worked** harder. If only I **hadn't failed** all my exams.* (Non-facts)

Hypothesizing about the present

The Past Simple is used in the second conditional, and with *wish, if only, would rather* and *it's time* to express unreal present and future.

*If I **had** enough money,*
   I'd buy a new car. (I don't have enough money.)
*I wish I **were** (or **was**) rich.* (I'm not rich.)
*If only I **had** a new car.* (I have an old one.)
*I wish I **could** come.* (I can't come.)
*I wish you **would** help*
   with the housework. (You won't/don't help.)
*I'd rather you **lived** nearer.* (You live miles away.)
*It's time you **knew** the truth.* (You don't know it.)

Hypothesizing about the past

The Past Perfect is used in the third conditional, and with *wish, if only,* and *would rather* to express unreal or imaginary past.

*If he'd **been** more careful, he **wouldn't have fallen**.*
(He wasn't careful. He fell.)
*I wish I'd **met** the President.*
(I didn't meet/I haven't met the President.)

Should + the perfect infinitive is used to refer to a past action that didn't happen. The action would have been a good idea. It is advice that is too late!
*You **should have taken** the medicine.*
(You didn't take it.)

📖 **Grammar Reference: page 158.**

● LISTENING AND READING

Things we never said

Listening

1 Friends often lose touch with each other. Do you have any friends you have lost touch with? What memories do you have of these friends? Would you like to meet them again?

2 **T 11.4** You are going to listen to a short radio play. It is about two friends, Peter and Amanda, who meet again after some years. They are in their home town. Listen and answer the questions.

a Did they arrange to meet? How do you know?
b Why have they returned to their home town?
c Where do they live now?
d Have they kept in touch over the years? How do you know?
e What ambitions did they have when they were younger? Did these ambitions become reality?

3 The play is based on a short story called *Things we never said*. What can you predict about the full story? Consider these questions in pairs.

– How old do you think Peter and Amanda were when they first knew each other?
– What was their relationship?
– Why did they lose touch? Did they miss each other?
– What are their families like?
– Are they now married?
– Are they happy with their present lives?
– Do they have any regrets?
– Will they meet again soon?

Reading

Read the complete story. Compare your ideas with what you learn in the story.
Do you feel sorry for Peter and Amanda, or angry with them? Why? What is tragic about them?

Things we never said
by Fiona Goble

He saw her from behind and recognized her immediately. He walked faster until he was just ahead of her, then turned round, wondering whether to smile. It didn't seem like fifteen years. She didn't see him at first. She was looking in
5 a shop window. He touched the sleeve of her jacket.

'Hello, Amanda,' he said gently. He knew he hadn't made a mistake. Not this time. For years he kept thinking he'd seen her – at bus stops, in pubs, at parties.

'Peter!' As she said his name, her heart quickened. She
10 remembered their first summer together. They'd lain together by the river at Cliveden. They were both 18 and he'd rested his head on her stomach, twisting grass in his fingers, and told her that he couldn't live without her.

'I'm surprised you recognize me,' he said, burying his
15 hands in the pockets of his coat.

'Really?' She smiled. In fact she'd been thinking about him a lot recently. 'You haven't moved back here, have you?' Surely not, she thought. She knew he loathed the place. Even at 18, he couldn't wait to leave and travel
20 the world.

'Good heavens no,' he said. 'I'm still in London.'
She looked at him. He looked the same. He hadn't begun to go bald like so many of the men she knew, but his shoulders were broader and his face slightly rounder.
25 'I came back for the funeral,' he continued. 'My father's. A heart attack. It happened very suddenly.'

'I'm sorry,' she said, though she wasn't really. She remembered him telling her about how his father used to beat him regularly until he was 16 and grew too tall.
30 'Thank you,' he said to her, though he felt nothing for his dead father, just relief for his mother. She'd be happier without him. She'd been trying to pluck up courage to leave him for years.

'And I take it that you're not living back here either?'
35 'I'm in London, too,' she said. She pushed her hair behind her ears in a gesture that he hadn't forgotten.

'Just back for my sister's wedding tomorrow.'

'That's nice,' he said, though his only memory of Amanda's sister was as a rather plump, boring 12-year-old.
40 'Yes,' she agreed, feeling that her baby sister's wedding only served to spotlight her own series of failed relationships.

'And your parents?' he asked. 'They're well?'

'Fine.' She remembered how he'd always envied
45 her middle-class parents, who ate foreign food and took exotic holidays.

'Are you rushing off somewhere?' he asked.

'No, I'm just killing time, really.'

'Then I suggest we kill it together. Let's grab a coffee.'
50 They walked towards Gaby's, a small café just off the high street. They had spent hours there when they had first met, laughing and holding hands under the table, and discussing their plans for the future over cups of coffee. They sat opposite each other. He ordered the coffee.
55 'And so, Peter, did you become a foreign correspondent?' she asked, remembering the places they dreamed of visiting together – India, Morocco, and Australia.

'Not exactly,' he said. 'I'm a lawyer, believe it or not.' She
60 looked at his clothes, and she could believe it. They were a far cry from the second-hand shirts and jeans he'd worn as a student.

'You enjoy it?' she asked.

'Yes,' he lied. 'And you? Are you a world famous artist?'
65 He'd always loved her pictures. He remembered the portrait of herself which she'd painted for him for his twentieth birthday. He still had it.

'Well, … no.' She tried to laugh. She wondered if he still had her self-portrait. She'd stopped painting years ago. He
70 looked at her hair, cascading in dark unruly waves over her shoulders. He could see a few white hairs now, but she was still very beautiful.

'So,' he said. 'What are you up to?'

'Nothing much,' she said. 'I've tried a few things.' She
75 didn't want to tell him about the succession of temporary jobs that she'd hoped might lead to something more permanent but never had.

'So you're not painting at all?'

'Only doors and walls,' she joked, and he laughed
80 politely. She remembered the evenings they'd spent in the small bedsit that they rented together in their last term at college. He'd sit for hours just watching her paint. She filled sketch book after sketch book.

'So where are you in London?' she asked.
85 'North,' he said. It was a three-bedroom flat in Hampstead. Nice in an empty kind of way. He thought

about all the evenings he wished he had someone to come home to.

'And you?' he asked, after a pause.

90 'South. It's okay, I rent a room.' She thought of the small room with the damp walls which she rented in an unfashionable part of Clapham. 'But I'm thinking of buying somewhere. It's one of the reasons I came home. I want to sort things out a bit,' she sighed, thinking about the letters 95 from him that she'd found in her old bedroom. She'd been reading them only yesterday.

'Oh, Peter, I don't know why I left that day,' she said at last. He looked up at her.

'It's all right,' he said, remembering the evening she 100 hadn't come back to the bedsit.

'We were young. Young people do things like that all the time,' he added, knowing that this wasn't true, knowing that he hadn't deserved such treatment. He thought of all the letters he'd sent to her parents' home. He'd written 105 every day at first, begging her to return or at least to ring him. He'd known even then that he would never meet anyone like her again.

'I suppose you're right.' She swallowed hard, trying to hide her disappointment and hurt that he seemed to have 110 no regrets.

'Well, I ought to be going,' she said.

'Already? I thought you had time to kill.'

'I did,' she said, blinking to hold back the tears. 'But I ought to get back now to help my mother with 115 the wedding.'

'I understand,' he said, though he didn't. Surely her parents would understand?

'Shall I give you my phone number. Perhaps we could meet up?'

120 'Perhaps,' she said.

He wrote his telephone number on the back of the bill and she tucked it into the zipped compartment of her handbag.

'Thanks. Goodbye, Peter.'

125 'Goodbye, Amanda.'

Years later, every so often, she still checked that compartment to make sure his number was there.

Comprehension check

1 Are the following statements true (✔) or false (✗)? Correct the false ones.

a Peter and Amanda used to be in love.
b They are now both 33 years old.
c They both still look exactly the same.
d His mother is distraught over his father's death.
e Amanda's sister is twelve years old.
f Amanda hasn't had another boyfriend since Peter.
g Only Peter has had the career that he planned.
h They both live alone now.
i Peter was broken-hearted when Amanda left him.
j Amanda is on the verge of tears because Peter seems so cold and dispassionate.
k He still loves her, but she doesn't love him any more.

2 Close your books. Listen again to the play. Your teacher will stop the tape after every few lines. How much of the full story can you recall?

Roleplay

1 Divide into two groups.

Group A Make a list of Peter's problems. What are his regrets?
Group B Make a list of Amanda's problems. What are her regrets?

2 Work with a partner. One of you is Peter and the other is Amanda. You meet again. This time you tell each other the truth about your lives. Begin like this:

Do you want to know the truth? Well, I wish we hadn't split up, I hate my job. I still think about you a lot. And what about you? How do you really feel? Are you happy?

Language work

1 The following parts of the body appear in the text. In what connection are they mentioned?

head	heart (x2)	stomach
shoulders (x2)	face	hands (x2)
hair (x2)	hairs	fingers	ears

2 What part of speech are these words? Which parts of the body are they connected with?

| bald | blink | waves | swallow | beat |
| tears | plump | | | |

VOCABULARY

Idioms

Use your dictionary to check new words and expressions.

1 Read the sentences and answer the questions.

I had time to kill	so I went to a café and had a coffee.
I was at a loose end	
I was early and needed to pass the time	
I was bored and had nothing else to do	

a Which of the sentences contain idioms? <u>Underline</u> them.
b Which sentences do not contain idiomatic expressions?
c Which pairs of sentences have the same meaning?
d Under which word did you find the idiom in your dictionary?

2 Work in pairs. Do the same with these groups of sentences.

a This house | is a far cry from | where we used to live.
| isn't nearly as nice as |
| is very different from |
| isn't a patch on |

b A lot of water has flowed under the bridge | since we last met.
I've become much more successful
So much has happened
I've gone up in the world

c After just six months' trading, my uncle's business | went down the drain.
| became very successful.
| went bankrupt.
| hit the jackpot.

d His name's on the tip of my tongue, | but I have such a terrible memory.
His name rings a bell,
I'll remember his name in a minute,
His name sounds familiar,

3 Match a cartoon in **A** with one of these idioms.

> get cold feet   go through the roof   bury your head in the sand
> have butterflies in your stomach   break someone's heart   break the ice
> fall head over heels in love   be over the moon

4 The idioms are illustrated literally in **A** and idiomatically in **B**. Try to work out the meanings of the idioms.

5 Complete the sentences with the correct idiom from Exercise 3. You will sometimes need to make changes to fit the context.

a When I won a trip for two to Venice I …
b She doesn't want to hear about her husband and his secretary, she just …
c The party was very tense until Ian told some of his funny stories. This …
d They have eyes for nobody else. When they met, they …
e I was so nervous when I went for the interview for that job. I …
f My father will be furious when he hears I've crashed his car. He …
g I didn't go on that blind date, because at the last minute I …
h When I discovered he'd been unfaithful, it …

A

● LISTENING AND WRITING

Family secrets

You are going to hear two unusual family stories.

Pre-listening task

1 Do you come from a big or small family? How many brothers, sisters, aunts, uncles, cousins do you have?

2 Study this family tree. Discuss these questions with a partner.

a What is the relationship between:
Deborah and Ralph?
Christine and Ruth?
Christine and Yuri?
Christine and Clive and Isuzu?

b In the story Deborah learns of a family secret. What do you think it might be?

c Why do you think Ralph is known as the 'black sheep' of the family?

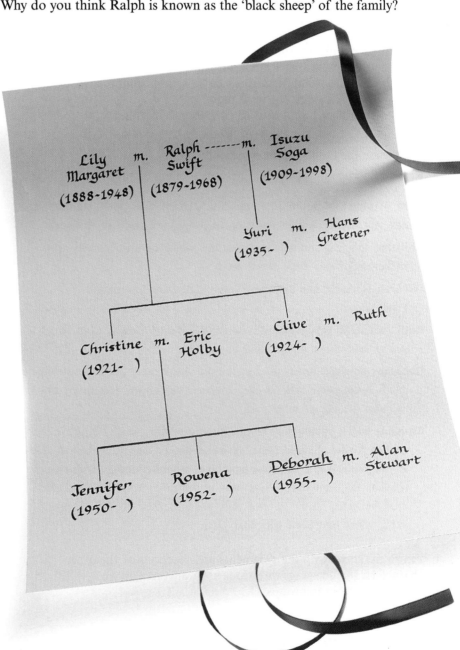

Listening and writing

Part 1

My Japanese aunt

T 11.5 Listen to Deborah talking about her family. As you listen, look at the family tree and circle the people she talks about. Most of them are not mentioned by name. Who are they in relation to Deborah?

Comprehension check

1 Answer the questions.

a Why does Deborah think that her grandfather is not really a 'black sheep'?

b Three jobs are mentioned. What are they? Whose are they?

c Whose is the baby mentioned? What's the name of the baby?

d Where and how did Deborah and her sisters learn the family secret?

e What is Christine's attitude to her father's behaviour?

f What does she wish that Ruth hadn't done?

g Why did Deborah find her visit to Japan so amazing?

h How old was she when she went there?

i How old were Isuzu and Yuri when Deborah met them?

2 This is a dramatic reconstruction of the conversation at the dinner table when the family secret came out.

a Read the scene and complete Christine's telling of the story.

> **Ruth** (wiping her mouth on a napkin) *Christine, I've been meaning to ask you. Did you ever hear again from Yuri and her mother?*
>
> **Christine** (coughs and splutters over her meal. Then replies icily.) *I'd rather we didn't talk about that.*
>
> **Deborah, Rowena, and Jennifer** (very puzzled and interested) *Who's Yuri?*
>
> **Ruth** (sounding very surprised) *Don't you know? Surely, Christine, you've told them about their Aunt Yuri?*
>
> **Deborah** (amazed) *Aunt? But you're our only aunt! We've never heard of an Aunt Yuri. Who is she, Mother?* (she turns accusingly to her mother) *You've got to tell us.*
>
> **Christine** (sighs deeply then laughs nervously) *Oh, well, I suppose you had to find out some time. It all happened many years ago. But if you really want to know* (she takes a deep breath) *I'll tell you.* (pause) *You remember that your grandfather was a silk dealer, and for many years he and your grandmother lived in Japan. Well, what happened was this ...*

b Finish the scene with the comments and reactions of the other characters. Include stage directions as in the piece above.

c Act out the scene in groups.

Part 2

My Canadian aunt

Listen to a lady called Connie talking about the birth of her great aunt.

Comprehension check

Answer the questions.

– Where and when was her great aunt born?

– Who was present at the birth?

– What was the problem? Who solved the problem and how?

– What would have happened if the oven had not been on?

Writing a play

Write a short play based on Connie's story with full stage directions.

Discussion

Do you know of any interesting stories about your family? Tell the rest of the class about them, but only if you want to!

PostScript

Moans and groans

1 Read the complaints in **A**. Match them with a response in **B**. Which of the items below do they refer to? Write a number in the box and an item on the line.

> a painting   a sweater   a tin opener   shoes   homework
> a meal   a TV programme   a washing machine   an exam

a ☐ _____   b ☐ _____   c ☐ _____
d ☐ _____   e ☐ _____   f ☐ _____
g ☐ _____   h ☐ _____   i ☐ _____

A	B
a So why didn't you hand it in on time? I'm not going to mark it now. b It's always the same. I hummed and hawed about getting it, then when I went back it had been sold and it was one of his best works. c Ouch! I've had it with this thing. It just doesn't work. d It's not fair. I'd been looking forward to watching it all day and then the phone goes and rings! e How many times do I have to tell you? Take them off *before* you come into the house! f This has gone beyond a joke. You promised you'd deliver it by Tuesday at the latest. Now you're saying next month! g I could kick myself. As soon as I'd handed in the paper, I remembered what the answer was. h Of course, they didn't have it in red. Apparently, it only comes in navy blue. i It's the last time I'll eat here.	1 Here, give it to me! Let me try. 2 Sorry. I forgot. I was in a hurry. 3 I'm awfully sorry, sir. I'm afraid there's nothing I can do about it. 4 You're not kidding! Massive prices and lousy food! 5 But, I'm really sorry. I just didn't have the chance to finish it at the weekend. 6 But do you think you've still passed? 7 You should have asked if you could put a deposit on it. 8 But wouldn't that go well with your white jeans? 9 And who was it? Anyone interesting?

2 **T 11.6** Listen and check your answers.

3 What are some of the events in a typical day in your life? For each event think of something to moan about.

4 What's happened recently? Do you have any moans and groans about the things that have happened?

12 Icons

Noun phrases
Adding emphasis
Linking and commenting

Match the words in the box with a picture. Then use the words to make one sentence about each picture.

Example
a *He's a grey-haired businessman with a rose in his button hole.*

> with a thatched roof   which expires in February 2020
> wearing a uniform   country   pair of
> roses growing round the front door   dirty
> ~~grey-haired~~   ~~business~~   ~~in his button hole~~
> giving someone a parking ticket   traffic   football
> ~~with a rose~~   sitting on a wall   driving
> licking an ice-cream   stuffed in a bag

a

b

c

d

e

f

LANGUAGE IN CONTEXT

Noun phrases and adding emphasis

1 Read text **A**. Your teacher will give you some questions.

Text A

Michelangelo (1475–1564) was one of the most inspired creators in the history of art. He had a tremendous influence on all his contemporaries, as a sculptor, an architect, a painter, and a poet.

He was born near Arezzo, but he considered Florence to be his home town. He loved the city's art, architecture, and culture above all.

He concentrated on sculpture initially. He began to carve a figure of David from a huge block of marble in 1501. He finished it in 1504, when he was 29. He shows David with a sling on his shoulder, looking into the distance.

Pope Julius II asked Michelangelo to paint the ceiling of the Sistine Chapel later. Michelangelo worked on this task every day for four years from 1508 till 1512, lying on his back at the top of high scaffolding, his neck stiff, with paint trickling onto his face.

Many buildings were designed by him. His work at St Peter's Basilica represented his greatest achievement as an architect. His dome became the model for domes all over the Western world. Its revolutionary design is difficult to appreciate nowadays.

Michelangelo belongs to that small group of artists such as Shakespeare and Beethoven, who have been able to express the deepest experiences of humanity through their work.

2 Read text **B**. Compare the two texts. The information is the same, but there are differences. Which one sounds better?

Michelangelo (1475–1564) was one of the most inspired creators in the history of art. As a sculptor, an architect, a painter, and a poet, he had a tremendous influence on all his contemporaries.

He was born near Arezzo, but it was Florence that he considered to be his home town. What he loved above all was the city's art, architecture, and culture.

Initially, he concentrated on sculpture. In 1501 he began to carve a figure of David from a huge block of marble. This was finished in 1504, when he was 29. David is shown with a sling on his shoulder, looking into the distance.

Later, Michelangelo was asked by Pope Julius II to paint the ceiling of the Sistine Chapel. Every day for four years, from 1508 till 1512, he worked on this task, lying on his back at the top of high scaffolding, his neck stiff, with paint trickling onto his face.

He designed many buildings, but it was his work at St Peter's Basilica that represented his greatest achievement as an architect. His dome became the model for domes all over the Western world. What is difficult to appreciate nowadays is its revolutionary design.

There is a small group of artists such as Shakespeare and Beethoven, who, through their work, have been able to express the deepest experiences of humanity. Michelangelo belongs to this group.

3 Close your book. Your teacher will give you a copy of Text **B** with gaps. Fill the gaps with one of the words in the box.

| a   an   the   (nothing = zero article)   his   all |
| this   its   every   their |

● Grammar questions

– How does word order change the emphasis in a sentence?

– Find sentences in Text **B** beginning *It was …* and *What …* that express emphasis. How are they different from those in Text **A**?

– Find examples of passive sentences with and without *by*. Where is the focus of attention in these sentences?

PRACTICE BANK

1 Adding emphasis

Rephrase the sentences to make them more emphatic.

Example
I like Tony's honesty.

| What
The thing | I like about Tony is | his honesty.
the way
the fact that | he always tells
the truth. |

a My daughter is very untidy. This annoys me.
b Tom's very generous. I like this.
c I can't stand my son's moodiness.
d I admire the Italians' love of life.
e The Germans' sense of duty makes them work hard.
f The reliability of Mercedes Benz cars makes them so popular.
g I can never resist chocolate desserts in a restaurant.

2 Emphasis and sentence stress

1 When we speak, we can stress the important part of a sentence with our voice.

T 12.1 Listen to the examples.

Examples
'*Who gave you that new car?*' '**Susan** *gave it to me.*'
'*Did she sell it to you?*' '*No, she* **gave** *it to me.*'
'*Did she give it to Peter?*' '*No, she gave it to* **me**.'
'*Is it second-hand?*' '*No, it's* **new**.'
'*Did she give you a new stereo?*' '*No, she gave me a new* **car**.'

T 12.2 Listen to the questions about these sentences. Then say the sentences with the correct stress. Change the sentences as necessary.

a Ann gave David a blue shirt for his birthday.
b James flew to Paris for a month to learn French.
c We go to Scotland every autumn because we like walking.
d My eldest son is studying law at Bristol university.

2 In pairs, ask similar questions about these sentences. Answer with the appropriate stress.

a Dave phoned me yesterday and invited me to his wedding.

b My wife and I are going to travel round Europe for three months by train.

c Mark lost a wallet with £50 in it while he was jogging in the park.

d I'm meeting Jane at half past seven outside the cinema.

3 Where is the stress in the second line of these dialogues?

a 'Why weren't you at school yesterday?'
  'I was at school.'

b 'Come on, Dave. It's time to get up.'
  'I am getting up.'

c 'It's a shame you don't like parties.'
  'But I do like parties!'

d 'I wish you'd tidy your room.'
  'I have tidied it.'

e 'What a shame you didn't see Tom.'
  'I did see Tom.'

T 12.3 Listen and check your answers. Note that if there is no auxiliary verb, we add *do/does/did*.

4 Your teacher will read out some sentences. Correct him/her.

Example
I never give you any homework.
*You **do** give us homework. Lots!*

3 Active or passive?

Complete the sentences. Use the verb in the active or the passive, depending where the focus of attention is.

a Yesterday, the murder trial of James Kent came to an end. _____ (sentence) to ten years' imprisonment.

b Judge Robert Henderson decided to make an example of Steve Phillips, who had been arrested for burglary for the thirtieth time. _____ (sentence) to four years' imprisonment.

c Flight attendants are always very busy. _____ (show) passengers how to put on a lifejacket, and _____ (serve) food and drinks.

d Every attempt is made so that airline passengers feel safe and comfortable. _____ (show) how to put on a lifejacket, and _____ (serve) food and drinks.

e Good luck with your new job in Italy. I'm sure _____ (tell) what you have to do when you arrive.

f Your new boss is Donatella Morno. _____ (tell) what you have to do.

4 Articles and determiners

1 Correct the mistakes in the sentences.

a I had the lunch with a colleague.

b Do you do business in States?

c I came here in one taxi.

d The unemployment is a world problem these days.

e I'm reading a book about life of Beethoven at the moment.

f My sister broke the leg skiing.

g Computer has changed our lives completely.

h I have only an ambition in life, and that is to be rich.

i She works as interpreter for United Nations.

j 'Where's your mother?' 'In a kitchen.'

k 'Would you like a drink?' 'Yes, I'd love it.'

l Tell me a truth. Do you love me or not?

m Last night we went to the restaurant. Food was good, but a service was terrible.

2 Have a class discussion. How are men and women different?

Men are more logical.
Women are more instinctive.
Men like talking about things.
Women like talking about people.

3 Match a line in **A** with a line in **B**.

A	B
Would you like Do all birds lay Where did I put	eggs? the egg? an egg?
I have two cars. Borrow I said goodbye to I have five nieces, I gave a present to	each one. everyone. either one.

A	B
Love A love The love	I have for you is forever. is everything. of animals is vital for a vet.
Both All Every	my friends like dancing. student in my class is friendly. my parents are Scottish.

5 Speaking

Each student should prepare a short talk on one of the following topics.

• A person you admire
• A hero or icon
• A pet hate

Try to include some of the ways of expressing emphasis.

LANGUAGE REVIEW

Noun phrases

1 Information can be added before and after a noun.

*a **grey-haired** businessman **with a rose in his button hole***
*a driving licence **which expires in 2020***

2 Articles and determiners refer to nouns.

*Cordoba is **a** city in the south of Spain.*
*My brother works in **the** City of London.*
(   ) Cities are (   ) exciting places. (= zero article)

each/every/either boy (singular noun)
both/all girls (plural noun)

this/that man
these/those women

Adding emphasis

There are many ways of adding emphasis to a text,
such as the passive, word order, using certain emphatic
structures, and auxiliaries.

***In 1504** Michelangelo finished the statue of David.*
***The statue of David was finished** in 1504.*

| **What** | **annoys me** is people who are always late. |
| **The thing that** | |

*It's people like you **who** are ruining the country.*

*I **did** tidy my room! Honest!*

📖 **Grammar Reference: page 158.**

● READING AND SPEAKING
It blows your mind!

Pre-reading task

1 Look at the photos. What do you know about the first atomic bomb test?

2 Work in pairs. Discuss whether this information is true or false.

a The atomic bomb was first tested just before the Second World War.
b The atomic bomb was developed by a team of American scientists.
c The first atomic explosion took place on an island in the Pacific.
d US marines were deliberately exposed to radiation to monitor its effects.
e It was hoped that the atomic bomb would end all wars.
f Albert Einstein was involved in the creation of the bomb.
g Atomic bombs were used against Japan just three weeks after the first test bomb.
h Everyone agreed that it was right to use the weapons against Japan.
i At the time German scientists were close to developing the atomic bomb.

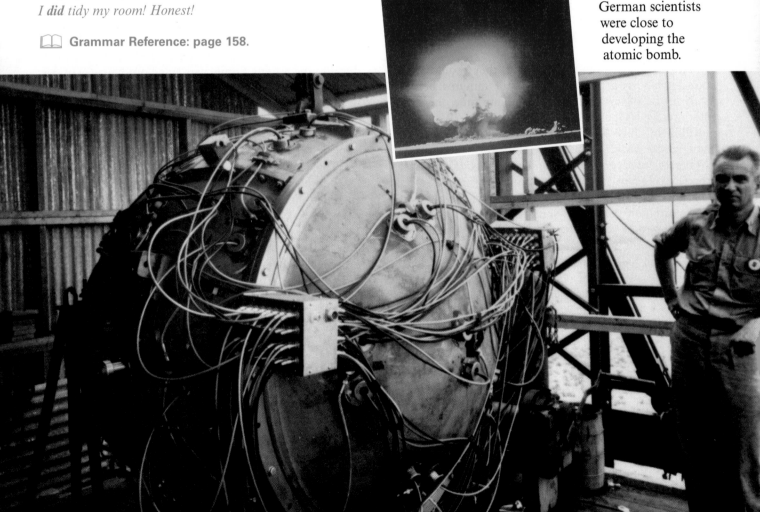

Read the article about the first atomic explosion. Which of the questions on page 121 can you now answer?

'I am become Death, the destroyer of worlds'

The first explosion of the atom bomb, on July 16, 1945, was summed up by Robert Oppenheimer with these words from a Hindu poem.

Peter Millar reports on the race led by Oppenheimer, the brilliant physicist, at Los Alamos, New Mexico, to create the weapon that would end the Second World War.

In the foothills of the New Mexican mountains, on a dusty desert plain known as the Jornada del Muerto – Dead Man's Journey – camped the greatest collection of scientific brains on earth. They were men who would redefine the 20th century: Robert Oppenheimer (American), Enrico Fermi (Italian), George Kistiakowski (Ukrainian), Otto Frisch (Austrian), General Leslie Groves (American), Edward Teller (Hungarian), and Klaus Fuchs (born in Germany, but a naturalized Briton).

Better than any men in the world, they should have known what to expect in those still minutes before dawn in the desert. But none of them knew for sure what would happen. The explosion at 05.29 on the morning of July 16, 1945, stunned its creators and changed the world: the atomic bomb worked.

There were several eye-witness accounts of that first atomic explosion. 'It blasted; it pounced; it bored its way right through you. It was a vision which was seen with more than the eye. It seemed to last forever. You longed for it to stop. Altogether it lasted about two seconds. Finally it was over.' Another observer wrote: 'It was like a ball of fire, too bright to look at directly. The whole surface of the ball was covered with a purple luminosity.' His report ends: 'I am sure that all who witnessed this test went away with a profound feeling that they had seen one of the great events in history.'

Los Alamos today supports a community of just over 18,000 people. On first impressions it is like many other small towns in western America: full of low two-storey buildings, dusty, with rather dingy shopping malls, a couple of banks, filling stations, Mexican and Chinese fast-food joints, a motel, and a McDonald's. But there are plenty of indications that this is no ordinary town. Big blue signs along State Highway 84 advise travellers that the road and land on either side belong to the US government. A notice declares that it is 'forbidden to remove dirt'. At one point a high watchtower stands sentry behind a twenty-foot barbed-wire fence.

Before 1942, however, Los Alamos had no history because it didn't exist. It was created for one purpose only, to house the technicians who would make the bomb before anyone else did. All mail was censored, and everyone was sworn to secrecy. The US government did not even trust its own protégés. Oppenheimer, who had mixed with left-wing groups in his youth, was tailed by FBI men. Einstein, who had written to President Roosevelt in 1939 urging him to develop the atomic bomb, was ruled out because of his outspoken pacifism and Zionism. Yet the real villain went undetected. Klaus Fuchs was revealed in 1950 as Stalin's spy.

What is interesting is that the scientists were much more interested in sharing the bomb with the Russians than the politicians were. Some physicists dreamed of the bomb as an end to all wars, a possible means of establishing global government. As it progressed from a theoretical possiblity to an experimental reality, concern grew among some of those involved about how it would be used. By early 1945, Germany, the original target, no longer needed an atomic explosion to force its surrender. Attention switched to Japan.

In 1943 Harold Argo was a graduate from Washington University when he was summoned to New Mexico. Now over 80, he describes his time at Los Alamos as 'the most exciting two years of my life'. He dismisses those whose consciences troubled them. 'I don't understand all those sceptics who had second thoughts. I had two brothers out there in the Pacific. If Harry Truman hadn't dropped the bomb, the war could have gone on forever.'

Carson Mark is more reflective. 'At the time, we thought it would put an end to organized war, because no one can put up with destruction on that scale. But

we didn't know how imminent it was that the Japanese would have to call it quits. Why kill all those people if you don't need to?'

85 In May 1945 nobody was sure just how devastating the bomb would be. There was general agreement that the simpler type of bomb would work, but the more complicated plutonium implosion device would need testing. Oppenheimer named the test Trinity, partly because of the Christian concept of God the Father,
90 the Son, and the Holy Spirit, but mainly because of the Hindu three-in-one godhead of Vishnu, Brahma, and Siva, the power of life, the creator, and destroyer.

The site selected was 33 miles from the nearest town. The VIP observation site was located 20 miles away.
95 The scientists had a bet with each other to guess how many tonnes' equivalent of TNT their bomb would produce. So imprecise was their knowledge that Oppenheimer conservatively suggested 300. Teller, wiser, speculated an incredible 45,000. Radiochemical
100 analysis revealed the blast had equalled 18,600 tonnes of TNT, four times what most of those involved on the project had guessed.

Even as they were celebrating at Los Alamos, hours after the explosion, the warship *Indianapolis* sailed out
105 of San Francisco harbour, carrying the atomic bomb nicknamed *Little Boy* on its fateful voyage to the island of Tinian in the Pacific. After unloading its deadly cargo, the ship sailed on towards the Philippines. On July 29 it was sunk by a Japanese submarine; of the 850
110 who survived the sinking, more than 500 were eaten alive by sharks.

On Tinian, group commander Paul Tibbets had his B-29 bomber repainted, and he gave it his mother's name, Enola Gay. In Hiroshima and Nagasaki, the
115 citizens slept.

Just three weeks after the test, the bomb was used for real. As the historian Richard Rhodes wrote in his book *The Making of the Atomic Bomb*, 'Once Trinity proved that the atomic bomb worked, men discovered reasons
120 to use it.'

Comprehension check

1 Explain the title of the article.

2 Answer the questions.
a Did the scientists know exactly what would happen when the first bomb exploded?
Did they expect it to be bigger or smaller?
b How did they feel when it went off?
c How did the eye-witnesses describe it?
d What are the indications that Los Alamos is no ordinary town?
e Why isn't the town on any map before 1942?
f Why did the scientists want to share their knowledge with the Russians?
Why do you think the politicians didn't agree with them?
g In what way do Harold Argo and Carson Mark have different opinions?
h What do you know about the warship *Indianapolis*?
i When and where was the first atomic bomb used in warfare?

3 Who are these people? What does the text say about them?
a the greatest collection of scientific brains (l. 7–8)
b none of them (l. 17)
c its creators (l. 19)
d a community (l. 33)
e travellers (l. 41)
f the technicians (l. 48)
g its own protégés (l. 51)
h the real villain (l. 56)
i the original target (l. 67)
j all those sceptics (l. 74)
k God (l. 89)
l VIP (l. 94)
m *Little Boy* (l. 106)
n Enola Gay (l. 114)

Language work

1 What is the subject of these sentences from the text?
a In the foothills of the New Mexican mountains … camped the greatest collection of scientific brains on earth. (l. 5–8)
b So imprecise was their knowledge that Oppenheimer conservatively suggested 300. (l. 97–8)
What is the effect of changing the normal word order?

2 Comment on the use of the passive in these sentences. Where is the focus of attention?
a All mail was censored, and everyone was sworn to secrecy. (l. 49–50)
b Oppenheimer … was tailed by FBI men. (l. 52–3)
c Klaus Fuchs was revealed in 1950 as Stalin's spy. (l. 57–8)
d … it was sunk by a Japanese submarine … (l. 109)
e … more than 500 were eaten alive by sharks. (l. 110–1)

What do you think?

1 How did the atomic bomb alter the course of history in the twentieth century?
2 Do you agree with the historian Richard Rhodes?

VOCABULARY

Homophones

1 Homophones are words with the same pronunciation but different spelling and different meaning.

/wɔː/   *war* and *wore*
/haɪə/   *higher* and *hire*

Think of two spellings for these words in phonemic script. One of the two words is in lines 5 to 24 of the text about the atomic bomb.

a /njuː/   _____   _____

b /pleɪn/   _____   _____

c /ʃɔː/   _____   _____

d /wʊd/   _____   _____

e /siːn/   _____   _____

f /θruː/   _____   _____

2 Think of two spellings for these words in phonemic script.

a /piːs/   _____   _____

b /kɔːt/   _____   _____

c /weɪ/   _____   _____

d /ˈweðə/   _____   _____

e /meɪl/   _____   _____

f /saɪt/   _____   _____

Homonyms

1 Homonyms are words with the same spelling and pronunciation but different meanings.

a dusty desert **plain**   the **plain** truth
a **plain** white blouse   **plain** food

Fill the pairs of gaps with the same word. Sometimes the word changes its form.
The words occur from the title to line 40 of the text about the atomic bomb.

a The film _____ an hour. It was great.

I came _____ in the race.

b There were several different _____ of the story in the newspapers.

My wife and I have a joint _____ at our bank.

c I was left a small _____ of money by my aunt.

Can I _____ up the meeting before we end?

d It is illegal to discriminate against people on grounds of sex, _____ , or religion.

I'm exhausted. I've been _____ around all day – working, shopping, and cooking.

e The queue was so _____ that I didn't wait.

Rain, rain, rain! I'm fed up with it. I'm _____ for some sunshine.

f _____ your name here, please.

What does that _____ on the wall mean?

g Keep _____ . Don't move.

She didn't do any revision, but she _____ passed the exam.

2 Think of two meanings for these words. Write sentences that illustrate the different meanings.

match	draw	cross	fine	fair	fit	suit
miss	mind	mark	sentence	point		

Children's jokes

T 12.4 A lot of jokes are made with homophones and homonyms because there is a play on words. Listen to these children's jokes.

LISTENING

Great events of the twentieth century

Pre-listening task

1 Look at the photos. What famous events of the twentieth century do they illustrate? Can you put a date to each photo?

2 Work in groups of four.
Think of the greatest event of the twentieth century for each of these categories.

Politics (P)	War (W)
Medicine (M)	Social changes (SC)
Transport (Tr)	Art and culture (AC)
Technology (Tech)	Sport (S)

3 Discuss your conclusions as a class.

Listening

T 12.5 You will hear people expressing opinions on the great events of the twentieth century. What is the event? What category of event is it? Put a letter from Exercise 2 opposite. Often you will need to write more than one letter.

Speaker	Event	Category
Pam		
David		
Alexa		
Penny		
Pam		
David		
Hilary		
Barry		

Comprehension check

1 Did any of them mention the same event as you?

2 Answer the questions.

a What is the image that Pam has in her mind?
How did the crowds feel?
How did *she* feel?

b What, for David, is the most surprising aspect of the collapse of communism?
Does he express a personal opinion on whether capitalism is preferable to communism?

c What does Alexa say is strange about conversations on the Internet?
In what way are they different from face-to-face conversations?

d How has Penny benefited from feminism?

e What is Pam's anecdote about penicillin?

f What, according to David, is the big problem for the twenty-first century?

g Why does Hilary say that the First World War was the main event of the century?
What does she say about life in the 1900s and life in the 1920s?

h What is silly about Barry's suggestion, and what is not?
What, according to Barry, did young people use to do?
What was different after Elvis?
Why was society ripe for a change?

WRITING

Focusing attention

1 Read the texts about Elvis Presley. Choose which version sounds better, a or b. Think about word order, and where the focus of attention is.

1 ☐ 2 ☐ 3 ☐ 4 ☐ 5 ☐ 6 ☐ 7 ☐
8 ☐ 9 ☐ 10 ☐

1	(a) **Elvis Presley** (1935–1977) was a rock and roll singer whose enormous success changed popular culture throughout the world.	(b) Popular culture throughout the world was changed by the enormous success of **Elvis Presley** (1935–1977), a rock and roll singer.
2	(a) His parents raised Presley in Memphis, where he sang at church services.	(b) Presley was raised in Memphis, where he sang at church services.
3	(a) As a teenager, he taught himself to play the guitar.	(b) He taught himself to play the guitar as a teenager.
4	(a) Sam Phillips was a rhythm and blues producer, and Presley recorded songs for him in July 1954.	(b) In July 1954 Presley recorded songs for Sam Phillips, a rhythm and blues producer.
5	(a) What earned him the nickname 'Elvis the Pelvis' was his charismatic style on stage.	(b) His charismatic style on stage earned him the nickname 'Elvis the Pelvis'.
6	(a) About this time Presley met Colonel Tom Parker, a promoter who managed the rest of his career.	(b) The rest of Presley's career was managed by a promoter, Colonel Tom Parker, who Presley met about this time.
7	(a) In 1956 Presley released *Heartbreak Hotel*, the first of 45 records that sold more than a million copies each.	(b) It was 45 records that Presley released that sold more than a million copies each, and the first of these was *Heartbreak Hotel* in 1956.
8	(a) Viewers saw him only from the waist up when he frequently appeared on television because people considered his dancing was too sexually suggestive.	(b) He frequently appeared on television, but because his dancing was considered too sexually suggestive, he was seen only from the waist up.
9	(a) Presley's personal life suffered desperately, and he fought battles with weight gain and drug dependence.	(b) Desperately Presley's personal life suffered, and battles with weight gain and drug dependence he fought.
10	(a) Before Presley, there were no teenagers, just young people without a voice. He was one of the founders of youth culture.	(b) Teenagers were just young people without a voice before Presley. Youth culture was founded by people like him.

2 **T 12.6** Listen and check your answers.

3 Write about the career of someone who interests you. It could be a sportsperson, an artist, a singer, an actor, a writer, a business person … anybody! Get some facts and dates about the person – their early life, how their career grew, what the high points of their professional life were/have been.

PostScript

Linking and commenting

1 Look at these extracts from tapescript 12.5. The expressions in italics link or comment on what has been said or what is going to be said. They are mainly adverbs.

I think it *somehow sort of* gets rid of the values, *possibly*,

... that can be covering up, *you know*, feelings.

... the advent of the Pill was *obviously* a great event as well ...

... life *certainly* was different after it than before ...

Probably because things were coming to an end before it, *anyway* ...

For me *personally* ... the greatest moment of change in the twentieth century was *actually* Elvis Presley.

2 In these dialogues, choose the correct linking or commenting expression.

a A Did you see the match last night?
  B No, I missed it, but **apparently/obviously** it was a good game. We won, didn't we?
  A **Probably/Actually**, it was a draw, but it was really exciting.

b A What do you think of Claire's new boyfriend?
  B **Personally/Ideally**, I can't stand him. I think she'll be let down by him. **Certainly/However**, that's her problem, not mine.
  A Poor old Claire! She always picks the wrong ones, doesn't she? **Anyway/Honestly**, I'll see you later. Bye!
  B Bye, Rita.

c A I don't know how you can afford to buy all those fabulous clothes!
  B **Still /Hopefully**, I'm going to get a bonus this month. I should do. My boss promised it to me. **After all/Presumably**, I did earn the company over £100,000 last year. **Basically/Actually**, it was nearer £150,000. I do deserve it, don't you think?
  A **Of course/In fact** you do.

d A She said some horrible things to me. I hate her! She called me names!
  B **Generally speaking/All the same**, I think you should apologize to her.
  A Me? Apologize? Never!
  B **Basically/Surely**, I think you're both being very childish. Why don't you grow up?
  A Oh, Mary! **Still/Honestly**, I never thought you'd speak to me like that. I hate you, too.

e A So, Billy Peebles. You say that this is the last record you're ever going to make?
  B **Surely/Definitely**.
  A But **surely/actually** you realize how upset your fans are going to be?
  B **Obviously/As a matter of fact**, I don't want to hurt anyone, but **certainly/basically**, I'm fed up with pop music. I'd like to do something else. **After all/Ideally**, I'd like to get into films.
  A Well, we wish you all the best.

3 T12.7 Listen and check your answers. Practise the dialogues.

Tapescripts

T1.1 See pp 6–7

T1.2

Kate

a How long has Kate been in Wales?
   For three days.
b Is she having a good time?
   Yes, she's enjoying it a lot.
c How long did the journey take?
   Twelve hours.
d What time do they have breakfast?
   At 7.30.
e Why was she nervous?
   Because she hadn't been on a horse before.
f What's she going to do tomorrow?
   She's going whitewater rafting.

Vicky

a What is Vicky studying at university?
   English.
b How long has she been going out with Luke?
   Two weeks.
c Where did they meet?
   At a dance.
d What sort of car has he got?
   A VW Beetle.
e Why is she tired?
   Because she's been getting ready for a tutorial.

Julie and Martin

a How long have Julie and Martin been in Mombasa?
   Since September.
b What time does Martin have to start work?
   At 7.00.
c Why did they decide to go to Amani?
   Because it's cooler.
d Where did they have lunch?
   At a friend's house.
e What has just happened?
   It's started to rain.

T1.3

a What does your sister do for a living?
b She's been working in advertising for a couple of years.
c What was she doing before that?
d She'd been out of work for a while.
e She won't be working next Monday.
f I'll leave at about 8.00 tomorrow morning.
g My car was made in Austria.
h I've had it for six months.
i It's being serviced today.
j Peter's sold his old car to his brother.
k It had done over 100,000 miles.
l This homework has to be given in tomorrow.

T1.4

1 A Aah! He's gorgeous! Look at those big, golden paws. When did you get him?
   B Yesterday. It's a she actually.
   A Oh, right. What kind is she?
   B A Labrador.
   A She's so cute. Is she house-trained yet?
   B No, of course not. She's only seven weeks old.

2 A Do you think you could possibly water my house-plants for me? I'm away on business for two weeks.
   B No problem. I'll be glad to. I'll keep an eye on your whole flat if you like.
   A That would be great.
   B Don't worry, I know how house-proud you are. I'll make sure everything stays clean and tidy.
   A I'll do the same for you any time, you know.
   B Thanks.

3 A Julie, have you heard? Anna's just been made managing director of the UK branch of her firm, so she's coming back from the States!
   B Oh, Mum, that's wonderful news. Let's give her a spectacular home-coming party when she gets back. Hmmm. She's certainly the career girl of the family.
   A My love, you don't envy her, do you?
   B Not me. I'm the original happy housewife, remember? Four kids, home-made cakes, home-grown vegetables!
   A And how are my fabulous grandchildren?

4 A We're having a house-warming party on the 12th. Can you come?
   B Yes, you bet. We'd love to! But I didn't know you'd moved.
   A Yeah, two weeks ago. It's much bigger than the old one. A huge kitchen and three big bedrooms.
   B It sounds wonderful.
   A Yeah. Mind you, there's much more housework to do!
   B That's a drag!

5 A Mu. u. . um? Mu. u. . um, I want to come home. I don't like it here.
   B Oh, Simon. Come on now. You were so looking forward to going to scout camp.
   A But ... but ... oh, Mu. u. . um, I hate it here. Why won't you and Dad come and get me?
   B Simon, we can't. I never thought you'd be so homesick, and you'll be home in two days.
   A TWO MORE DAYS! Oh, no!

T1.5

Hello Muddah, Hello Fadduh
Here I am at Camp Grenada.
Camp is very entertaining,
And they say we'll have some fun if it stops raining.

I went hiking with Joe Spivey
He developed poison ivy;
You remember Leonard Skinner?
He got ptomaine poisoning last night after dinner.

All the counsellors hate the waiters
And the lake has alligators.
And the head-coach wants no sissies,
So he reads to us from something called *Ulysses*.

Now I don't want this should scare ya,
But my bunk-mate has malaria;
You remember Jeffrey Hardy?
They're about to organize a searching party.

Take me home, oh Muddah, Fadduh
Take me home, I hate Grenada.
Don't leave me out in the forest where
I might get eaten by a bear.

Take me home, I promise I will not make noise
Or mess the house with other boys.
Oh please don't make me stay.
I've been here one whole day.

Dearest Fadduh, darling Muddah,
How's my precious little bruddah?
Let me come home if you miss me,
I would even let Aunt Bertha hug and kiss me.

Wait a minute, it's stopped hailing,
Guys are swimming, guys are sailing.
Playing baseball, gee that's better.
Muddah, Fadduh, kindly disregard this letter.

T1.6

a A Have you got a reference number?
   B Yes. 304556.
   A Credit card number?
   B 4929 901 520 401.

b A Three take away three is nought.
   B In America, we say three minus three is zero.

c ... and we're in the closing minutes of the second half, and Liverpool are winning one-nil, but can they hold onto this lead as Barcelona attack again?

d What a beautiful backhand! That shot gives Smith three match points. She's one set up at 6-0, 5-4 and it's 40-0 in what could be the final game.

e There will be widespread frosts tonight, with temperatures at or below nought degrees Celsius.

f A My phone number is 0171 498 7032. That's a London number.
   B My New York number is 212 70 65449.

T1.7

Here is the news.
There are fears for the safety of a Boeing 747 on its flight from Lima to Los Angeles. The plane, Bel Air flight 409 with 280 passengers on board, left Peru at 10.40 in the morning local time. It had completed three quarters of the four thousand-mile trip when radio contact was lost. Postal workers are on strike. Their demand for a five and a half per cent pay rise has been rejected. Management say they can only afford

to offer 3.2 per cent spread over the next sixteen months.

A man armed with a shotgun held up a jeweller's in central Birmingham yesterday. He escaped with rings and bracelets worth £55,000. Police are appealing for witnesses. The number to phone is 0151 324408.

Unemployment figures were released today. Last month there were 2,876,000 registered unemployed. This is an increase of 32,000 on the previous month.

Finally, the weather. It will be cold and windy today, with gales up to seventy miles an hour and temperatures dropping to minus 7 degrees Celsius.

And that's all from me.

UNIT 2

T2.1

David Livingstone, African explorer

David Livingstone was one of the most important Victorian explorers. He spent thirty years travelling in Africa.

He was born in Scotland in 1813. He studied medicine, and in 1841 he sailed to South Africa to join a Christian mission in Botswana. He married soon after he arrived, and with his wife he travelled into regions where no Europeans had ever been. He went to the Kalahari Desert, the Zambezi River, and the Victoria Falls.

His second expedition, up the Zambezi River by canoe, was a disaster. His wife, Mary, died of a fever, and many other lives were lost.

A few years later he set out to discover the source of the River Nile on foot. He vanished, and some people thought he had died. In 1871 the American journalist Henry Morton Stanley greeted him on the shore of Lake Tanganyika with the famous words 'Dr Livingstone, I presume.'

He died in 1873, in modern Zambia. His followers buried his heart at the foot of the tree where he died. His remains were buried at Westminster Abbey, in London.

Mick Watts, backpacker in Asia

Mick Watts is in Melbourne. He is on a nine-month backpacking trip round Australia and south-east Asia.

He flew into Bangkok five months ago. Since then he has been to Kuala Lumpur, Singapore, Java, and Bali. He has visited temples in Thailand, and seen giant turtles in Indonesia. He's been staying in cheap hostels, along with a lot of other young people. 'I've met a lot of great people, but it hasn't all been easy,' said Mick. 'I've had diarrhoea a few times, and I've been mugged once, which was really scary.' Apart from that, his only worry is the insects. He has been stung all over his body.

He's been travelling mainly by public transport – bus, train, and ferry – except in Bangkok, where he got around by river taxi.

For him, the best part of the trip so far has been learning to scuba dive on the Great Barrier Reef.

He's looking forward to taking things easy for another week, then setting off again to New Zealand. 'Once you've got the travel bug, it becomes very hard to stay in the same place for too long,' he said.

T2.2

a   What did he study?
b   Why did he go to South Africa?
c   When did he get married?
d   What did his wife die of?
e   Where were his remains buried?
f   How long has he been away from home?
g   Which countries has he been to?
h   Where has he been staying?
i   How often has he had diarrhoea?
j   Has he been mugged?

T2.3

Part 1 Childhood

I = Interviewer   N = Natalie

I   First of all tell me what your earliest memory is.

N   'Course, I was born just before the First World War, and my earliest memory, I think, is my third birthday party. Everything was very short, but I did have a birthday cake and all the lights were out and I was told to go into the room first and there was this beautiful cake with the candles on it.

I   When you were small what did you want to be when you grew up?

N   Well, I thought, perhaps, I would be one of the first people ever to fly the Atlantic but it didn't quite work out like that. After a time I became rather an indifferent glider pilot, which wasn't quite the Atlantic.

I   And what did you actually expect would be the story of your life? What did you expect to be when you grew up?

N   I had no idea. I couldn't believe that I'd end up as a lavender farmer in Shropshire! Certainly not that! I did think I might be an MP but in the end I was a librarian in Wolverhampton, again not quite Westminster!

I   You lived abroad for a while when you were young in Paris and in Dresden. What are your most vivid memories of those two cities?

N   In Paris I heard *Boris Godunov* sung by Schalliapin and that is something that has always lived in my memory, and in Dresden I went to every single Wagner opera in the order he wrote them.

I   Were you there to learn French and German?

N   I was. Er ... I learnt many other things, not too much French or German. A bit.

Part 2 The war years

I   You were in Germany before the Second World War began. Are there memories of the seriousness of the political situation developing?

N   Well, I was young so I didn't really take it in but there were days when we were not allowed to go out, because there were these torchlight processions and the Jews' shop windows were broken, and one knew it was serious but certainly I didn't realize how serious.

I   During the Second World War you were involved in political warfare, sending misinformation to the enemy, and then after the war you worked in London in naval intelligence. You must have had to keep completely secret the work that you were doing. It must have been years before you were able to tell anybody about the work you did during the war.

N   We did have to take an oath of secrecy, but I think that one of the ... tiresome things that happened from that was, that when I wrote to my husband, who as I said was away for four years, I wasn't allowed to say where I worked, who I worked with, or what I did, and after three or four years it gets quite difficult to write letters, without saying these things.

Part 3 The best is yet to come

I   How long have you lived in this lovely house in Shropshire with its magnificent gardens?

N   We came here in 1953. We didn't really mean to come to a house as big as this but we saw the garden one night by moonlight, and the moon was coming up behind this beautiful cedar tree and we said we really must have the cedar tree, never mind the house.

I   And how do you fill your time here?

N   Er ... very well. I'm very busy. I have five acres of garden, four acres of lavender, twenty hives of bees, eight grandchildren and one step-grandchild. Er ... really, time goes quite fast.

I   You've travelled a great deal during the course of your life. Where in the world have you most enjoyed visiting?

N   Well, I've enjoyed going almost everywhere. But I think that Machu Picchu, the lost city of the Incas, is something quite special. It's quite a spiritual place. It was their holy place. And then of course you go to the Grand Canyon. I went there, ... quite modern there. I went in a helicopter along the edge of the Grand Canyon and that's magnificent too. India, China, the Great Wall, you say it, there are so many places – Madagascar with their incredible lemurs and the animals that are being driven to extinction. Each place has its charm and I'm hoping to see lots more!

I   I was going to ask you whether you have plans to make more journeys. Are there places in particular that you know you want to visit as soon as you can?

N   Well, I haven't been to Egypt which is a terrible miss, and I always want to go back to Jerusalem, which has ... I've been there two or three times, and I don't know why, I find it a most compelling city. I don't think it's changed, it's still violent and cruel and divided and beautiful, and you meet a camel where you least expect it round the corner and the little streets are the same and you feel you could see Jesus of Nazareth there still today.

I think I also like to look forward, too. I'm just as interested in the future as I am in the past and what I really want is for us to find life in outer space before I die. I should like that.

I   Your work here fills up almost all of your time ...

N   All of my time.

I   All of your time, not almost all of your ...

N   Rather more than my time!

I   But do you sometimes manage to fit in other activities? For example, is it correct that you enjoy waterskiing?

N   I ... I think I enjoy waterskiing, but it's always anxious because I'm never quite sure if I'll get up. But I do enjoy it and once up I think it's great, brilliant!

I   Does it ever occur to you that it's an unusual pastime for a lady in her eighties to be going waterskiing?

N   Well, I never really had thought of it like that. I think if you do something you just go on doing it, as long as you can and hope that nothing dreadful happens to stop you.

I   You mentioned that you are a glider pilot. Do you still get the chance to fly?

N   I don't ever go alone any more, I go up with somebody else in a two-seater, but when I started to learn, before the war, there were no two-seaters. You always had to go alone.

I   As you look back on a very rich, colourful, interesting life, which seems to you to have been the best part? Which was your golden age?

N   Well, I don't know that there is a golden age. I look forward with just as much pleasure as I look back. I've got lovely things to look back on, but I hope I've got lovely things to look forward to.

T2.4

1   We went to dinner with some friends on Saturday evening. We had a lovely time, but the meal was awful! We had sheep's heart with rice and bananas!

2   We were all going on holiday to Spain next week. We were really looking forward to it, but my father's been quite ill so we've had to cancel the holiday.

3   A   Has Annie had the baby yet? It must be due any time now.
    B   Oh, yes. Haven't you heard? She didn't have one. She had three. Tom's the father of triplets!

4   Careful with that knife. Mind you don't cut yourself. It's very sharp.

5   Do be careful. That bowl's really heavy!

6   How's your steak? Is it OK?

7   Look! Isn't that Peter Wilson over there, sitting on his own?

8   Sarah told me that you hated me. She said that you didn't want to see me ever again!

9   So anyway, in the middle of the meeting the manager, you know ... Keith Matthews, well, he suddenly got up out of his chair and started walking around the room ... Darling, are you listening to me?

T2.5

1   We went to dinner with some friends on Saturday evening. We had a lovely time, but the meal was awful! We had sheep's heart with rice and bananas!
    Yuk! How disgusting! Did you eat any of it?

2   We were all going on holiday to Spain next week. We were really looking forward to it, but my father's been quite ill so we've had to cancel the holiday.
    Ah! What a shame! You must be so disappointed!

3   A   Has Annie had the baby yet? It must be due any time now.
    B   Oh, yes. Haven't you heard? She didn't have one. She had three. Tom's the father of triplets!
    A   Wow! Triplets! How amazing! That'll keep them busy.

4   Careful with that knife. Mind you don't cut yourself. It's very sharp.
    Ouch! I've just cut my finger. I don't think it's very deep, but I'd better put a plaster on it.

5   Do be careful. That bowl's really heavy! Whoops! I've dropped it! Don't worry. I'll get you a new one.

6   How's your steak? Is it OK?
    Mmm! It's absolutely delicious! Just the way I like it.

7   Look! Isn't that Peter Wilson over there, sitting on his own?
    Hey, Peter! Come over here and sit with us. We'd really like you to join us.

8   Sarah told me that you hated me. She said that you didn't want to see me ever again!
    Uh? That's crazy! What a stupid thing to say! You know it's not true.

9   So anyway, in the middle of the meeting the manager, you know ... Keith Matthews, well, he suddenly got up out of his chair and started walking around the room ... Darling, are you listening to me?
    Uh-huh. Of course I'm listening to you. You're talking about Keith whatsisname and some meeting or other.

UNIT 3

T3.1

L = Laura   J = John

L   Did I ever tell you that story about my friend Mandy?

J   No, I don't think so. Why, what happened?

L   Well, Mandy's an air-hostess, except they don't call them that any more ...

J   What is it now? Member of the cabin staff ...

L   Flight attendant or something. Well, it was quite a long flight ... it was a long-haul flight going to ... somewhere. And it was quite a long way into it and ... erm ... I think ... it was ... in the night-time so most people were sleeping and ... what happened was Mandy suddenly saw this man stand up out of his seat and fall over into the aisle, and he was just lying there. And so they ... all the stewards and stewardesses thought 'Oh my God! He's had a heart attack or something', and went running over to him, and so ... they were trying to ... they wanted to know if he was unconscious, so they were trying to find out what was wrong, what had happened. And then they smelt this smell of alcohol on him, so they thought 'Oh, he's had too much to drink on the plane, too much whisky or whatever, and he's drunk.' So, they reckoned that that was why he'd fallen over.

J   Oh dear!

L   Mmm. So anyway, they started to feel less sympathetic to him, and told him ... 'Come on! Get back in your seat!' and everything, helping him back up, you know, back into his seat. And it was only then that they found out what had happened ... well, he managed to tell them what had happened. He'd been fast asleep, and ... a bottle of whisky or gin or something in the overhead compartment had started ... it had broken and it had started leaking and dripping out of the overhead compartment onto his head ...

J   Poor guy!

L   Yeah. And it was the alcohol that had woken him up with such a start. He'd been in quite a deep sleep. He stood up and ... the thing is he only had one leg and he'd forgotten ... that he'd taken off his false leg, his wooden leg or whatever, and put that in the overhead compartment with the bottle of whisky. So he was completely off balance, and he'd stood up so quickly but with only one leg he'd fallen right over onto the aisle ...

J   Oh no!

L   ... and that's what happened. They all thought he'd had a heart attack or something, but ... it was because it was so sudden when he woke up that he didn't have time to remember that he didn't have his false leg on.

J   What I don't understand is why he'd taken it off in the first place.

L Well, I don't know. Maybe because it's quite cramped on planes ... I've no idea why he'd taken it off.

T3.2

This is the BBC news at six o'clock.
Three climbers, missing for thirty hours, have been found safe and well by rescue teams in Scotland. The three, two men and a woman, who are all from Glasgow, had been climbing in the Highlands when they were forced to take shelter by the bad weather. They were found early this morning. They are recovering in hospital, and are said to be doing well. Rescue organizations have been warning walkers and climbers of the dangers of going out onto the mountains at this time of year since the deaths of five young men last month.

T3.3

The death has been announced of one the world's best-selling novelists. Saskia Lane was found on Sunday evening by her ex-husband in the bedroom of her apartment overlooking Central Park in New York. He was bringing back their twelve-year-old daughter who had been spending the weekend with him. A post-mortem revealed that she had taken a large quantity of sleeping pills. Miss Lane had been depressed since the break-up of her fifth marriage. Her last novel *Ex-wives of Manhattan*, was published two years ago. She also leaves a nineteen-year-old son from her second marriage.

T3.4

Yesterday afternoon five million pounds was stolen from a security van in North London. Three men on motorcycles attacked two security guards as they were carrying the money from the bank. The men were all wearing masks. Shots were fired but no one was hurt. The police were given a good description of one of the men, whose mask had been pulled off in the fight. It is believed that the gang had been watching the bank for several weeks.

T3.5

MH = Michael Henchard
SH = Susan Henchard
A = Auctioneer   S = Sailor   M = Man

MH I don't see why men who have got wives who don't want 'em shouldn't get rid of 'em as these ... these gipsy fellows do their horses. Why, I'd sell mine this minute if anyone would buy her! Well, then, now is your chance; I am open to an offer.

SH Michael, you have talked this nonsense in public places before. A joke is a joke, but you may make it once too often, mind!

MH I know I've said it before, and I meant it. All I want is a buyer. Here ... here ... here, I'm waiting to know about this offer of mine. This woman is no good to me. Who'll have her?

SH Come, come, it's getting dark, and this nonsense won't do. If you don't come along, I shall go without you. Come!

MH I asked this question and nobody answered to it. Will anybody buy her?

SH I wish somebody would! Her present owner is not to her liking!

MH Nor you to mine! Now stand up Susan, and show yourself. Who's ... who's the auctioneer?

A I be. Who'll make an offer for this lady?

M Five shillings!

MH No insults! Who'll say a guinea? Set it higher, auctioneer!

A Two guineas!

MH If they don't take her for that, in ten seconds they'll have to give more. Very well. Now, auctioneer, add another!

A Three guineas. Going for three guineas!

MH I'll tell ye what. I won't sell her for less than five. I'll sell her for five guineas to any man that will pay me the money and treat her well; and he shall have her for ever. Now then, five guineas and she's yours. Susan, you agree?

A Five guineas. Do anybody give it? The last time. Yes or no?

S Yes!

MH You say you do?

S I say so.

MH Saying is one thing, and paying is another. Where's the money?

S One ... two ... three ... four ... five.

SH Now, before you go further, Michael, listen to me. If you touch that money, I and this girl go with the man. Mind, it is a joke no longer.

MH A joke? Of course it is not a joke! I take the money, and the sailor takes you.

S Come along! The little one, too. The more the merrier!

SH Mike, I've lived with thee a couple of years, and had nothing but ill-temper! Now I'll try my luck elsewhere. 'Twill be better for me and Elizabeth-Jane, both. So, good-bye!

T3.6

Joey

I = Interviewer

I You really enjoy reading, Joey, don't you?

J No, I do very much. I'm a prolific reader.

I Erm ... can you tell me the title and the author of one of your favourite books?

J Well, it's very difficult to kind of pinpoint a favourite book, but I suppose erm ... *The Woman in White*, by Wilkie Collins particularly erm ... sticks in my mind.

I Wilkie Collins?

J Yes. That's right.

I And when was that written?

J Er .. it was just in the nineteenth century. So it's erm ...

I And what kind of a book is it?

J It's er ... it's a detective story with a bit of romance thrown in, so you've got it all there, really, a complete package. But it's a very good detective story ...

I I think I've heard of it. I think it's called the very first detective story that was ever written.

J Oh, really? Considering ...

I I think so.

J Considering it's the first one, it's jolly good.

I And so ... and what ... what's it about?

J Well, it's basically about mistaken identity. The woman in white erm ... looks very like this young lady called Miss Fairlie. Erm ... basically it's ... the main character's Walter Hartwright, who's a young artist, and he goes up to the north of England to instruct these two ... these two young ladies in the ... the art of how to ... you know ... in how to paint. And erm ... he falls in love with Miss Fairlie ...

I Mmm huh.

J Erm ... but he's too poor, so she can't marry him, so she marries somebody else.

I Oh, dear!

J And then he hears that she's died, so he goes up to her gravestone, and he's weeping erm ... on her gravestone and ... when she suddenly appears. So she pretended to die, so she could escape from her ...

I Is this because she has a look-alike, somebody who looks like ...

J Yes.

I ... her twin?

J It was the woman in white that had actually died, not Miss Fairlie.

I Ah! So I mean they look so alike like ...

J They look so alike, yes.

I ... like identical twins.

J As if, yes.

I What a wonderful theme for a detective story.

J Mmm, indeed.

I Where does it take place, this story?

J Erm .. it takes place in London and the north of England because that's where he goes to ... to teach these two young ladies.

I Mmm huh. And er ... you really ... obviously you enjoyed reading it very much. I mean, why particularly? Why did you like it so much?

J Well, you know, it's ... it's so important when you look forward to reading the present book, you can't wait to go to bed ...

I Yeah.

J ... because you want to carry on reading it, and that's what it was like with this book. I couldn't wait to go to bed, so I could carry on reading it, and I would ...

I So you read it all night ...

J ... read it in the early hours of the morning ...

I ... couldn't put it down!

J No, absolutely not. It was ... it was very good.

I Page after page. I think it's the best, yeah, the ... the best kind of book, isn't it?

J Definitely.

I That's great. Thanks very much.

Ken

I Right Ken, what kinds of books do you enjoy reading?

K Actually I enjoy reading quite a range of books, but I suppose if I had to choose one as it were for my desert island I would choose autobiography and I think mainly because I just enjoy reading about other people's lives, and the adventures they've got into, the ups and downs of the ... er you know, character of their lives, ... er, and because they're always very weighty and somehow you get to know the people very well and perhaps with more insight than you might otherwise ... you may hear about them on the radio or television and so on but suddenly you get behind all that and see what it is that makes the person tick and that always fascinates me.

I What about a particular book that you've read recently that you've really enjoyed?

K Well I think the book that I always come back to is Laurie Lee's *Cider with Rosie* ... er it's a favourite, it's one that I'm always recommending to young students to read. It's extremely good quality. He is of course a poet and this comes through in the language and his observations. It never fails to please me. I always find something new in it to enjoy... He expresses himself so very well, lots of humour, acute observations and generally here's a writer who I think is a real writer in that he conveys his enthusiasm for writing itself and his life and the things he sees.

I What's it about, *Cider with Rosie*?

K *Cider with Rosie* is an autobiography. It tells of his life in the Cotswolds, in a little village and it starts when he's about three years of age and it tells of the village, its people ... er the way the society works and about his growing up in this rather countrified quiet little community ... erm ... which ... he stays there until he's about eighteen and then off he goes around ... I believe in the first case on his journey ... was around Spain. So it's ... it's his childhood in this little village. And it describes the village of course and its characters and the way he feels about it and the way it's shaped his life ... erm and it's called *Cider with Rosie* because the one event that he remembers particularly well ... was a little encounter with Rosie in the bushes with some cider. And you're left to think about what that may mean.

Kate

I Kate, do you like reading?

K Yes.

I Good. Erm ... what about telling me about erm ... just one of ... one of your favourite books ... erm ... what about its title and its author?

K It's called *The Valley of Adventure*, and it's written by Enid Blyton.

I And ... and what kind of a book's that?

K It's an adventure book.

I An adventure book. *The Valley of Adventure*. I suppose it would be. And erm ... can you tell me a bit about it? Can you tell me about the people who are in it, and what it's about?

K There are four children, called Phillip, Dinah, Lucy-Ann, and Jack, and they go on ... they get on a plane. But they're meant to be getting on their friend's plane, but they get the wrong one.

I Just the children?

K Yeah.

I The four of them? Just them?

K They get on the wrong plane. And they end up in this deserted valley, where there's this hut, full of food, and they break in ...

I That's fortunate ...

K Yeah.

I ... with food.

K And they break in, and get the food. And they see ... they see that there's someone else living on the island, and they follow them. And they find a map ... this old man gives Phillip ...

I Yeah.

K And they find a huge cave of treasures and gold and ...

I So it's a treasure map?

K Mmm.

I Wow! And er ... is it exciting?

K Very.

I Have you read lots of stories with these characters?

K Yeah, I've read about twelve of them.

I And is it just the four children in the stories? Any ... any ...?

K There's a man called Bill, who's their friend, and their Mum, but the mum doesn't get very involved.

I And what about the ending of the story? What happens in the end?

K They erm ... find their friend, and erm ... and he ... he gets to the police, and the police take the treasure, and they put it in a museum, and they give some of the money back to the villagers who lost it.

I Mmm. No, it sounds very good. What about if ... what about if you met someone who didn't know Enid Blyton stories, and er ... wondered ... about that story. Would you recommend it? What would you ... what's your opinion of the story? Why ... why did you like it?

K I liked it because it was really exciting ... like ... it kept you on the edge of your seat.

I Page after page.

K Yeah.

I Ah, right. Any other reason why you liked it?

K It was funny.

I Which ... which bits are funny in the story?

K Erm ... when some of the children are speaking ... and the parrot, they have a pet parrot.

I They have a pet parrot? What's it called?

K Kiki.

I Kiki.

K And it's really funny, 'cos it answers back. And it keeps these men erm ... wondering what ... he keeps ... the parrot keeps talking, and the men don't know who's talking, so they get scared and run away.

I They don't know it's a parrot?

K No.

I It sounds great. It sounds really good. So ... exciting and funny, that's why you like it. Thanks very much. That's terrific.

T3.7

A Meg's got a new boyfriend.

B A new boyfriend?

A Yes. He lives in a castle.

B A castle?

A Yes. She met him in Mauritius.

B In Mauritius?

T3.8

A Meg's got a new boyfriend.

B Has she?

A Yes. He lives in a castle.

B Does he?

A Yes. She met him in Mauritius.

B Did she?

T3.9

a

A Sam wants to apologize.

B Does he?

A Yes. He's broken your mother's Chinese vase.

B My mother's Chinese vase? Oh, no!

b

A We had a terrible holiday.

B Did you?

A Yes. It rained all the time.

B Did it?

A Yes. And the food was disgusting!

B Was it? What a drag!

c

A Look! Bob's drunk.

B Is he?

A Yes. He's had six glasses of whisky.

B Six glasses of whisky?

A Yes. He doesn't like parties.

B Doesn't he? How strange!

A The poor chap can't walk straight.

B Can't he? How's he going to get home?

A I don't know. I never have too much to drink.

B Don't you?

A No. I can't stand hangovers.

d

A It took me three hours to get here.

B Did it?

A Yes. There was a traffic jam ten miles long.

B Ten miles long? That's awful!

A Now I've got a headache!

B Have you? Poor darling. I'll get you something for it.

e

A I've met the love of my life!

B Have you?

A Yes. We're getting married next Saturday in Barbados.

B Next Saturday? In Barbados?

A Yes. We've booked a flight on Concorde.
B Have you? You lucky thing!
f
A I'm on a mobile phone.
B Are you?
A Yes. And I've got something very important to tell you.
B Have you? What is it? I can't wait!
A You'd better sit down ... I'd like to marry you.
B Marry me? Blimey!

UNIT 4

T4.1

a Scotland imports a lot of its food from other countries. Its exports include oil, beef, and whisky.
b I'm very pleased with my English. I'm making a lot of progress.
c Ministers are worried. There has been an increase in the number of unemployed.
d But the number of crimes has decreased, so that's good news.
e How dare you call me a liar and a cheat! What an insult!
f There was a demonstration yesterday. People were protesting about blood sports.
g People usually buy CDs these days. Not many people buy records any more.
h Don't touch the video! I'm recording a film.
i Britain produces about 75% of its own oil.

T4.2

a He takes away our refuse.
b An unidentified flying object.
c A desert.
d Presents!
e The contents pages.
f Con'tent. A 'contract. In'valid. Mi'nute. To ob'ject. To re'fuse.

T4.3

a This programme is coming to you live from Mongolia.
b Mind that nail! You'll tear your shirt. Oh!
c Listen to that wind howling outside.
d The use of mobile phones is strictly forbidden in this library.
e Listen to the neighbours! They're having a terrible row.
f Where do these stairs lead?
g I hate mornings! I'm not used to getting up so early.

T4.4

I = Interviewer   T = Tom   S = Sue

I All over France the city of Lyon is regarded as a gastronomic paradise. 'You're going to Lyon? *Vous allez très bien manger* – you'll eat very well,' say the French. And it's true. Lyon has hundreds of fine restaurants. Given this situation, would it be wise to open an English restaurant there? After all, we all know that the French consider British cuisine to be inedible. But that is exactly what Tom and Sue Higgins have done. They've opened an English restaurant and called it 'Mister Higgins'. How did they get the idea? Why did they do it?
T Well, I had been working as a translator in Geneva and Sue had just finished her medical training in England. So you see, we needed to live near Geneva for my work, but in the EU for Sue's qualifications to be recognized, so Lyon seemed a good choice.
S Yes. The only one, really. Then one night, after we moved here, some French friends came for dinner and we gave them meat loaf. They loved it, and we were laughing and joking and they said 'You should open a restaurant and serve things like this.' And we laughed, too. We knew we were quite good cooks, but we thought 'Oh yeah! An English restaurant in Lyon!'
T But then ... I mean it was me, bit by bit, I just became obsessed with the idea. 'Cos our new house had once been a bakery, so it seemed to ask to be converted into a restaurant. But the formalities were horrendous! I went to the Lyon Chamber of Commerce and came back exhausted with all the papers and the details ... we almost gave up ... but not quite ...
S ... no ... the the next stop was the bank. Of course, we had to borrow the money. And Monsieur Dufour, the bank manager, didn't laugh at us. He even said he would consider an application from us. We were thrilled ...
T ... but the documents and the bureaucracy! It was a nightmare. I couldn't believe it when Monsieur Dufour finally gave us the cash. And then ... er ... when we started rebuilding ... it took two and a half months to rebuild ... passers-by were fascinated, they simply couldn't believe what we were doing. '*Un restaurant anglais? Ce n'est pas possible!*'
I And how did you decide on the name? Or was it just obvious to call it by your name?
T No, we tried lots before it seemed obvious. But then we thought, 'Well, *Higgins* sounds very British, and it's quite easy for the French to pronounce, apart from one letter, H, and they all understand *mister* just as we understand *monsieur*, so ...
I And did you have an opening party?
S Oh yes. We invited everybody we could think of. British friends, obviously, and all the workmen who had helped build it ...
T Yeah, and absolutely everyone we saw in the street for days before, and of course we had free wine. The restaurant was really crowded ... almost impossible to move. We were so busy. Oh, my goodness! In my memory, the whole first year is just a grey blur of exhaustion and tiredness, but with some wonderful moments.
S Yes. D'you remember once we had to turn away a couple because we were full and Madame was furious! She said '*What! An English* restaurant, and you have to make reservations?! Pah!*'
T Mmm, we were often full, but we still only earned £2 a week each for ourselves in that year! I had to carry on doing translations for a while.
S But ... what we had right from the start and we still have ... is curiosity value. Customers told their friends about our amazing meat loaf. '*Le meat loaf! Vraiment délicieux!*' Nowadays they know they have to book and ...
T ... and some even admit that the food is good!
S Yes, but they won't admit it's British! Their reasoning goes: English cooking is bad therefore this can't be English. Actually I think it's a big compliment, coming from the French!
I Well, I loved every bit of my meal. But then I am English!

T4.5

a Could I use your phone for a moment?
  By all means. Help yourself.
b What film would you like to see tonight?
  I don't mind. Whatever you want.
c Everyone says you're mad. Did you know that?
  I don't care what other people think. That's their problem, not mine.
d I'll give you £6,000 for your car. That's my final offer.
  It's a deal! It's yours!
e When he told me he'd smashed my car, I was furious!
  I bet you were. I'd have hit him.
f Oh, no! The photocopier's jammed again!
  Has it? Let me have a look. I'll try and fix it.
g Can we meet next Thursday?
  Let me see. Yes, I can make the morning.
h Bye! I'm off now!
  Hang on a sec. Where are you going?

T4.6

a I'm really sorry, but I can't go out to the cinema with you this week.
  Never mind. Let's try again next week.
b I walked out of my job. I just couldn't take it any more.
  I don't blame you. I'd have done the same thing myself.
c What if I forget everything in the exam? What if my pen runs out?
  For goodness' sake stop worrying! You'll be fine. Just don't panic!
d Have you applied for that job?
  No, there's no point. I'm not qualified for it. I wouldn't stand a chance.
e Are you going to phone Andy again?
  I can't be bothered. I've left five messages for him, and he's never replied.
f I don't know what to do. Do I tell her the truth, or do I say nothing?
  I see what you mean. You're in a very difficult position.
g We aren't having a holiday this year.
  How come? Can't you afford it?
h Why did you tell everyone that I'm in love with Mike? It's not true!
  Hey! I was kidding. It was just a joke.

UNIT 5

T5.1

1 What am I doing tomorrow, you say? Well, my daughter will be here. She'll be bringing the little 'uns, and we'll all have a cup of tea and a good old chat. And I'll bake a cake, a ginger cake. They like that.

2 In the next few years? I hope I'll be earning a lot of money. And with a bit of luck I'll be living in my own flat, as well!

3 I'm waiting for my exam results at the moment. I did my 'A' levels a few weeks ago, and if I get good results I'm going to study medicine at Newcastle University. If I don't get the grades I need, I don't know what I'll do. I haven't really thought about it.

4 My Mom's a marine in the US Navy, and we move every couple of years. Next July we're all moving to Hawaii, and we'll be there for a year or two, then move on again.

5 It's Saturday tomorrow, isn't it, so I'm going to see a football match with me son and some mates from work, aren't I? It's Arsenal versus Manchester United.

6 Marie's having a baby soon, so we're both very excited. The baby's due in four weeks.

7 In ten years' time? I'll have finished school by then. Wey-hey! I'm going to have a toy factory.

8 Tomorrow morning I'm going to France for the day. It's a school trip. I have to be at school at five in the morning, my Dad's giving me and a few of my friends a lift. Then we're going by coach to Waterloo and we're going on Eurostar to Paris. The train leaves at 9.30.

T5.2

Good morning, ladies and gentlemen. Welcome on board this British Airways flight to Rome. In a very short time, just as soon as we have received permission, we'll be taking off. When we have reached our cruising speed of 550 miles an hour, we will be flying at 35,000 feet. Our flight time today is two and a half hours, so we will be in Rome in time for lunch! The cabin crew will be serving refreshments during the flight, so just sit back and relax. We hope you will enjoy the flight. If you need any assistance, just press the button and a flight attendant will come to help you.

If you look out of the right-hand side of the plane, you will see Mont Blanc. In a few moments' time, the crew will be coming round with duty-free goods. We will also be giving out immigration forms. When you have filled them in, please place them in your passport. They will be collected as you go through passport control.

In twenty minutes' time we will be landing. Please put your seats into the upright position. You are requested to remain seated until the plane has come to a complete standstill. Before you leave the plane, please look around to make sure you haven't left any of your possessions behind you.

We hope you will fly again soon with British Airways.

T5.3

a
Do you think you'll ever be rich?
I hope so.
I might one day.
It's possible, but I doubt it.
I'm sure I will.
I'm sure I won't.

b
Are you going out tonight?
Yes, I am.
I think so, but I'm not sure.
I might be.

c
Do you think the world's climate will change dramatically in the next fifty years?
I don't think so.
I hope not.
Who knows? Maybe.

T5.4

A = Alan S = Sarah

S Hello. 267890.
A Hello. Is that Sarah?
S Speaking.
A Hi, Sarah. It's Alan, Alan Cunningham.
S Alan! Hi! How are you? How are things?
A OK, yeah, not too bad, thanks. And you? How's the family?
S Oh, we're surviving! Dave's away at the moment at a conference, which leaves me running the house and looking after the kids on my own.
A That's tough. It takes a lot out of you, doesn't it?
S You're not kidding. I tell you, at 9.00 in the evening I just collapse into an armchair in front of the telly. Still, Dave's back soon, thank goodness. Anyway, how are things with you? What are you up to? We haven't spoken for a while.
A No, that's right. Well, we went through a very quiet period at work, but right now things are looking up and I've got a lot on. I'm a bit snowed under at the moment. It's OK, but I need a break. Speaking of which, I'm phoning about our reunion ...
S ... our what?
A You know, in Durham, ten years on, with James.
S Oh, of course! No, I hadn't fogotten. On the fourteenth, right? Friday night. No, I can't wait. I'm really looking forward to it.
A Have you any ideas where we can meet? A restaurant somewhere?
S Well, what do you fancy? Indian? A bar meal? A Chinese? There's a really good Chinese where we used to go in Clay Path.
A Oh, yes. What's it called?
S The Lotus Garden.
A That's right. Now, I'm driving from the Midlands, so I'll be coming into Durham from the A1(M). How do I get to the restaurant?
S Well, you come in on the A177. You go past the sports centre on your right, and you come to a roundabout. Left takes you on the A1051. Don't take that, go straight on into town. It's called Hallgarth Street, if I remember rightly.
A Uh huh.
S Then you come into New Elvet, past the police station on your right, over the river and you come to another roundabout.
A Right. Got it. And I take a left there, don't I?
S No, you can't. Well, you can, but not to get where you need to go. You need to go right, up Leazes Road, past St Bede's College on your right, and up to the roundabout, then you take a very sharp left into Clay Path. Go down a couple of hundred yards and you see the restaurant, the Lotus Garden on your left. It's bang opposite a car park. That's handy for you.
A Right, I've got it. That's great. I'll be leaving about 3.00 in the afternoon, so I should be in Durham about 5, 6 o'clock depending on the traffic.
S Where are you staying?
A In The County. What about you?
S Oh, that's good. I'm staying in The Three Tuns, just down the road. We can meet up for a drink.
A Sounds great! How are you getting there?
S By train. It's direct from here, so it's easy. The journey takes less than an hour. Why don't I come to The County at about 6.30? I'll see you in the bar.
A All right. That sounds great. Will you phone James, or shall I?
S Erm ... No, don't worry. I'll phone him.
A OK. So I'll see you on the fourteenth in the bar of The County. I presume there's only one.
S Well, it's not that big. I'm sure we won't lose each other!
A That's right. OK, then. See you then.
S About 6.30.
A That's it. Bye.
S Bye. See you soon.

T5.5

S = Sarah J = James

J Hello. Simpson's Travel Agents.
S Hello, James. This is Sarah Jackson. How are you?
J Sarah! Hello! How lovely to hear from you!
S Sorry to disturb you at work.
J Oh, don't worry. I'm only too pleased to be interrupted. Anything to stop me having to deal with customers and their complaints! Never mind! How's everything with you?
S Oh, fine. Have you got a lot on at the moment?
J Well, it's our busy time of year, you know, coming up to the summer. Everyone booking their holidays. Still, I mustn't complain.
S That's right. Business is business! Anyway, James, I spoke to Alan yesterday, you know,

about our get-together in Durham ...

J Now there's something to look forward to.

S ... on the fourteenth, and I'm just ringing to let you know what's happening.

J Great!

S We've decided to meet in The Lotus Garden, the er ... Chinese restaurant ...

J You mean the one in Clay Path?

S Yes.

J Where we all used to go?

S Yeah.

J Oh.

S Why? Is that no good?

J It closed about three years ago.

S Oh, dear. Are you sure?

J Uh huh. Absolutely. But it doesn't matter. There's the other one, the Kwai Lam. It's just as good, better, in fact.

S Now where is that? I've forgotten.

J How are you getting to Durham?

S My train leaves Leeds at five o'clock.

J Well, when you come out of the station, go down the path to the roundabout, and go down North Street towards the town centre.

S Uh huh. I'm with you.

J Cross over Framwellgate Bridge and go up Silver Street. There's Fairbrother's jeweller's on the right, on the corner as you go up. Remember? Big place.

S Yes, I do.

J Up into the Market Place, where the Town Hall is. Then you go right into Saddler Street, and then the road divides. Saddler Street goes down to the left over Elvet Bridge, and right is North Bailey, which goes up to Palace Green and the cathedral. Got it?

S Yeah, yeah.

J That's right. Well, the Kwai Lam is on the corner of Saddler Street and North Bailey.

S OK. Now, what time are you coming from Sunderland? How are you getting there?

J Well, I'm so close, I'll be catching the bus. The office closes at 6.00, and I'll go straight to the bus station. There's a bus to Durham every twenty minutes, so I'll get the first one, probably about 6.30.

S So you'll be there at about ... what? Seven?

J Yeah, something like that.

S Well, look. Why don't we see you in the Kwai Lam? I'm meeting Alan in The County before that, because we both get in earlier than you. I need to phone Alan to tell him about the Lotus Flower ...

J ... Lotus Garden.

S Lotus Garden. Sorry.

J No, I'll phone Alan. I haven't spoken to him for ages.

S OK. Yeah, you phone him then. What about if we see you in the Kwai Lam between seven and half past? How does that sound?

J Fine. That'll give me enough time, I'm sure. Shall I phone and book a table?

S That would be great. By the way, where are you staying that night?

J I'll be coming back here, I suppose.

S Can't you stay in Durham so we can have more time together? You don't want to rush back to Sunderland, do you?

J I guess I could give a friend of mine a ring to see if he can put me up. Yeah, I'll do that.

S Great! Well, we'll see you on the fourteenth, then, around 7.15.

J In the restaurant, that's it. And you know where it is, don't you?

S Yeah, yeah, I've got it. Bye, now, James.

J Bye, Sarah. Thanks for phoning.

T5.6

A Hello. TVS Computer Services. Darren speaking. How can I help you?

B Good morning. Could I speak to your customer services department, please?

A Certainly. Who's calling, please?

B This is Keith Jones.

A One moment, Mr Jones. I'm trying to connect you.

B Thank you.

A I'm afraid the line's busy at the moment. Will you hold?

B Er ... yes, please.

A OK. You're through now. Go ahead.

B Hello. Is that customer services? I was wondering if you could tell me ...

T5.7

A So, Barry. It was good to talk to you. Thanks very much for phoning.

B My pleasure. By the way, how's your golf these days? Still playing?

A No, not much. I just don't seem to find the time these days. Anyway, Barry ...

B What a shame! You used to enjoy it so much.

A It's true. Right, Barry. I must fly. I'm late for a meeting.

B OK. I don't want to keep you. So, you'll give me a ring when you're back, right?

A I certainly will. And you'll send me a copy of the report?

B It'll be in the post tonight.

A That's great, Barry. Have a good weekend!

B Same to you, too! Bye, Andy.

A Bye, Barry.

UNIT 6

T6.1

a The area of London I like best is Soho.

b People who smoke risk getting all sorts of illnesses.

c I met a man whose main aim in life was to visit every capital city in the world.

d Charlie Chaplin, who made over fifty films, won an Oscar in 1973.

e George Orwell's most famous book is *Nineteen Eighty-Four*, which he completed the year before he died.

f Charles passed his driving test first time, which surprised everybody.

T6.2

a The book I'm reading at the moment is fascinating.

b It's called *The Shell Seekers*, and it's about a family who live in Cornwall.

c It was written by Rosamunde Pilcher, who has been writing all her life.

d It's over six hundred pages, which put me off starting it for a long time.

e The name of the main character is Penelope Keeling, whose father was a famous painter.

f Penelope was married with three children, but the man she really loved died in the war.

g The children, who are grown up when the story takes place, are all very different.

h The thing that most impressed me was the portrayal of the characters.

T6.3

a

A Have you heard about Doug and Maggie?

B No. Tell me, tell me!

A Well, last week they went to a party, and Maggie ditched him in front of all these people and went off with another bloke!

B Really! How interesting!

b

A How did you do in your maths test?

B Oh! Don't ask!

A Oh, dear. What did you get?

B Twenty per cent. I came last. I thought I was going to do really well.

c

A Did you have a good holiday?

B It was lovely, thanks.

A Did you do much?

B No, we sat by the pool, read books, and took it easy for two whole weeks.

d

A Are you sure you saw a ghost?

B Absolutely convinced. It walked through the wall and came over to my bed.

A What did you do?

B I screamed and screamed and screamed.

e

A Come on in and sit down. You must be exhausted!

B Oof, I am. I've been travelling for the past thirty hours. Oh, how wonderful to be back home.

A Just relax now.

f

A How's your new job?

B Good, thanks, very good. It's quite difficult, and I have to concentrate very hard, but I'm enjoying meeting so many famous people and travelling all over the world.

A I know what you mean.

B It's great to be doing something that's so satisfying.

g

A So anyway, at the end of the evening I had to walk back home because I'd lost the car keys and I didn't have any money for a taxi. I didn't get home until three.

B That's the funniest thing I've heard for ages. Oh, poor you. I'm sorry I'm laughing.

h
A What's the programme about?
B The life of frogs.
A Is it any good?
B No. Absolute rubbish.

i
A Did you have a nice weekend?
B Yes. Some friends of ours came for supper, but it was spoilt by their kids.
A What did they do?
B They made so much noise, they were always interrupting, and they ate nothing but crisps.
A That's terrible. Did you say anything?

j
A What's the matter with you?
B I've done something awful.
A What?
B I just asked that lady over there when her baby was due, and she said she wasn't pregnant.
A Oh, no!

T6.4

a Would you prefer red wine or white?
b Are you sure she was telling you the truth?
c When are you going to mend that door? You've been saying you're going to do it for ages.
d I hate the way he eats with his mouth open. Don't you?
e What's up with Kathy? She looks pretty unhappy, doesn't she?
f Your daughter can dance, sing, speak French, and act! She's so clever.
g What's your ambition in life?
h What were you and James rowing about last night?
i Did you confess that you'd lied?
j That woman who won £2 million says she's going to give it all away. Don't you think she's mad?

T6.5

95.8 Capital FM

DJ OK, folks, time for a break. We'll be back soon.

a

J = John   M = Mike

M Anyway, John, how's business?
J Not bad. Just me and Maggie, and the computer. I'll tell you what, though. I could really use a printer. Have you got any ideas?
M Pass.
J And a fax, and a copier. A scanner! Any suggestions?
M Pass.
J I thought you were supposed to know about these things. A bit of an expert.
M Pass. Flexipass from Zubichi. Attach it to your PC, and it'll print, fax, copy, and scan. It's even compact enough to fit into your office. Anyway, John. Your turn to buy lunch?
J Pass.

For more information, just Freephone 0800 541001. With a Zubichi Flexipass, you and Zubichi can.

b

J = Juliet   R = Romeo

And now, the Soup-in-a-box Players proudly present *Romeo and Juliet*, by William Shakespeare.

J Oh, Romeo, Romeo, wherefore art thou, Romeo? But that you were with me now, to share the pleasures and delights of my chicken supreme.
R She speaks. Oh, speak again, bright angel.
J For I have fried two boneless, skinless chicken breasts until they hath browned, adding one small sliced onion, one hundred grammes of mushrooms, and cooking until soft.
R Shall I hear more, or shall I speak at this?
J A goblet of white wine hath been lovingly added, and boiled, until the liquid hath been reduced by half. Then, a packet of Soup-in-a-box Cream of Chicken Soup poured in.
R Oh, temptation! Fair maid! Let me taste thy dish. Has it yet simmered until the meat is as tender as my love?
J The dish is as warm as thy lips, dear Romeo. Five fluid ounces of single cream hast been stirred in, and it awaits you.

The recipe featured in this production of the condensed works of Shakespeare is now available on the back of a box of new Soup-in-a-box Cream of Chicken Soup.

c

W = Woman   I = Inspector

W Who's there?
I Inspector R21. Our records show you have an unlicenced television on the premises. Please open the door. You have forty seconds to comply.

If you're still watching TV without a licence, be warned. There may come a time when our enquiries are no longer carried out by humans.

W But my husband bought the telly.
I Thirty seconds.

Already, we're equipped with computerized records of every unlicensed home in the country.

W He said he'd get the licence.
I Twenty seconds.

So, our eight hundred enquiry officers will track you down sooner or later, wherever you are.

W Why are you picking on me?
I Ten seconds.

Last year we caught 260,000 offenders.

W Go away.
I Five seconds.

So, even without robots, the future looks pretty bad for licence evaders.

I Time's up!

Get a licence. Or get a visit.

d

S = Sarah   M = Mummy

Sarah is five, and this is her favourite play shirt. It's pink, with fluffy yellow ducks. Sarah loves her play shirt.

S It's my favourite.

And she wears it to play in the garden.

S Look what I've found, Mummy!

And you wash it at low temperature. And she wears it to play in the garden.

S Mummy! Look what I've made.

And you wash it. And she wears it to play in the garden.

M Sarah! What on earth ...?

And after a while, the dirt builds up, so the pink isn't quite as pink, and the yellow ducks aren't as fluffy. New System Sudso Automatic can help. Its advanced formula can remove ground-in dirt even at low temperatures. So the pink stays very pink, and the fluffy yellow ducks are happy again. Wash ...

S Mummy! Look what I've made.

... after wash ...

S Look what I've found, Mummy!

... after wash.

M Sarah! Don't you dare bring that in here!

New System Sudso Automatic. It's all you could want from a powder.

e

P = Presenter   M = Minister

P I'm challenging Britain's disposable users to experience the extraordinary comfort of the Sure Grip Supreme. Today I'm with Stephen Hobson, Minister for Frozen Fish. Good morning, Minister.
M It is.
P And why is that?
M Well, since coming to power, the policies we've put in place have enabled ordinary people to go up ...
P Minister, what disposable razor do you use?
M Tom, I hardly think what I choose to do in my own home is what is important here.
P Because the Sensor Excel's protective micro-fins ensure a more comfortable shave every time. Why not try it?
M In the fullness of time it ...
P Just try it!
M Mmm. Mmm! Mmm!
P Minister. Is that as close a shave as you've ever had?
M Yes.
P Is that it, then. What, you don't wish to expand?

Take the Sure Grip Supreme challenge. One shave, and we bet you don't go back to disposables. Sure Grip – you're never unsure with Sure Grip!

f

D = Daughter   F = Father

D Well, Dad. I've decided which new car I'm getting.

F It's all right for some. When I was your age ...

D ... you counted yourself lucky to have a bike, and that was second-hand.

F Now, well, that's where you're wrong, Miss Smartypants. I was going to say that I was twenty-two, I couldn't even have afforded to insure a new car.

D Neither can I.

F Well, don't expect me ...

D ... and I don't have to. 'Cos all new Ford Escorts now come with one year's free insurance, for anyone between 18 and 80. Which rules you out, anyway.

See your Thames Ford dealer now, as offer ends soon. Free insurance, subject to age and status.

F Just like your mother. Always have to have the last word.

D No, I don't.

g

What do you think is harder, going into a quiet peaceful community and causing trouble, or going into a troubled fighting community and making peace? As an infantry soldier, making and keeping the peace is what you're paid to do. It's a daunting task, but with training and full military back-up, you can get the job done. If you're between 16 and 24 and would rather be known as a peacemaker than a trouble-maker, visit your local army career's office, or call 0345 421 633.

UNIT 7

T7.1 See p 68

T7.2

Dear Sean

My dear Sean,
How lovely to get your letter! Mummy is right! I will really enjoy helping you with your schoolwork, and I will try very hard to remember what it was like when I was a little girl all those years ago.
When the war started, I was just five and I'll never forget watching my grandfather dig a big black hole in the back garden. This was our air raid shelter. At first I was really scared of going into it. Every time the siren went off, I started trembling and I was sick, actually sick with fear. I refused to leave my bed. I didn't find it easy to get used to sleeping in that shelter. But soon, living in the cities was so dangerous that the government decided to send all the children away to the countryside. I think I was lucky because I was able to go away to my aunt's. Some children were forced to stay with total strangers. My aunt lived in a small town, called Alston, high in the hills, not too far from Newcastle. And guess what Sean, she had a sweet shop! Mrs Crozier's Sweet Shop. But, oh dear me, at first I was so unhappy, I couldn't stop crying because I couldn't help worrying about my mother back home. My aunt let me have as many sweets as I wanted, but I was too

miserable to eat many. Silly me! Most children didn't have the chance of getting lots of sweets because sweets were rationed. That meant that you couldn't buy all you wanted. You were only allowed to buy a small amount. Lots of other things were rationed, too. It was almost impossible to get butter, cream, meat, fruit, vegetables, and petrol. We did without a lot of things during the war. Can you believe that just after it ended someone gave me a banana and I didn't know what to do with it?
Sean, I hope this is useful. I'm longing to see you all. Give my love to Mummy, Daddy and Liam. Don't worry, he'll be much more fun soon.

Lots of love and kisses,
Grandma

T7.3

a A Are we going to have a break?
  B No, we don't have time to.

b A Can I smoke in here?
  B No, you're not allowed to.

c A I can't help you do your homework this evening. Sorry.
  B Oh, but you promised to!

d A Why did you do Exercise 2?
  B Because you told us to.

e A You said you'd phone me last night.
  B I'm really sorry, I meant to, but I forgot.

f A Have you finished marking the homework yet?
  B Sorry, I haven't had a chance to.

T7.4

a 'There's no way I'm going to give up using my car!'
b 'It's a beautiful morning, isn't it dear?'
c 'No, I haven't ironed your white shirt yet! I haven't had the time.'
d 'Come on! Stop gazing at that blank screen. Let's have a game of Scrabble.'
e 'Well, I'm not doing it! I did it last night. Anyway I want to mend the puncture on my bike.'
f 'Damn! I forgot to buy sugar!'
g 'If it were up to me, I'd throw the lot out!'
h 'Personally, I think life was much harder fifty years ago.'
i 'Never again! That was the longest three days of my life!'

T7.5

You've got a fast car
I want a ticket to anywhere
Maybe we (can) make a deal
Maybe together we can get somewhere
Any place is better
Starting from zero we've got nothing to lose
Maybe we'll make something
But me myself I've got nothing to prove.

You've got a fast car
And I've got a plan to get us out of here
I've been working at a convenience store
Managed to save just a little bit of money

We won't have to drive too far
Just cross the border and into the city
You and I can both get jobs
And finally see what it means to be living.

You see my old man's got a problem
He lives with the bottle, that's the way it is
He says his body's too old for working
His body's too young to look like his
My mama went off and left him
She wanted more from life than he could give
I said somebody's got to take care of him
So I quit school and that's what I did.

You've got a fast car
But is it fast enough so we can fly away?
We've got to make a decision
We leave tonight or live and die this way.

I remember when we were driving driving in your car
The speed so fast I felt like I was drunk
City lights lay out before us
And your arm felt nice wrapped round my shoulder
And I had a feeling that I belonged
And I had a feeling I could be someone, be someone, be someone.

You've got a fast car
And we go cruising to entertain ourselves
You still ain't got a job
Now I work in a market as a checkout girl
I know things will get better
You'll find work and I'll get promoted
We'll move out of the shelter
Buy a bigger house and live in the suburbs.

I remember when ... etc.

You've got a fast car
And I've got a job that pays all our bills
You stay out drinking late at the bar
See more of your friends than you do of your kids
I'd always hoped for better
Thought maybe together you and me would find it
I've got no plans and I ain't going nowhere
So take your fast car and keep on driving.

I remember when ... etc.

You've got a fast car
But is it fast enough so you can fly away?
You've got to make a decision
You leave tonight or live and die this way.

T7.6

1
OK, folks. Don't go away now. We'll be back in a few minutes, just after the break.

2
A It's not fair! Everyone else is allowed to go.
B I don't care about everyone else. You're not, and that's all there is to it.

3
A Open wide and say 'Ah'. Oh, dear.
B Ish it bad newsh?

4
A A big Mac with regular fries and a strawberry milkshake.

B Eat here or take away?

5

Mummy! I need a wee-wee!

6

Has Kelly Jones' latest album been released yet?

7

Well, I'm just going to put my feet up and have a nap, if that's all right with you.

8

Let passengers off first. Move right down inside the car.

9

Thanks for having me!

10

'scuse fingers!

11

A With respect to my Right Honourable friend, I have to say that I find his statement to be inconsistent with the truth.
B Ooh!
C Hear, hear!

12

A Things aren't what they used to be.
B You can say that again. It was different in our day, wasn't it?

13

Will passengers in rows A to K please board now?

14

A I can't find my gym kit.
B Think. Where did you last have it?

15

News is coming in of a major hold-up on the A45 Colchester bypass. Drivers are advised to avoid this area if at all possible.

16

A Could you develop this for me?
B Normal six by four?
A Yeah, that's fine.
B When do you want them by?
A This time tomorrow's all right.

UNIT 8

T8.1 See p 80

T8.2

R = Rod   M = Miranda

R Hello. Kingsbridge 810344. Rod speaking.
M Hi, Rod. It's me, Miranda. I've got to talk to you.
R Oh, hi Miranda. Why all the excitement?
M Well, can you remember that competition I entered, just for a laugh, a few weeks ago?
R Yes, I can. I remember you doing it in the coffee bar. It was the one in the *Daily Express*, wasn't it? Didn't you have to name loads of capital cities?
M Yes, that's it. You've got it. Well, get this, I've won it! I came first!
R You can't have! I don't believe it! What's the prize?

M A trip to New York.
R You must be kidding! That's brilliant. For how long?
M Just three days – but it's three days in the Waldorf Astoria, of all places!
R Well, you should be able to do quite a lot in three days. And the Waldorf Astoria! I'm impressed! Isn't that on Park Avenue?
M Yes, it is.
R I thought so. Not that I've been there of course.
M And Rod, there's something else, even better than that.
R And what could possibly be even better than that?
M Well, you won't believe it ... but the journey there and back is on Concorde!
R Wow! That's fantastic. That's something I've always wanted to do. D'you know it only takes three and a half hours, so you arrive before you've left ..., if you see what I mean.
M I know. And another thing Rod. It's a trip for two and I'd really love it if you would come with me. Will you?
R You can't be serious? You know I'd love to! But why me? Surely you should be taking Richard.
M Haven't you heard? Richard and I have split up. You must have known it had been going wrong between us for ages.
R Oh, sorry! I didn't know. I really am sorry. When did this happen?
M Well, a couple of weeks ago. We ...

T8.3

a A Oh no! I've lost my passport.
   B Well, you could have left it in the taxi.
   A Oh, thank goodness! Here it is at the bottom of my bag.

b A It's an early start for us tomorrow.
   B Really? What time do we have to set off?
   A Well, the taxi's arriving at six o'clock. We have to be at the airport at seven.

c A The traffic's not moving. We'll never get to the concert.
   B Don't worry, don't worry. We should still be there in plenty of time.
   A But I'd hate to miss the beginning.

d A I've brought you some flowers. I hope you like tulips.
   B Oh, how kind of you, you needn't have. I love all spring flowers.
   A I thought you might.

e A All the teachers are going on strike!
   B What? That's brilliant, we don't have to come to school tomorrow.
   A The bad news is that they're setting us loads of homework!

T8.4

A That film was very good, wasn't it?
B Good? It was absolutely fantastic!

A You must have been quite pleased when you passed your exam.
B Pleased? I was absolutely delighted!

T8.5

The Oscar ceremony

'I am absolutely delighted to receive this award, and I am sincerely grateful to all those wonderful people who voted for me. *Kisses and Dreams* was a fantastic movie to work on from start to finish. And I thank all those brilliant and talented people involved in the making of this absolutely fantastic film. Nobody could have possibly known that it would be such a huge success, especially those who told us at the start that the plot was boring and ridiculous. They have now been proved quite wrong. My particular thanks go to Marius Aherne my marvellous director; Julietta Brioche my gorgeous co-star; Roger Sims for writing such a hilarious and thrilling story. I absolutely adore you all.'

T8.6

[two extracts from musicals]

T8.7

I = Interviewer   TR = Tim Rice

I I went to interview Tim Rice in his London home by the Thames, and we discussed how he came to create a musical about a religious figure.
I What a subject to choose! Why did you choose to write about Jesus Christ?
TR In a way I guess it's rather an obvious subject, I mean so many people have written versions of the Jesus story, whether it be in serious music, straight plays, movies and in our case pop music or rock music. And I can't really remember why, other than the fact that when I was at school, and I went to a school that placed a great emphasis on religion and going to chapel, the character of Judas Iscariot always intrigued me, because here was a guy who was central to the whole Jesus story, without him there wouldn't be much of a story, if he hadn't betrayed Jesus, and yet the sketch of him in the Bible is just that. And the idea of Judas Iscariot seemed to be rather a good one, but of course once we got into it, once I began drafting out the story line as seen from Judas's point of view it became clear that really the piece should be called *Jesus Christ* or as it became *Jesus Christ Superstar* because Jesus is the most important character by far.
I But how did he come to decide on the term 'superstar'?
TR It was ... originally that song was just *Jesus Christ, Jesus Christ, who are you? What have you sacrificed?* And I can remember working in my parents' house, and it was one Sunday morning before lunch and I thought 'Gosh! Superstar, da da dum, ba ba bom', and I just put it in and it seemed to work.
I I then asked Tim if he was surprised by the reaction of certain church people who

hammered him for it, and hammered the show for being too simplistic, even blasphemous.

TR Well, I suppose we were surprised by the fact that it was noticed at all. When we wrote it ... erm ... we didn't really contemplate what reaction it would have with the world outside because, certainly I didn't ever think it would hit the world outside. I thought ... well, this is quite good but other people have hits, this ... this isn't the sort of thing that's going to be known ... erm ... and then when it did come out and particularly in America, when it was a huge overnight smash on record, we then did get some reaction, but the reaction that surprised me more was the churchmen who quickly took it up as ... as a thing to help their congregations, their causes. I remember going to one church service in New York and seeing a baby being christened in the name of Jesus Christ Superstar.

T8.8

I = Interviewer   PN = Paul Nicholas

The actor, Paul Nicholas, played the part of Jesus in the first-ever production.

I What do you think it was in the show that made it so successful?

PN Well I think the subject was somewhat taboo therefore it made it sort of slightly risky and interesting ... er ... I think from their point of view they were young when they wrote it, Andrew and Tim, and therefore had the courage to write lyrics that were perhaps a little near the knuckle and music that certainly was, was ... very strong and youthful and brave.

I It must have been a bit strange for you to suddenly be in this part of Jesus.

PN No, I think, I think the strange part for me was playing such a recognizable figure ... er ... a figure that meant so much to so many people and trying to do it justice for them and in some ways it was very moving. I remember the first time that ... we did the crucifixion, and I went up on the cross and there's a wonderful piece of music that Andrew played, or composed at that point, which I was very overcome with ... with the vulnerability of actually hanging there on a cross with this music going on, and it made me cry, I remember ... erm ... but thereafter ... after eight performances a week for about two or three weeks it became like a job, and most of the time I ... I was more concerned that I may sneeze ... in ... while I was up on the cross, which would have slightly ruined the evening for ... for many people. Indeed the problem for me with the show was that there weren't really enough laughs ... er the only time I managed to crack a joke was, I remember at the beginning of the second act, a gentleman in the front row sneezed, and I couldn't resist saying 'God bless you my son' which was ... I realized about that point that perhaps it was time I moved on.

I Say you were playing the part now ... erm how would you be different from twenty-five years ago?

PN If I were playing it ... erm ... I think I'd do probably much the same thing as I did before but probably better. I'd probably sing better, I would understand it better. The only thing is I probably wouldn't ... wouldn't look as slim on the cross! If the truth be known.

T8.9

a A I'm starving. I could eat a horse.
  B Yes, I'm a little peckish, too.

b A I'm absolutely dying for a drink.
  B Yes, my throat's a bit dry, I must say.

c A His family are pretty well off, aren't they?
  B You can say that again. They're absolutely loaded!

d A You must have hit the roof when she told you she'd crashed your car.
  B Well, yes, I was a bit upset.

e A I think Tony was a bit tipsy last night.
  B What! He was totally smashed out of his brain!

f A I can't stand the sight of him.
  B I must admit, I'm not too keen on him, either.

g A He isn't very bright, is he?
  B You're not kidding. He's as thick as two short planks.

h A Look at the weather! It's vile again.
  B I know. It is a bit wet, but we mustn't grumble, must we?

i A What a fantastic holiday!
  B Yes, it was a nice little break, but all good things must come to an end.

j A I'm knackered. Can we stop for a rest?
  B OK. I feel a bit out of breath, too.

k A He invited quite a few friends to his party.
  B I'll say. We had to fight our way through millions of people to get to the drinks.

l A Well, that journey was absolute hell!
  B I suppose it did take rather a long time to get here.

m A They've got this huge great dog called Wizzer. I'm terrified of it.
  B What? That little thing wouldn't hurt a fly!

UNIT 9

T9.1

1 I'm not really going babysitting. I just don't want to go out with Mark. I can't stand him. I don't know why he keeps asking me to go out with him. If he rings again, I'm not in, right?

2 I didn't actually trip over the cat. I was in a fight. I can't even remember what it was all about.

3 It's awful! It doesn't suit her at all! I don't know why she bought it.

4 I'm not going to Laura's to watch telly. I'm going out with a bloke called Max. I daren't tell my Dad about him 'cos he's 25. I think my Dad would kill me if he knew.

5 Actually, I hate being at college. I haven't made any friends and I'm really homesick, but I don't want to upset Mum and Dad.

6 I'm not ill at all. I just want a day off work. I'm going to play golf.

7 Miss Jones isn't out of the office. She's sitting right there, but she doesn't want to be disturbed at the moment.

T9.2

a Who did she give her money away to?
b What do you want to have a word with me about?
c Who did you dance with?
d What do you need £5,000 for?
e What's he writing a book about?
f Who did you get a present from?
g Who did you buy a birthday card for?
h What are you thinking about?
i Where do you want me to give you a lift to?
j What do you want me to clean the sink with?

T9.3 See p 90

T9.4 See p 90

T9.5

a Don't you think it's time to go home?
b Can't they understand what they have to do?
c Aren't you coming to the cinema with us?
d Hasn't she ever been abroad?
e Isn't that Peter sitting over there?
f Haven't I met you somewhere before?
g Hasn't the postman been yet?
h Weren't you in my class at school?
i Didn't you want to watch the football tonight?

T9.6

This is Radio 4. This week in 'File on Life': *Saying 'I won't'* or *What stopped the wedding?* The photographer may be booked, the cake may be iced, and the dress may fit perfectly, but suddenly it's all off. What stops the wedding and forces one half of the happy couple into saying 'I won't'? Listen to the stories of Elizabeth, George, and Nicole.

Elizabeth

The nearer it got to the date, there ... there was more pressure. I felt more and more pressure on me because everybody'd been out and bought their wedding gear and I'd had the final fitting for the dress. It was ivory, and everyone said how great it looked. And ... and ... the printing of the stationery'd been done and the cake'd been made. There was so much pressure and it was awful 'cos deep down inside I knew ... I knew it was wrong. But the pressure was to go through with it just for the sake of keeping everyone happy. I felt inside ... I can't, I can't, I can't go through with this, but I've got to because of all the expense ... I mean the cost of everything. The whole thing was confused in my head. In the end I tried to say something to my mum, but she kept saying 'Come on, it's just nerves'. She said she'd felt the same before marrying dad, they all said it was just nerves, but I knew ... I knew it wasn't. I knew I had to pluck up courage and speak out ... it, it wasn't fair on anybody, 'specially Paul. I just didn't love him any more. We'd been going out since we were sixteen. Kids really. He was like my brother.

Afterwards it was such relief, it was like a cork coming out of a bottle. It all just poured out. Paul was upset, yes, of course he was, but not distraught, not really. Not as much as I'd thought anyway. It was my little sister, she was distraught, 'cos she had the dress and was going to be bridesmaid and everything. I felt worse for her ... terrible. But in fact my family were brilliant ... er ... in the end, and actually we wore the dresses, me and my sister, we went to a fancy dress party, yes, we went as the brides of Frankenstein! Wasn't that awful?

George

It was the rehearsal. We had a rehearsal a week before the wedding. Everything was fine. Vicky and I went to the church and we met the best man and the bridesmaids ... and it was all fine. And we went through the ceremony and, and we were all very happy and everything was fine and then ... then, it was just sort of after that, and we had to fill in some forms and we were all sitting down and filling in the forms and then, Vicky, she couldn't fill the forms in, and she had this ... er ... panic attack. She was just sitting down crying and screaming and saying 'I can't do it, I just can't do it, I can't face it'. I was just sitting there holding her hand really, comforting her. At that point I think I was more concerned for her really, rather than for me. I was upset that she was upset and I said ... in the end ... I said to her and to the minister that maybe it would be better to postpone it. And then ... then it was amazing, just amazing. From the moment she knew the wedding was off she was perfectly normal and the relationship was perfectly normal. In fact a week later on the actual day when we should have been getting married, we went for a drive by the lake and it was a super hot day, and we had a picnic and it was a really smashing day. I really enjoyed it. I don't think we'll ever marry now ... not to each other anyway.

Nicole

I was just getting out of the white Rolls Royce. I was sitting in my wedding dress outside a Greek cathedral in downtown Manhattan. And then, then suddenly someone came out of the church, I dunno who this guy was, but he thrust a piece of paper in my hand and ran. I didn't know what it was, I opened it, and read it ... seven words, just seven words and the end of my world! It said 'I can't go through with it. Michael.' Can you believe it? Not even '*Love Michael*'. I was in shock. I ... I felt ... it felt like I was in a movie. So I thought, 'What would they do in a movie?' And I figured ...er ... I could see it all in my head, so I got out of the car and I went into the church ... it was packed. I just went in and I walked slowly down the aisle, all by myself, like in slow-motion, then I turned and ... it was real dramatic ... I announced, 'Michael's not coming but let's have a party anyway.' So that's what we did. I had a non-wedding reception. It was spectacular. I'm afraid I got pretty drunk ... very drunk in fact. All I can remember is dancing non-stop to 'I Will Survive'. *I will survive, oooh yeah I will survive.*

I haven't heard a word from him since that note. I think I'm angrier now than I was then. I just want him to tell me, in person, why he did this to me. He could at least tell me the reason. He's a sh ... shameful human being. I can't believe he's the same man I met last year on that beach in Greece. We talked the same language, we had so much in common. You see, we're both Greek, at least our parents are Greek, but he was born and raised in London and I was born in New York. Last March he proposed to me on the telephone. I was in heaven. I just believed he was my destiny.

You know, I spent $25,000 on this wedding and he wasn't even there. I've kept the ring, it cost $6,000. The dress cost $2,000. No, I don't know where he is now. It wouldn't surprise me if he'd gone to Tahiti where we'd planned to have our honeymoon. Actually nothing would surprise me. Maybe he's already married. Who cares?

T9.7

There was I waiting at the church, waiting at the church, waiting at the church,
When I found he'd left me in the lurch.
Lor, how it did upset me!
All at once he sent me round a note.
Here's the very note, this is what he wrote,
'Can't get away to marry you today. My wife won't let me!'

I'm in a nice bit of trouble, I confess.
Somebody with me has had a game.
I should by now be a proud and happy bride,
But I've still got to keep my single name.
I was proposed to by Obadiah Binks
In a very gentlemanly way.
Lent him all my money so that he could buy a home,
And punctually at twelve o' clock today,

There was I waiting at the church, waiting at the church, waiting at the church,

When I found he'd left me in the lurch.
Lor, how it did upset me!
All at once he sent me round a note.
Here's the very note, this is what he wrote,
'Can't get away to marry you today. My wife won't let me!'

T9.8

a 1   I'm sorry to bother you, but could you possibly change a five-pound note?
  2   Have you got change for a five-pound note?

b 1   Where's the station?
  2   Could you tell me where the station is, please?

c 1   A   This is a present for you.
      B   For me! Oh, how kind! You shouldn't have, really. Thank you so much.
  2   C   This is a present for you.
      D   Thanks.

d 1   A   Can you come to a party on Saturday?
      B   No, I can't.
  2   C   Can you come to a party on Saturday?
      D   Oh, what a pity! I'm already going out, I'm afraid.
      C   Never mind!
      D   Thanks for the invitation.

e 1   A   Excuse me! Do you mind if I sit down here?
      B   No, not at all.
  2   C   Is anyone sitting here?
      D   No.

f 1   A   You forgot to post my letter.
      B   Sorry.
  2   C   You've spilt red wine on my dress!
      D   I am SO sorry. I do apologize, Madam. I don't know how it happened. Let me get a cloth.

g 1   A   Can you give me a hand? I need to carry this box upstairs.
      B   OK.
  2   C   I wonder if I could possibly ask you a favour? You see, I need to get this box upstairs. Would you mind helping me?
      D   No, not at all.

h 1   A   So I said ...
      B   Pardon? What was that?
  2   C   So I said ...
      D   What?

i 1   A   Goodbye. It was a lovely evening. Thank you so much. We had a wonderful time.
      B   We enjoyed it, too. So glad you could make it. Safe journey back. See you soon.
      C   Bye.
      D   Good night. Take care.
  2   E   Goodbye. Thanks for the meal.
      F   Bye. See you.

T9.9

a A Hi! Listen, can you come round for a meal tomorrow evening? I'm cooking Chinese.

b A Can you help me with my maths homework? We're doing algebra.

c A Would you like me to babysit this evening so you can go out for a meal?

d A Can you tell me where the nearest post office is, please?

e A Hi, it's Susan here. Could I ask you a big favour? Could you look after my dog next week? I have to go away.

T9.10

a A Hi! Listen, can you come round for a meal tomorrow evening? I'm cooking Chinese.

   B Oh, I'd love to, but I'm afraid I'm already going out. Oh, what a shame!

b A Can you help me with my maths homework? We're doing algebra.

   B Believe me, I would if I could, but I don't know the first thing about algebra. Sorry.

c A Would you like me to babysit this evening so you can go out for a meal?

   B That's very kind of you, but we've arranged for my sister to come over. Thanks for the offer, though.

d A Can you tell me where the nearest post office is, please?

   B I'm afraid I don't know. Sorry.

e A Hi, it's Susan here. Could I ask you a big favour? Could you look after my dog next week? I have to go away.

   B I'm terribly sorry, Susan, but I can't. I'd love to have Molly, you know I adore dogs, but I'm going away myself for a few days.

T9.11

A and B = Hostess and Host   H = Henry

A Pat! Hello! How lovely to see you. Come on in. Let me take your coat.
 – *Give the flowers to your host.*

A How kind of you! They're lovely. Thank you so much. Now, do you know everybody? Let me introduce you to Henry. Henry, this is Pat.

H Hello, Pat. Nice to meet you.
 –

H Where are you from, Pat?
 –

H That's interesting. And what are you doing in London?
 –

H And how do you find London, Pat? Is it like home, or is it very different?
 –

A Now, Pat. What would you like to drink?
 –

A Right. I'll just get that for you.

B Pat, do have some nuts.
 –

A Right, everybody. Dinner's ready. Come and sit down. Pat, you sit here next to me.
 –

B Has everyone got a drink? Cheers, everybody!
 –

A Pat, help yourself. Would you like some roast parsnips?
 –

A Roast parsnips. It's a vegetable. Maybe you don't have them in your country. Would you like to try some?
 –

A Pat, what about some more to eat?
 –

B Another glass of wine, perhaps?
 –

B I hope you enjoyed your meal, Pat.
 –

A Well, Pat. We're so glad you could come. It's a shame you have to leave so early.
 –

B Thank you, Pat. Safe journey back. Bye now!

UNIT 10

T10.1

Rosemary Sage is 100 years old. She lives in the village of Hambledon, Surrey. Many people commute daily from Hambledon to work in London. Rosemary has only been to London once in her life, when she went to the zoo sixty years ago!
Her daily routine goes back to a time before there were any commuters in the village.
It never varies. At the start of each day, she gathers and chops wood for the fire, on which she'll boil a large kettle of water. Then she'll carry some of the water to her wash-house in the garden and she'll get washed. Next she'll make herself a cup of tea. She has no means of heating or cooking apart from the open fire.
Her home is like a working museum, and her clear memory is a precious source of knowledge of old country ways. She's always telling stories of when she was young.
In those days, the Lord and Lady of the Manor used to own all the cottages and they rented them to the villagers for 2s 9d (14p) a week. Every winter the village pond would freeze over and she'd go skating with her six brothers and sisters. Every summer they'd spend one day at the seaside. Other than that and her one trip to London, she has hardly ever left the village. She is perfectly content with her life. She has no bath, no fridge, and no telephone. 'I could never get used to such 'modern' appliances at my age,' she says. 'I'm used to the old ways. I'm far too old to change.'

T10.2

My first friend? Well, ... I suppose my first *best* friend was when I was about eight. It was a girl in our street. She lived up the road in a big white house, ... er ... it was a much bigger house than ours. We went to the same school but we didn't use to see much of each other at school 'cos we were in different classes. She was a bit older than me. Oh, ... her name ... she was ... oh, Gillian Milne. Her dad had a really good job with the local brewery. I suppose we had a lot in common but we used to fight a lot, too. We both loved going to the cinema, 'specially to see musicals. We'd learn all the words of the songs by heart, and we'd come home and we'd act it all out in the field at the end of the road. Yuk! I mean it sounds really nauseating now! But I have to say it seemed really good fun at the time, ... but then we were always having these huge rows about nothing. You see, I used to think that she was spoilt rotten. Honestly, she just got everything she wanted. When the ice-cream van came round she'd get four flavours *and* an ice lolly and she was so mean. She wouldn't share a thing, and she'd just burst into tears and run home to mummy! Actually, when I think of it now, I'm not really sure why we were friends. Oh, I once went on holiday to Blackpool with her and her Auntie Ethel and it was a disaster.

T10.3

a How often do you get homework?
  Well, we usually get it twice a week.

b Do you read many books in English?
  Well, yes, I do now, but I didn't use to.

c Do you find it easy to use your monolingual dictionary?
  I didn't at first, but I soon got used to it.

d Do you look up every word that you can't understand?
  Well, I don't now, but I used to when I was a beginner.

e How can you understand English when it is spoken so quickly?
  Well, I suppose I'm used to it.

f Did you do much pronunciation practice when you were first learning English?
  Oh, yes we did. We used to do it every lesson.

g How do you find using the telephone in English?
  It's not easy, but I think that gradually I'm getting used to it.

T10.4

Part 1

O = Oliver McGechy   I = Interviewer

I Hello, and welcome to 'Worldly Wise'. In today's edition, we look at the problem of homelessness.
  Why is it that, even in the richest countries in the world, there are so many homeless people? Someone who has experienced the

problem first hand, as a homeless person himself, is Oliver McGechy, a former journalist and publisher and a reformed alcoholic. He now works to help others in the same position.

I asked Oliver if he could tell us something about the work he does, and the problems of homeless people.

O I run a project for people who have a long-term commitment to alcohol recovery and who basically are homeless and ... er ... who ... who need help. It was put to me the other day that in Europe at the moment that the average lifespan is for someone who's street homeless is only 42. So you're actually moving back to almost Victorian days and Victorian principles in terms of how people can expect to live and what quality of life they can expect. But the people you see sleeping on the streets, the people you see sleeping in ... in shop doorways represent only the tip of the iceberg, they represent ... represent only a very, very small proportion of the ... the overall number of people, who ... who are actually homeless.

I I asked Oliver what had gone wrong in these people's lives.

O You're looking at someone who's not only lost their home, they've probably lost their partner, their children, their family, all of the social contact which they've had ... they've probably lost all of the network which has supported them within society, their doctors ... their GP, ... erm their dentist, their job. They become unemployed, and because they're into a downward spiral all of these things combine to make it very, very difficult to move back into society. Therefore they become lost. They tend to be forgotten. There's little political gain in supporting homeless people.

I Who exactly are these people, Oliver?

O It ... it's impossible to say. I mean ... I've worked with people who have been accountants, I've worked with people who have been doctors, I've worked with a number of members of the clergy ... erm ... I've worked with people who have worked in factories, I've worked with people who have never worked in their life at all. I've worked with postmen, I've worked with ex-service men. The spread of people who ... who are affected by homelessness, or who have become homeless, is ... is infinite, is as wide as society itself.

I But are there problems that all of these people have in common?

O One of the biggest problems which homeless people face in fact is drug addiction and alcoholism, but let me ask you a question. If you were homeless and you had nowhere to live, and you'd lost your family, you'd lost your job, ... life had fallen round ... er fallen down roundabout you, and you could escape just a little by using alcohol, would you?

I Absolutely ... I take the point.

Part 2

C = Chris Caine

I Chris, can you tell us why it was that you ended up homeless?

C Well, I 'ad a house wiv a woman that I ... er took on, wiv 'er kids and I 'ad a job 'n' all, workin' at the Royal Mail Post Office ... erm I dunno about .. ... what ... two, two years it was into the relationship and all of a sudden, like, she just wanted out, so ... er I tried to patch fings up which really didn't work, yer know, so I ended up going back to the woods, well, yer know, where I was before ...

I Back to the woods?

C Yeah.

I How d'you mean? Literally to the woods?

C Yeah. I used to lived out in the woods.

I Did you?

C Yeah.

I What ... er .. you mean ... living rough (Yeah, living rough in the woods) or in a tent, or how?

C Just in a 'bivvy' bag, Goretex 'bivvy' bag, 'n' sleeping bag and stuff, in the woods, for a while, lighting fires 'n' havin' my grub out there, yer know. There's just summink about the woods .. yer free out there ... you, yer can't do it round the towns 'cos there's ... you know ... erm ... you're too at risk in towns, too many people ... yer know ... too much ... too much hassle in towns. Best fing to do is get out and, and get ... get where you feel safe, so I feel safe in the woods all the time yer know ... erm ...

I So why aren't you in the woods now?

C 'Cos I 'ad a breakdown out there, and I went to the doctor's 'n' that and he give me some tablets for that, and I ended up comin' here ... was the best solution ... yer know ... to ... er ... get meself back on my feet ... sort of thing ... yer know.

I But ... so living in the woods, although as you say ... it was ... you know, you were free, free from the hassles and so on, I mean ... it's not the ideal way of life for you?

C Erm ... no and yes. It was my job once ... (upon) a time.

I Living in the woods?

C Yeah, I was a survival instructor, teaching the army and stuff.

I So you like the woods?

C ... the woods, the mountains is fine for me. But coming into towns I find very stressful ... erm I'm here now but each time, here now, I'm still fightin'. I've been here six months, so each day now I'm still fighting to stay here, which is hard for me ... I'd be safe out there, yer know, instead of here, but ... all I'm trying to do is get me act togever and start again really. It's ... it's hard work.

I What does it mean to you not to have a home?

C Devastating, really. I miss the family feeling or the family comfort, not ... not the television but having a woman there to care for, and someone to talk to. You get very lonely. I mean, in here you've got friends 'n' 'at ... but I admit I get very lonely when you're on your own, an' it takes its toll because if you're used to that way of life, it's hard to comprehend what it's all about ... yer know the worst fing is, when yer think about that which hurts most, is to see people holding hands going down the street with their wife and kids and you've had that once and you've lost it, and you'd like that again but it's going to take time to get that back ... yer know so ... erm, yeah I find it really hard, actually.

I And what's it like when you're actually on the road?

C When yer roamin' round the country yer see so many of yer people like yerself ... erm on the street, sleepin' in doorways, parks, benches, yer know, and ... erm yeah, yer kind of get used to it after a while, it takes about a week to get used to being on the road but then it takes about seven ... seven to eight months trying to get used to getting back into society again, you know. I find it hard anyway, even now.

Part 3

I Chris is just one of a growing army of people of all ages and positions in life who have become homeless and have ended up sleeping rough. Throughout the ages there have always been homeless people. For some, a life without obligations and responsibilities has its attractions. But, for most homeless people, like Chris, the everyday world of homelessness is very grim indeed.

C Well, when you get to rock bottom, you either turn yourself to drink or drugs. An' you can get drunk as much as you want but the next day it's still there. You got the same problem as you did the day before.

UNIT 11

T11.1

a I wish I lived somewhere warm, preferably the Mediterranean, and ideally the island of Gozo, near Malta.

b If only I weren't such a quick-tempered person. If I hadn't shouted at George the other day, we'd still be friends.

c I wish I could read faster, 'cos there's so many books I want to read and there's never enough time, 'cept when you're on holiday. I wish I had longer holidays, but I still wouldn't get through them all.

d If only animals could talk, I'd be able to really know what our dogs think of us.

e If only I hadn't parked my car on the double yellow line I wouldn't have got that ticket. I knew it was a mistake ... it was a very busy Saturday and the traffic wardens are often out on the High Street, but I thought, well, if I just park it round here, just round the corner, just off the main High Street, I'm sure that I'll be OK, it's only for twenty minutes.

f I wish I'd listened to my grandmother more before she died. She was full of stories about all kinds of weird and wonderful people in our family. And now ... now, I'm trying to draw up our family tree, so you see I'd be really interested in it all.

g I wish I hadn't studied business and politics at university. I should have studied languages, I'd love to be able to speak French and Spanish fluently. But if I hadn't studied politics ... I suppose ... I might never have met Andy.

h I shouldn't have eaten that huge slice of chocolate cake last night. I'm going to Tenerife in two months' time, and I want to try and lose weight so I can wear my bikini.

T11.2 See p 109

T11.3

1 If only you'd told me earlier.
2 I wish you'd help more with the housework.
3 I wish you'd helped me with my homework.
4 I'd have passed the exam if you'd helped me.
5 If you'd turned left not right, we'd be there by now.
6 She'd come if he weren't coming.
7 If she'd come, I'd have introduced you to her.
8 I'd rather you'd asked me before you'd written to complain.

T11.4

P = Peter   A = Amanda

P Hello, Amanda.
A Peter!
P I'm surprised you recognize me.
A Really? You haven't moved back here, have you?
P Good heavens no ... erm ... I'm still in London. I came back for the funeral. My father's. A heart attack. It happened very suddenly.
A I'm sorry.
P Thank you. And I take it that you're not living back here either?
A No, I'm in London, too, just back for my sister's wedding tomorrow.
P That's nice.
A Yes.
P And ... er ... your parents? They're well?
A Fine.
P Er ... are you rushing off somewhere?
A No, I'm just killing time, really.
P Then I suggest we kill it together. Let's grab a coffee.
A Er . . . and so, Peter, did you become a foreign correspondent?
P Not exactly. I'm a lawyer, believe it or not.
A You enjoy it?
P Yes. And you? Are you a world famous artist?
A Well ... er ... no.
P So. What are you up to?

A Nothing much. I've tried a few things.
P So you're not painting at all?
A Only doors and walls. So ... where are you in London?
P North. And you?
A South. It's okay, I rent a room, but I'm thinking of buying somewhere. It's one of the reasons I came home. I want to sort things out a bit. Oh, Peter, I don't know why I left that day.
P It's all right. We were young. Young people do things like that all the time.
A I suppose you're right. Well, ... I ... I ought to be going.
P Already? I thought you had time to kill.
A I did, ... but I ought to get back now to help my mother with the wedding.
P I understand. Shall I give you my phone number. Perhaps we could meet up?
A Perhaps. Thanks. Er ... goodbye, Peter.
P Goodbye, Amanda.

T11.5

Part one

My grandfather was not a black sheep in the sense that he was ... erm ... sent away by his family but he was rather a naughty man ... erm ... he was a silk dealer in Japan, and ... erm ... I'm trying to think of ... well the early part of this century and as was the custom with European families in Japan, they had servants in the family and my grandfather had an affair with the maid of the household, and, from that affair a daughter was born, and in fact unlike many black sheep my grandfather took responsibility for the ... his offspring, and kept her in the house and in the family and in fact made sure that she had an education. And when his wife eventually died ... erm ... he did marry this Japanese maid ... erm ... I found out about this story through my mother who was in her teens at the time that the baby was born and of course was still alive and living at home when her mother died and when her father married again. And, it was obviously something very distressing for my mother because she had never mentioned it to me or any of my sisters until one dramatic day when her sister-in-law at the dinner table, with us present, asked my mother if she'd ever heard from Yuri, and we innocently asked 'Who is Yuri?' And this tale came out. I think it took my mother a long time to forgive her sister-in-law for this indiscretion. The indiscretion was totally innocent my ... my aunt had no idea that we were in the dark about this or that my mother was so sensitive about it but ... erm ... the interesting follow-up for me was that when I went to Japan about sixteen years ago, with my husband, my mother's step-sister, half-sister was actually living in Japan at that time having married a Swiss businessman, who had business in Japan. So I met my ... I call her my half-aunt, and I even met her mother who was still alive living in Tokyo, and the amazing thing for me was to go to a country as foreign as Japan and find that I actually had Japanese family as a result of the ... the black sheep adventures of my grandfather.

Part two

This is the main story in my family, actually ... erm ... it's the story of my great aunt's birth. She was born in Winnipeg, in 1900, in December, on December 13th and ... when ... she was born at home, and when she was born she was blue and wasn't breathing ... and the midwife said to the mother, 'Well, I'm ... I'm terribly sorry, there's nothing that we can do about this ... erm ... the child isn't breathing.' And the grandmother, who was present at the birth, said, 'Stuff and nonsense! Give me that child!' And she grabbed the baby, and she went downstairs, and she opened the door to the oven of the wood stove and she put my great aunt in the oven. And lo and behold a few minutes later a great cry came from the oven and my great aunt had been born. And my great aunt is still alive and is still able to tell this story.

T11.6

a A So why didn't you hand it in on time? I'm not going to mark it now.
    B But, I'm really sorry. I just didn't have the chance to finish it at the weekend.

b A It's always the same. I hummed and hawed about getting it, then when I went back it had been sold and it was one of his best works.
    B You should have asked if you could put a deposit on it.

c A Ouch! I've had it with this thing. It just doesn't work.
    B Here, give it to me! Let me try.

d A It's not fair. I'd been looking forward to watching it all day and then the phone goes and rings!
    B And who was it? Anyone interesting?

e A How many times do I have to tell you? Take them off before you come into the house!
    B Sorry. I forgot. I was in a hurry.

f A This has gone beyond a joke. You promised you'd deliver it by Tuesday at the latest. Now you're saying next month!
    B I'm awfully sorry, sir. I'm afraid there's nothing I can do about it.

g A I could kick myself. As soon as I'd handed in the paper, I remembered what the answer was.
    B But do you think you've still passed?

h A Of course, they didn't have it in red. Apparently, it only comes in navy blue.
    B But wouldn't that go well with your white jeans?

i A It's the last time I'll eat here.
    B You're not kidding! Massive prices and lousy food!

UNIT 12

T12.1

A Who gave you that new car?
B Susan gave it to me.

A Did she sell it to you?
B No, she gave it to me.

A Did she give it to Peter?
B No, she gave it to me.

A Is it second-hand?
B No, it's new.

A Did she give you a new stereo?
B No, she gave me a new car.

T12.2

a Did Ann give James a blue shirt?
   Did she give him a white shirt?
   Did she give him a blue jumper?
   Was it a Christmas present?

b Did James fly to Rome?
   Did he go to Paris by Eurostar?
   Did he want to do some shopping in Paris?
   Did he go there just for the weekend?

c Do you go to Scotland in summer?
   Do you go to Ireland in the autumn?
   Do you go there to relax?

d Is your daughter at Bristol university?
   Is it your youngest son that's studying at Bristol?
   Is he studying modern languages?

T12.3

a A Why weren't you at school yesterday?
   B I was at school.

b A Come on, Dave. Its time to get up.
   B I am getting up.

c A It's a shame you don't like parties.
   B But I do like parties!

d A I wish you'd tidy your room.
   B I have tidied it.

e A What a shame you didn't see Tom.
   B I did see Tom.

T12.4

1 How do you keep cool at a football match?
  Sit next to a fan.

2 Why do Swiss cows have bells?
  Because their horns don't work.

3 Customer: Waiter, waiter! I'm in a hurry. Will my pancake be long?
  Waiter: No, sir. It'll be round.

4 Mother: You spend too much money. Money doesn't grow on trees, you know.
  Daughter: Well, why do banks have so many branches, then?

5 What's the difference between a sailor and someone who goes shopping?
  One goes to sail the seas, the other goes to see the sales.

6 What's the difference between a jeweller and a jailer?

One sells watches and the other watches cells.

7 What did the sea say to the beach?
  Nothing. It just waved.

8 What sort of crisps can fly?
  Plain crisps.

9 A prisoner is locked in a cell with only a chair. How does he escape?
  He rubs his hands until they are sore, he uses the saw to cut the chair in half. Two halves make a whole. He climbs through the hole and shouts himself hoarse. Then he gets on the horse and gallops away.

T12.5

Pam
For me, one of the most special moments of the twentieth century was the end of apartheid in South Africa, which I watched as much as possible on television, and I have a marvellous image in my mind of the morning Nelson Mandela was released, and he walked, as it were, to freedom, with Winnie by his side, and there were crowds of wonderfully excited people. It was a very moving moment.

David
I think the collapse of the Berlin Wall was one of the seminal events of the twentieth century. Er ... it led to erm ... an astonishingly fast collapse of communism across East Europe, the Soviet Union ... well, it didn't lead to it, but it all happened very, very quickly after that. So we had er ... a social system, a political system which had covered large parts of the ... of the world, erm ... over a period of fifty or sixty years erm ... and then within the space of two or three years it had gone and what ... been ... sort of washed away, and erm ... led to erm ... the introduction of ... of capitalism erm ... good or bad, but it all happened incredibly quickly. So it has to count as one of the great events, human events as well as political events, of the twentieth century.

Alexa
Oh, I think that the Internet has changed erm ... quite a lot of people's perspective of the world. You can have conversations ... decent conversations with people from Australia, from America. And it's ... it's quite strange. Erm ... there is the thing, though, that the people you are talking to may not be the people they seem, I mean, they can lie about their age, what they look like. They even lie about their personality, try and pretend to be someone else. And it's ... it's very strange, the way that I think ... you would talk ... you can talk to someone on the Internet, in a way that you would never dream of talking to someone to their face, or on the telephone. If you met them in the street, you would not say the things you say to them on the Internet ... er ... to their face. And it's ... I think it somehow sort of gets rid of the values, possibly, that you hold for people that you meet, because you treat them in a totally different way because you can't ... you can't see them, you can't see how they're reacting. You just go by what they say, and that ... that can be covering up, you know, feelings.

Penny
Well, I think the advent of feminism in the early sixties ... I'm a sort of late fifties baby, so I have really benefitted from that. Er ... I found it really fascinating, I can see obviously it's gone too far in some ways, but for me it's given me the right to have my own life, my own job, a career plus being a mother, ... erm ... the advent of the Pill was obviously a great event as well, ... erm ... which made women feel they have ... they had more control over their bodies, what they wanted to do with their bodies, ... erm ... and that there was a life after children.

Pam
I think a really significant event in this century was the discovery of penicillin. I was told when my first child was born that ... that if I hadn't had antibiotics, I would have died in childbirth, like so many women did before me.

David
Well, the arrival of the motor car erm ... the ... the ... the growth of motoring throughout the twentieth century has ... has changed people's lives. It's changed the whole way that people interact with their relatives, with their friends, business. And, really only in the past ... like in the last twenty years of ... of the century has it been realized that it also brings with it enormous amounts of problems, er .. through er ... pollution, congestion, erm ... through making people feel too ... too er ... reliant on motor power rather than cycling or walking or erm ... using public transport, even. The balance between using er ... using the car properly, and letting it take over our lives hasn't really been found yet, and that is the big problem for the twenty-first century.

Hilary
It would be very easy to be flippant ... about it, and say it was the Beatles, or something like that, or Elvis. But I suspect it was probably the First World War. I know that was very early ... quite early on in the century, but erm ... I think everybody's life was ... from what I've read, not from personal experience, everybody's life was so changed by that. And the whole structure of society was so changed by that. I think that must be the main change ... the main event of this century. The Second World War was dreadful. It should never have happened and ... but life ... and life certainly was different after it than before, from what I've heard. But not so hugely si ... hugely different as it was before and after the ... Even though the First World War was only four years, it just revolutionized everything. Probably because things were coming to an end before it, anyway, the sort of Edwardian society was rather in decay, anyway, and was ready for a change, but er ... I think life in the 1920s compared with the life in the 1900s was like a different century.

Barry
For me personally ... and don't laugh, because in a way this is silly, but in a way it isn't ... the greatest moment of change in the twentieth century was actually ... Elvis Presley. I remember

so well hearing *Heartbreak Hotel*. The first time you heard that – ah! And then suddenly ... I mean, it was more than just a pop record, it was more than just a ... singer ... you know ... a pop singer who's new and different. Suddenly it was ... it was the beginning of youth ... I mean, the whole culture of youth, taking over, which has gone on and on ever since. Suddenly, instead of young people being like and dressing like their mums and dads, and doing what their mums and dads did and gradually drifting into their way of life, nothing very different, suddenly youth had an identity. And it rebelled and challenged and said 'Hey, we're here. You'd better listen to us, because we're going to do what we want for a change.' Youth was nothing before Elvis, was it? I mean, our elders and betters had led us into the Second World War, had ... had created disasters left, right, and centre, had invented the atomic bomb and killed cities full of people, and ... er ... society was ripe for a change. Young people said, 'Right, now it's our turn.'

T12.6

Elvis Presley (1935–1977) was a rock and roll singer whose enormous success changed popular culture throughout the world.

Presley was raised in Memphis, where he sang at church services.

As a teenager, he taught himself to play the guitar.

In July 1954 Presley recorded songs for Sam Phillips, a rhythm and blues producer.

His charismatic style on stage earned him the nickname 'Elvis the Pelvis'.

About this time Presley met Colonel Tom Parker, a promoter who managed the rest of his career.

In 1956 Presley released *Heartbreak Hotel*, the first of 45 records that sold more than a million copies each.

He frequently appeared on television, but because his dancing was considered too sexually suggestive, he was seen only from the waist up.

Presley's personal life suffered desperately, and he fought battles with weight gain and drug dependence.

Before Presley, there were no teenagers, just young people without a voice. He was one of the founders of youth culture.

T12.7

a A Did you see the match last night?
   B No, I missed it, but apparently it was a good game. We won, didn't we?
   A Actually, it was a draw, but it was really exciting.

b A What do you think of Claire's new boyfriend?
   B Personally, I can't stand him. I think she'll be let down by him. However, that's her problem, not mine.
   A Poor old Claire! She always picks the wrong ones, doesn't she? Anyway, I'll see you later. Bye!
   B Bye, Rita.

c A I don't know how you can afford to buy all those fabulous clothes!
   B Hopefully, I'm going to get a bonus this month. I should do. My boss promised it to me. After all, I did earn the company over £100,000 last year. Actually, it was nearer £150,000. I do deserve it, don't you think?
   A Of course you do.

d A She said some horrible things to me. I hate her! She called me names!
   B All the same, I think you should apologize to her.
   A Me? Apologize? Never!
   B Basically, I think you're both being very childish. Why don't you grow up?
   A Oh, Mary! Honestly, I never thought you'd speak to me like that. I hate you, too.

e A So, Billy Peebles. You say that this is the last record you're ever going to make?
   B Definitely.
   A But surely you realize how upset your fans are going to be?
   B Obviously, I don't want to hurt anyone, but basically I'm fed up with pop music. I'd like to do something else. Ideally, I'd like to get into films.
   A Well, we wish you all the best.

Grammar Reference

UNIT 1

The tense system

There are three classes of verbs in English.

1 Auxiliary verbs

The auxiliary verbs are *be*, *do*, and *have*.

Be is used ...

1 with verb + *-ing* to make continuous verb forms.
You're lying. (present)
They were reading. (past)
I've been swimming. (present perfect)
We'll be having dinner at 8 o'clock. (future)
You must be joking! (infinitive)

2 with the past participle to make the passive.
These books are printed in Hong Kong. (present)
Where were you born? (past)
The car's been serviced. (present perfect)
The city had been destroyed. (past perfect)
This work should be done soon. (infinitive)

Do/does/did are used ...

in the Present Simple and the Past Simple.
Do you smoke? (question)
She doesn't understand. (negative)
When did they arrive? (question)

Have is used ...

with the past participle to make perfect verb forms.
Have you ever tried sushi? (present)
My car had broken down before. (past)
I'll have finished soon. (future)
I'd like to have met Napoleon. (infinitive)
Having had lunch, we tidied up. (participle)

Auxiliary verbs are also used ...

1 in question tags.
It's cold today, isn't it?
You don't understand, do you?
You haven't been to China, have you?

2 in short answers. *Yes* or *No* alone can sound abrupt.
'Are you hungry?'   *'No, I'm not.'*
'Do you like jazz?'   *'Yes, I do.'*
'Did you have a nice meal?' *'Yes, we did.'*
'Has she seen the mess?'   *'No, she hasn't.'*

3 in reply questions. These are not real questions. They are used to show that the listener is paying attention and is interested. They are practised on page 37 of the Student's Book.
'The party was awful.'   *'Was it? What a pity.'*
'I love hamburgers.'   *'Do you? I hate them.'*
'I've bought you a present.'   *'Have you? How kind!'*

2 Modal auxiliary verbs

These are the modal auxiliary verbs.

can	could	may	might	will	would
shall	should	must	ought to	need	

They are auxiliary verbs because they 'help' other verbs. They are different from *be*, *do*, and *have* because they have their own meanings.
He must be at least 70. (= probability)
You must try harder. (= obligation)
Can you help me? (= request)
She can't have got my letter. (= probability)

I'll help you. (= willingness)
(Ring) That'll be the postman. (= probability)

Modal auxiliary verbs are dealt with in Units 5, 8, 10, and 11.

3 Full verbs

Full verbs are all the other verbs in the language.

run	walk	eat	love	go	talk	write

The verbs *be*, *do*, and *have* can also be used as full verbs with their own meanings.
Have you been to school today?
I want to be an engineer.
I do a lot of business in Russia.
The holiday did us a lot of good.
They're having a row.
Have you had enough to eat?

English tense usage

English tenses have two elements of meaning: time and aspect.

The simple aspect

1 The simple aspect describes an action that is seen to be complete. The action is viewed as a whole unit.
The sun rises in the east. (= all time)
When I've read the book, I'll lend it to you. (= complete)
She has red hair. (= permanent)
He always wore a suit. (= a habit)
It rained every day of our holiday. (= the whole two weeks)
This shop will close at 7.00 this evening. (= a fact)

2 The simple aspect expresses a completed action. For this reason we must use the simple, not the continuous, if the sentence contains a number that refers to 'things done'.
She's written three letters this morning.
I drink ten cups of tea a day.
He read five books while he was on holiday.

Simple tenses are dealt with further in Units 2, 3, and 5.

The continuous aspect

1 The continuous aspect focuses on the duration of an activity. We are aware of the passing of time between the beginning and the end of the activity. The activity is *not* permanent.
I'm staying with friends until I find a flat. (= temporary)
What are you doing on your hands and knees? (= in progress)
I've been learning English for years. (And I still am.)
Don't phone at 8.00. We'll be eating. (= in progress)

2 Because the activity is seen in progress, it can be interrupted.
We were walking across a field when we were attacked by a bull.
'Am I disturbing you?' 'No. I'm just doing the ironing.'

3 The activity may not be complete.
I was writing a report on the flight home. (I didn't finish it.)
He was drowning, but we saved him. (He didn't die.)
Who's been drinking my beer? (There's some left.)

4 The action of some verbs, by definition, lasts a long time, for example, *live*, *work*, *play*. The continuous gives these actions limited duration and makes them temporary.
Hans is living in London while he's learning English.
I'm working as a waiter until I go to university.
Henman has been playing well recently. Maybe he'll win Wimbledon.

5 The action of some other verbs lasts a short time, for example, *lose*, *break*, *cut*, *hit*, *crash*. They are often found in the simple.
I lost all my money.
She's cut her finger.
I've crashed your car. Sorry.
He hit me.

In the continuous, the action of these verbs seems longer or habitual.

I've been cutting the grass. (= for hours)
He was hitting me. (= again and again)

Note

We cannot say a sentence such as *I've been crashing your car because it suggests an activity that was done deliberately and often.

Continuous tenses are dealt with further in Units 2, 3, and 5.

The perfect aspect

The perfect aspect expresses two ideas.

1 The action is completed *before* another time.
Have you ever been to America? (= some time before now)
When I arrived, Peter had left. (= some time before I arrived)
I'll have finished the report by 10.00. (= some time before then)

2 The exact time of the verb action is not important. The perfect aspect refers to indefinite time.
Have you seen my wallet anywhere? I've lost it. (= before now)
We'll have arrived by this evening. (= before this evening)

The exception to this is the Past Perfect, which can refer to definite time.

I recognized him immediately. I had met him in 1992 at university.

Perfect tenses are dealt with further in Units 2, 3, and 5.

Active and passive

1 Passive sentences move the focus of attention from the subject of an active sentence to the object.
Shakespeare wrote Hamlet in 1599.
Hamlet, one of the great tragedies, was written in 1599.

2 In most cases, *by* and the agent are omitted in passive sentences. This is because the agent is not important, isn't known, or is understood.
My car was stolen yesterday.
This house was built in the seventeenth century.
She was arrested for drink-driving.

3 Sometimes we prefer to begin a sentence with what is known, and end a sentence with the 'news'. In the passive, the news can be the agent of the active sentence.
'What a lovely painting!' 'Yes. It was painted by Canaletto.'

4 In informal language, we often use *you* or *they* to refer to people in general or to no person in particular. In this way we can avoid using the passive.
You can buy anything in Harrods.
They're building a new airport soon.

5 There are many past participles that are used more like adjectives.
I'm very impressed by your work.
You must be disappointed with your exam results.
I'm exhausted! I've been on my feet all day.

Passive sentences are dealt with further in Unit 12.

UNIT 2

Present Perfect

Introduction

Many languages have a past tense to refer to past time, and a present tense to refer to present time. English has these, too, but it also has the Present Perfect, which relates past actions to the present.
The use of the Past Simple roots an action in the past, with no explicit connection to the present. When we hear or read a verb in the Past Simple, we want to know *When?* The use of the Present Perfect always has a link with the present. When we come across a verb in the Present

Perfect, we want to know *How does this affect the situation now?*

Compare these sentences.

I lived in Rome. (But not any more.)
I've lived in Rome, Paris, and New York. (I know all these cities now.)
I've been living in New York for ten years. (And I'm living there now.)
She's been married three times. (She's still alive.)
She married three times. (She's dead.)
Did you see the Renoir exhibition? (It's finished now.)
Have you seen the Renoir exhibition? (It's still on.)
Did you see that programme on TV? (I'm thinking of the one that was on last night.)
Did you enjoy the film? (Said as we're leaving the cinema.)
Have you enjoyed the holiday? (Said near the end of the holiday.)
Where have I put my glasses? (I want them now.)
Where did I put my glasses? (I had them a minute ago.)
It rained yesterday. (= past time)
It's been snowing. (There's snow still on the ground.)

Present Perfect simple and continuous

See the introduction to the perfect aspect and the continuous aspect on p 9.

These tenses have three main uses.

1 Unfinished past

The verb action began in the past and continues to the present. It possibly goes on into the future, as well.
We've lived in this house for twenty years.
Sorry I'm late. Have you been waiting long?
I've been a teacher for five years.
I've been working at the same school all that time.

Notes

• There is sometimes little or no difference between the simple and the continuous.

I've played
I've been playing | *tennis since I was a kid.*

• The continuous can sometimes suggest a more temporary situation. The simple can sound more permanent.
I've been living with a host family for six weeks.
The castle has stood on the hill overlooking the sea for centuries.

• Certain verbs, by definition, suggest duration, for example, *wait, rain, snow, learn, sit, lie, play, stay.* They are often found in the continuous.
It's been raining all day.
She's been sitting reading for hours.

• Remember the state verbs that rarely take the continuous.
I've known Joan for years. *I've been knowing
How long have you had that car?* *have you been having
I've never understood why she likes him.* *I've never been understanding

2 Present result

The verb action happened in the past, usually the recent past, and the results of the action are felt now.
You've changed. What have you done to yourself?
I've lost some weight.
I've been doing some exercise.
I'm covered in mud because I've been gardening.

In this use, the simple emphasizes the completed action. The continuous emphasizes the repeated activities over a period of time.

Notes

• Certain verbs, by definition, suggest a short action, for example *start, find, lose, begin, stop, break, die, decide, cut.* They are more often found in the simple.

*We've **decided** to get married.*
*I've **broken** a tooth.*
*I've **cut** my finger.*

In the continuous, these verbs suggest a repeated activity.

*I've **been stopping** smoking for years.*
*You've **been losing** everything lately. What's the matter with you?*
*I've **been cutting** wood.*

- The use of the simple suggests a completed action.

*I've **painted** the bathroom.*

The use of the continuous suggests a possibly incomplete action.

*I'm tired because I've **been working**.* (Finished? Not finished?)
*Someone's **been drinking** my beer.* (There's some left.)

- The continuous can be found unqualified by any further information.

*I'm wet because I've **been swimming**.*
*We're tired because we've **been working**.*
'Why are you red?' *'I've **been running**.'*

The simple sounds quite wrong in this use.
*I've swum. *We've worked. *I've run.

- Sometimes there is little difference between the Past Simple and the Present Perfect.

| Where | **did** you **put** | my keys? |
| | **have** you **put** | |

- American English is different from British English. In American English, these sentences are correct.

Did you hear the news? The President resigned!
Did you do your homework yet?
Your father just called you.
I had breakfast already.

3 Indefinite past

The verb action happened at an unspecified time in the past. The actual time isn't important. We are focusing on the experience at some time in our life.

*Have you ever **taken** any illegal drugs?*
*She's never **been** abroad.*
*Have you ever **been flying** in a plane when it's hit an air pocket?*

Note
Here is an example of the indefinite past.
*She's **been** to Spain.* (At some time in her life.)

Here is an example of present result.
*She's **gone** to Spain.* (And she's there now.)

UNIT 3

Narrative tenses

Past Simple and Present Perfect

See the introduction to the perfect aspect and the simple aspect on p 9.

The Past Simple differs from all three uses of the Present Perfect.

1 The Past Simple refers to **finished past**.
*Shakespeare **wrote** plays.* (He's dead.)
*I've **written** short stories.* (I'm alive.)

2 There is **no present result**.
*I **hurt** my back.* (But it's better now.)
*I've **hurt** my back.* (And it hurts now.)

3 It refers to **definite past**.

| I saw him | **last night**. | **on Monday**. |
| | **two weeks ago**. | **at 8.00**. |

Compare this with the indefinite adverbials found with the Present Perfect.

| I've seen him | *recently*. |
| | *before*. |

I haven't seen him	*since January*.
	yet.
	for months.

| I've | *never* | seen him. |
| | *just* | |

Even when there is no past time adverbial, we can 'build' a past time in our head.

Did you have a good journey? (The journey's over. You're here now.)
Thank you for supper. It was lovely. (The meal is finished.)
Where did you buy that shirt? (when you were out shopping the other day.)

Past Simple

The Past Simple is used:

1 to express a finished action in the past.
*Columbus **discovered** America in 1492.*

2 to express actions which follow each other in a story.
*I **heard** voices coming from downstairs, so I **put on** my dressing-gown and **went** to investigate.*

3 to express a past state or habit.
*When I **was** a child, we **lived** in a small house by the sea. Every day I **walked** for miles on the beach with my dog.*

This use is often expressed with *used to*.
*We **used to** live ...*
*I **used to** walk ...*

See Unit 10 for more information on this use.
See Unit 11 for information on the Past Simple used for hypothesis.

Past Continuous

See the introduction to the continuous aspect on p 9.

The Past Continuous is used:

1 to express an activity in progress before and probably after a time in the past.
*I phoned at 4.00, but there was no reply. What **were** you **doing**?*

2 to describe a past situation or activity.
*The cottage **was looking** so cosy. A fire **was burning** in the grate, music **was playing**, and from the kitchen **were coming** the most delicious smells.*

3 to express an interrupted past activity.
*I **was having** a bath when the phone rang.*

4 to express an incomplete activity in the past.
*I **was reading** a book during the flight.* (But I didn't finish it.)
*I **watched** a film during the flight.* (the whole film)

5 to express an activity that was in progress at every moment during a period of time.
*I **was working** all day yesterday.*
*They **were fighting** for the whole of the holiday.*

Notes
- The Past Simple expresses past actions as simple, complete facts. The Past Continuous gives past activities time and duration.
'What did you do last night?'
*'I **stayed** at home and **watched** the football.'*
'I phoned you last night, but there was no reply.'
*'Oh, I **was watching** the football and I didn't hear the phone. Sorry.'*

- Notice how the questions in the Past Continuous and Past Simple refer to different times.

When we arrived, Jan was ironing. She stopped ironing and made some coffee.
*What **was** she **doing** when we arrived?   She was ironing.*
*What **did** she **do** when we arrived?   She made some coffee.*

Past Perfect

See the introduction to the perfect aspect and the continuous aspect on p 9.

The Past Perfect is used to look back to a time in the past and refer to an action that happened before then.

*She was crying because her dog **had died**.*
*I arrived to pick up Dave, but he **had** already **left**.*
*Keith was fed up. He**'d been looking** for a job for months, but he**'d found** nothing.*

Notes
- The continuous refers to longer actions or repeated activities. The simple refers to shorter, complete facts.
  *He**'d lost** his job and his wife **had left** him. Since then he**'d been sleeping** rough, and he**'d been drinking** far too much.*
- The Past Perfect can refer to definite as well as indefinite time.
  *I knew his face immediately. I**'d** first **met** him **in October 1993**.*
  (= definite)
  *I recognized her face. I'd **seen** her somewhere **before**. (= indefinite)*

Past Perfect and Past Simple

Verbs in the Past Simple tell a story in chronological order.

*John **worked** hard all day to prepare for the party. Everyone **had** a good time. Even the food **was** all right. Unfortunately, Andy **got** drunk and **insulted** Peter, so Peter **left** early. Pat **came** looking for Peter, but he **wasn't** there.*
*It **was** a great party. John **sat** and **looked** at all the mess. He **felt** tired. It **was** time for bed.*

By using the Past Perfect, the speaker or writer can tell a story in a different order.

*John sat and looked at all the mess. It **had been** a great party, and everyone **had had** a good time. Even the food **had been** all right. Unfortunately, Andy got drunk and insulted Peter, so Peter left early. Pat came looking for Peter, but he**'d** already **gone**.*
*John felt tired. He**'d been working** all day to prepare for the party. It was time for bed.*

Note
For reasons of style, it is not necessary to have every verb in the Past Perfect.

*... Andy **got** drunk and **insulted** ...   Peter **left** ...*

Once the time of 'past in the past' has been established, the Past Simple can be used as long as there is no ambiguity.

Time clauses
1 We can use time conjunctions to talk about two actions that happen one after the other. Usually the Past Perfect is not necessary in these cases, although it can be used.
   *After I**'d had**/ **had** a bath, I **went** to bed.*
   *As soon as the guests **left**/**had left**, I **started** tidying up.*
   *I **sat** outside until the sun **had gone**/**went** down.*

2 The Past Perfect can help to make the first action seem separate, independent of the second, or completed before the second action started.
   *When I **had read** the paper, I **threw** it away.*
   *We **stayed** up until all the beer **had gone**.*

3 Two verbs in the Past Simple can suggest that the first action lead into the other, or that one caused the other to happen.
   *When I **heard** the news, I **burst** out crying.*
   *As soon as the alarm **went** off, I **got** up.*

4 The Past Perfect is more common with *when* because it is ambiguous. The other conjunctions are more specific, so the Past Perfect is not so essential.
   *As soon as all the guests **left**, I tidied the house.*
   *Before I **met** you, I didn't know the meaning of happiness.*
   *When I **opened** the door, the cat jumped out.*
   *When I**'d opened** the mail, I made another cup of tea.*

See Unit 11 for information on the Past Perfect used for hypothesis.

UNIT 4

Expressing quantity

Quantifiers

1 The following can be used before a noun.

some/any	*much/many*	*each/every*	
more/most	*a little/little*	*a few/few*	*both*
fewer/less	*several*	*all/no*	*enough*

With count nouns only	With uncount nouns only	With both count and uncount nouns
(not) many cigarettes a few cars very few trees fewer books several answers	(not) much luck a little cheese very little experience less time	some money some eggs (not) any water (not) any friends more/most rice more/most people all/no work all/no children enough food enough apples

With singular count nouns only	With plural count nouns only
each boy every time	both parents

2 Most of the quantifiers can be used without a noun. *No, all, every,* and *each* cannot.

Have you got any money?	***Not much/a little/enough***.
Are there any eggs?	***A few/not many***.
Have some wine.	*I don't want **any**.*
How many people came?	*Very **few**.*
Have some more tea.	*I've got **some**.*
Did Ann or Sam go?	***Both**.*

3 Most of the quantifiers can be used with *of + the/my/those*, etc. + noun. *No* and *every* cannot.
   *They took **all of my money**.*
   *Take **a few of these tablets**.*
   ***Some of the people** at the party started dancing.*
   *Were **any of my friends** at the party?*
   *Very **few of my friends** smoke.*
   *Not **much of the food** was left.*
   *I've missed too **many of my French lessons**.*
   *I couldn't answer **several of the questions**.*
   *I'll have **a little of the strawberry cake**, please.*
   ***Both of my children** are clever.*
   *I feel tired **most of the time**.*
   *I've had **enough of your jokes**.*

4 For *no* and *every*, we use *none* and *every one* or *all*.
   ***None of the audience** was listening.*
   ***All of the hotels** were booked.*

   In formal, written English, *none* is followed by a singular form of the verb.
   ***None** of the guests **has** arrived yet.*

But in informal English, a plural verb is possible.
*None of my friends **smoke**.*
*None of the lights **are** working.*

Note
When we use *none* with a plural noun or pronoun, the verb can be singular or plural. Grammatically, it should be singular, but people often use the plural when they speak.
*None of my friends **is** coming.*
*None of my friends **are** coming.*

Some, any, somebody, anything

1 The basic rule is that *some* and its compounds are used in affirmative sentences, and *any* and its compounds in negatives and questions.
*I need **some** help.*
*I need **somebody** to help me.*
*Give me **something** for my headache.*
*I don't need **any** shopping.*
*We can't go **anywhere** without being recognized.*
*Is there **any** sugar left?*
*Did **anyone** phone me last night?*

2 *Some* and its compounds are used in requests or invitations, or when we expect the answer 'yes'.
*Have you got **some** money you could lend me?*
*Would you like **something** to eat?*
*Did **someone** phone me last night?*
*Can we go **somewhere** quiet to talk?*

3 *Any* and its compounds are used in affirmative sentences that have a negative meaning.
*He **never** has **any** money.*
*You made **hardly any** mistakes.*
*I made the cake myself **without any** help.*

4 *Any* and its compounds are used to express *It doesn't matter which/who/where.*
*Take **any book** you like. I don't mind.*
***Anyone** will tell you 2 and 2 makes 4.*
*Sit **anywhere** you like.*
*I eat **anything**. I'm not fussy.*

Nobody, no one, nowhere, nothing

1 These are more emphatic forms.
*I saw **nobody** all weekend.*
*I've eaten **nothing** all day.*

2 They are used at the beginning of sentences.
***No one** was saved.*
***Nobody** understands me.*
***Nowhere** is safe any more.*

Much, many, a lot of, lots of, a great deal of, a large number of, plenty of

1 *Much* and *many* are usually used in questions and negatives.
*How **much** does it cost?*
*How **many** people came to the party?*
*Is there **much** unemployment in your country?*
*I don't have **much** money.*
*Will there be **many** people there?*
*You don't see **many** snakes in England.*

2 We find *much* and *many* in affirmative sentences after *so*, *as*, and *too*.
*He has **so much** money that he doesn't know what to do with it.*
*She hasn't got **as many** friends as I have.*
*You make **too many** mistakes. Be careful.*

3 In affirmative sentences, these forms are found.
Spoken/informal
*There'll be **plenty of food/people**. (uncount and count)*
*We've got **lots of time/friends**. (uncount and count)*
*I lost **a lot of my furniture/things**. (uncount and count)*

Written/more formal
***A great deal of money** was lost during the strike. (uncount)*
***A large number of strikes** are caused by bad management. (count)*
***Many world leaders** are quite young. (count)*
***Much time** is wasted in trivial pursuits. (uncount)*

4 These forms are found without nouns.
*'Have you got enough socks?'   '**Lots**.'*
*'How many people were there?'   '**A lot**.'*
*Don't worry about food. We've got **plenty**.*

little/few/less/fewer

1 *A little* and *a few* express a small amount or number in a positive way. Although there is only a little, it is probably enough.
*Can you lend me **a little sugar**?*
***A few friends** are coming round tonight.*

2 *Little* and *few* express a small amount in a negative way. There is not enough.
***Very few** people passed the exam.*
*There's **very little milk** left.*

3 *Fewer* is the comparative of *few*; *less* is the comparative of *little*.
***Fewer people** go to church these days. (= count noun)*
*I spend **less and less time** doing what I want to. (= uncount noun)*

It is becoming more common to find *less* with a count noun. Many people think that this is incorrect and sounds terrible.
*~~Less people~~ go to church. *You should smoke ~~less cigarettes~~.

all

1 We do not usually use *all* to mean *everybody/everyone/everything.*
***Everybody** had a good time.*
***Everything** was ruined in the fire.*
*I said hello to **everyone**.*

But if *all* is followed by a relative clause, it can mean *everything.*
***All** (that) I own is yours.*
*I spend **all** I earn.*

This structure can have a negative meaning, expressing ideas such as *nothing more* or *only this.*
***All I want** is a place to sleep.*
***All I had** was a couple of beers.*
***All that happened** was that he pushed her a bit, and she fell over.*

2 Before a noun with a determiner (for example *the*, *my*, *this*) both *all* and *all of* are possible.
*You eat **all (of) the time**.*
***All (of) my friends** are coming tonight.*

Before a noun with no determiner, we use *all.*
***All people** are born equal.*

3 With personal pronouns, we use *all of.*
***All of you** passed. Well done!*
*I don't need these books. You can have **all of them**.*

UNIT 5

Future forms

There is no one future tense in English. Instead, there are several verb forms that can refer to future time. Sometimes, several forms are possible to express a similar meaning, but not always.

will for prediction

1 The most common use of *will* is as an auxiliary verb to show future time. It expresses a future fact or prediction – *at some time in the future this event will happen.* This use is uncoloured by ideas such as intention, decision, arrangement, willingness, etc.

I'll be thirty in a few days' time.
It will be cold and wet tomorrow, I'm afraid.
Who do you think will win the match?
You'll feel better if you take this medicine.
I'll see you later.

This is the nearest English has to a neutral, pure future tense.

2 *Will* for a prediction can be based more on an opinion than a fact or evidence. It is often found with expressions such as *I think ..., I hope ..., I'm sure ...*

I think Labour will win the next election.
I hope you'll come and visit me.
I'm sure you'll pass your exams.

3 *Will* is common in the main clause when there is a subordinate clause with *if, when, before,* etc. Note that we don't use *will* in the subordinate clause.

You'll break the glass if you aren't careful.
When you're ready, we'll start the meeting.
I won't go until you arrive.
As soon as Peter comes, we'll have lunch.

going to for prediction

Going to can express a prediction based on a present fact. There is evidence now that something is sure to happen. We can see the future from the present.

Careful! That glass is going to fall over. Too late!
Look at the sky! It's going to be a lovely day.

Notes

- Sometimes there is little or no difference between *will* and *going to.*
  We'll
  We're going to | *run out of money if we aren't careful.*

- We use *going to* when we have physical evidence to support our prediction.
  She's going to have a baby. (Look at her bump.)
  Liverpool are going to win. (It's 4–0, and there are only five minutes left.)
  That glass is going to fall. (It's rolling to the edge of the table.)

- We can use *will* when there is no such outside evidence. Our prediction is based on our own personal opinion. It can be more theoretical and abstract.
  I'm sure you'll have a good time at the party. (This is my opinion.)
  I reckon Liverpool will win. (Said the day before the match.)
  The glass will break if it falls. (This is what happens to glasses that fall.)

  Compare the sentences.
  I bet John will be late home. The traffic is always bad at this time. (= my opinion)
  John's going to be late home. He left a message on the answerphone. (= a fact)

  Don't lend Keith your car. He'll crash it. (= a theoretical prediction)
  Look out! We're going to crash! (= a prediction based on evidence)

Decisions and intentions – will and going to

1 *Will* is used to express a decision or intention made at the moment of speaking.
I'll phone you back in a minute.
Give me a ring some time. We'll go out together.
'The phone's ringing.' 'I'll get it.'

2 *Going to* is used to express a future plan, decision, or intention made before the moment of speaking.

When she grows up, she's going to be a ballet dancer.
We're going to get married in the spring.

Other uses of will and shall

1 *Will* as a prediction is an auxiliary verb that simply shows future time. It has no real meaning.
Tomorrow will be cold and windy.

2 *Will* is also a modal auxiliary verb, and so it can express a variety of meanings. The meaning often depends on the meaning of the main verb.
I'll help you carry those bags. (= offer)
Will you marry me? (= willingness)
Will you open the window? (= request)
My car won't start. (= refusal)
I'll love you for ever. (= promise)
'The phone's ringing.' 'It'll be for me.' (= prediction about the present)

3 *Shall* is found mainly in questions. It is used with *I* and *we.*
Where shall I put your tea? (I'm asking for instructions.)
What shall we do tonight? (I'm asking for a decision.)
Shall I cook supper tonight? (I'm offering to help.)
Shall we eat out tonight? (I'm making a suggestion.)

Present Continuous for arrangements

1 The Present Continuous is used to express personal arrangements and fixed plans, especially when the time and place have been decided. A present tense is used because there is some reality in the present. The event is planned or decided, and we can see it coming. The event is usually in the near future.
I'm having lunch with Brian tomorrow.
What time are you meeting him?
Where are you having lunch?
What are you doing tonight?

2 The Present Continuous for future is often used with verbs of movement and activity.
Are you coming to the dance tonight?
I'm meeting the director tomorrow.
I'm just taking the dog for a walk.
We're playing tennis this afternoon.

3 The Present Continuous is used to refer to arrangements between people. It is not used to refer to events that people can't control.
It's going to rain this afternoon. *It's raining this afternoon.*
The sun rises at 5.30 tomorrow. *The sun is rising ...*

Notes

- Sometimes there is little or no difference between the Present Continuous and *going to* to refer to the future.
  We're seeing
  We're going to see | *Hamlet at the theatre tonight.*

- When there is a difference, the Present Continuous emphasizes an arrangement with some reality in the present; *going to* expresses a person's intentions.
  I'm seeing my girlfriend tonight.
  I'm going to ask her to marry me. *I'm asking ...*

  What are you doing this weekend?
  What are you going to do about the broken toilet? (= What have you decided to do?)

Present Simple

1 The Present Simple refers to a future event that is seen as unalterable because it is based on a timetable or calendar.
My flight leaves at 10.00.
Term starts on 4 April.
What time does the film start?
It's my birthday tomorrow.

2 It is used in subordinate clauses introduced by conjunctions such as *if, when, before, as soon as, unless*, etc.
*We'll have a picnic if the weather **stays** fine.*
*When I **get** home, I'll cook the dinner.*
*I'll leave as soon as it **stops** raining.*

Future Continuous

1 The Future Continuous expresses an activity that will be in progress before and after a time in the future.
*Don't phone at 8.00. We**'ll be having** supper.*
*This time tomorrow I**'ll be flying** to New York.*

2 The Future Continuous is used to refer to a future event that will happen in the natural course of events. This use is uncoloured by ideas such as intention, decision, arrangement, or willingness. As time goes by, this event will occur.
*Don't worry about our guests. They**'ll be arriving** any minute now.*
*We**'ll be going** right back to the football after the break.* (said on television)

Future Perfect

The Future Perfect refers to an action that will be completed before a definite time in the future. It is not a very common verb form.
*I**'ll have done** all my work by this evening.*

UNIT 6

Relative clauses

Introduction

It is important to understand the difference between two kinds of relative clauses.

1 Defining relative (DR) clauses qualify a noun, and tell us exactly which person or thing is being referred to.
*She likes people **who are good fun to be with**.*
*Politicians **who tell lies** are odious.*
*A corkscrew is a thing **you use to open a bottle of wine**.*

She likes people on its own doesn't mean very much; we need to know which people she likes.
who tell lies tells us exactly which politicians are odious. Without it, the speaker is saying that all politicians are odious.
A corkscrew is a thing doesn't make sense on its own.

2 Non-defining relative (NDR) clauses add secondary information to a sentence, almost as an afterthought.
*My friend Andrew, **who is Scottish**, plays the bagpipes.*
*Politicians, **who tell lies**, are odious.*
*My favourite plane is Concorde, **which has been flying for over twenty-five years**.*

My friend Andrew is clearly defined. We don't need to know which Andrew is being discussed. The clause *who is Scottish* gives us extra information about him.
The clause *who tell lies* suggests that all politicians tell lies. It isn't necessary to identify only those that deceive – they all do!
We all know which plane Concorde is. The following clause simply tells us something extra.

3 DR clauses are much more common in the spoken language, and NDR clauses are more common in the written language. In the spoken language, we can avoid a NDR clause.
My friend Andrew plays the bagpipes. He's Scottish, by the way.

4 When we speak, there is no pause before or after a DR clause, and no commas when we write. With NDR clauses, there are commas before and after, and pauses when we speak.
I like the things you say to me. (No commas, no pauses)
My aunt (pause), *who has been a widow for twenty years* (pause), *loves travelling.*

Defining relative clauses

1 Notice how we can leave out the relative pronoun if it is the object of the relative clause. This is very common.

> **Pronoun left out**
> *Did you like the present (   ) I gave you?*
> *Who was that man (   ) you were talking to?*
> *The thing (   ) I like about Dave is his sense of humour.*

2 We cannot leave out the pronoun if it is the subject of the clause.

> **Pronoun not left out**
> *I met a man **who** works in advertising.*
> *I'll lend you the book **that** changed my life.*
> *The thing **that** helped me most was knowing I wasn't alone.*

3 Here are the possible pronouns. The words in brackets are possible, but not as common. ____ means nothing.

	Person		Thing	
Subject	who	(that)	that	(which)
Object	____	(that)	____	(that)

Notes

- *That* is preferred to *which* after superlatives, and words such as *all, every(thing), some(thing), any(thing)*, and *only*.
  *That's the **funniest** film **that** was ever made.*
  ***All that**'s left is a few slices of ham.*
  *Give me **something that**'ll take away the pain.*
  *He's good at **any** sport **that** is played with a ball.*
  *The **only** thing **that**'ll help you is rest.*

- *That* is also preferred after *it is* ...
  *It is a film **that** will be very popular.*

- Prepositions usually come at the end of the relative clause.
  *Come and meet the people I work **with**.*
  *This is the book I was telling you **about**.*
  *She's a friend I can always rely **on**.*

Non-defining relative clauses

1 Relative pronouns cannot be left out of NDR clauses.

> **Relative pronoun as subject**
> *Paul Jennings, **who** has written several books, addressed the meeting.*
> *His last book, **which** received a lot of praise, has been a great success.*

> **Relative pronoun as object**
> *Paul Jennings, **who** I knew at university, addressed the meeting.*
> *His last book, **which** I couldn't understand at all, has been a great success.*

2 Look at the possible pronouns. *Whom* is possible, but not as common.

	Person	Thing
Subject	... , who ... ,	... , which ... ,
Object	... , who (whom) ... ,	... , which ... ,

Note
Prepositions can come at the end of the clause.
*He talked about theories of market forces, which I'd never even heard **of**.*

In a more formal written style, prepositions come before the pronoun.
*The privatization of railways, **to which** the present government is committed, is not universally popular.*

which

Which can be used in NDR clauses to refer to the whole of the sentence before.

*She arrived on time, **which** amazed everybody.*
*He gambled away all his money, **which** I thought was ridiculous.*
*The coffee machine isn't working, **which** means we can't have any coffee.*

whose

Whose can be used in both DR clauses and NDR clauses.

*That's the woman **whose son was killed recently**.*
*My parents, **whose only interest is gardening**, never go away on holiday.*

what

What is used in DR clauses to mean *the thing that*.

*Has she told you **what**'s worrying her?*
***What** I need to know is where we're meeting.*

why, when, where

1   Why can be used in DR clauses to mean *the reason why*.

*I don't know **why** we're arguing.*

2   When and where can be used in DR clauses and NDR clauses.

*Tell me **when** you expect to arrive.*
*The hotel **where** we stayed was excellent.*
*We go walking on Mondays, **when** the rest of the world is working.*
*He works in Oxford, **where** my sister lives.*

Participles

1   When present participles (-*ing*) are used like adjectives or adverbs, they are active in meaning.

*Modern art is **interesting**.*
*Pour **boiling** water onto the pasta.*
*She sat in the corner **crying**.*

2   When past participles (-*ed*) are used like adjectives or adverbs, they are passive in meaning.

*I'm **interested** in modern art.*
*Look at that **broken** doll.*
*He sat in his chair, **filled** with horror at what he had just seen.*

3   Participles after a noun define and identify in the same way as relative clauses.

*I met a woman **riding** a donkey.* (= who was riding ...)
*The car **stolen** in the night was later found abandoned.* (= that was stolen ...)

4   Participles can be used as adverbs. They can describe

*   two actions that happen at the same time.
    *She sat by the fire **reading** a book.*
*   two actions that happen one after another.
    ***Opening** his case, he took out a gun.*

    If it is important to show that the first action is completed before the second action begins, we use the perfect participle.
    ***Having finished** lunch, we set off on our journey.*
    ***Having had** a shower, she got dressed.*
*   two actions that happen one because of another.
    ***Being** mean, he never bought anyone a Christmas present.*
    ***Not knowing** what to do, I waited patiently.*

5   Many verbs are followed by -*ing* forms.

*I **spent** the holiday **reading**.*
*Don't **waste** time **thinking** about the past.*
*Let's **go swimming**.*
*He **keeps on asking** me to go out with him.*

Infinitive clauses

In indirect speech, we can use an infinitive after certain question words and *whether*. This expresses ideas such as obligation and possibility.

*I don't know **who to speak to**.*
*Tell me **where to go**.*
*Show me **how to make** this dish.*
*You need to tell me **when to arrive**.*
*I can't decide **whether to go** to the party or not.*

UNIT 7

Verb patterns

Uses of the -*ing* form

1   The -*ing* form (gerund or present participle) is used after prepositions.

*I'm good **at running**.*
*We're thinking **of living** abroad.*
*I'm interested **in seeing** your book.*
***After having** lunch, we tidied up.*
*I'm looking forward **to meeting** you.*
*We can't get used **to driving** on the left.*

Notice that in the last two examples, *to* is a preposition, so it is followed by -*ing*. It is NOT part of the infinitive.

2   The -*ing* form is used after certain verbs.

*I **enjoy visiting** my relatives.*
*She **denies stealing** the money.*

Here are some other verbs followed by -*ing*.

avoid	admit	finish	can't stand	don't mind
adore	give up	keep on	can't stop	can't help

3   There are some verbs that are followed by an object + -*ing*.

*I **hate people telling** me what to do.*
*You can't **stop me doing** what I want.*
*I can **hear someone playing** the violin.*
*I **spent the weekend gardening**.*
*Don't **waste time doing** nothing.*

4   The -*ing* form is used as the subject or object of a sentence.

***Living** in a big city is exciting.*
***Smoking** is bad for your health.*
*I find **working** in the garden a real bore.*

5   The -*ing* form is used after certain idiomatic expressions.

*It's no use **talking** to her. She never listens.*
*This book is **worth reading**.*
*There's no point in **doing** it your way. It won't work.*
*It's no good **saying** you're sorry. It's not enough.*

Note

suggest can be followed by -*ing* or a *that* clause.

*He suggested **going** to London to look for work.*
*I suggest **(that)** we all go to bed.*

Forms of the infinitive

Present Simple

*I want **to have** a bath.*
*It's time **to go**.*

Present Continuous

*It's nice **to be sitting** here with you.*
*I'd like **to be lying** next to a swimming pool.*
*They seem **to be having** a few problems.*

Perfect

*I'd like **to have seen** his face when you told him.*

*He seems **to have forgotten** about our date.*
*I hope **to have retired** by the time I'm fifty.*

Passive

*I'd like **to be promoted** to sales manager.*
*There's a lot of tidying up **to be done**.*
*I asked **to be informed** as soon as there was any news.*

Note

- These infinitives are used after modal auxiliary verbs without *to*.
  *You should **be working**, not watching TV.*
  *She must **have gone** home early.*
  *This essay must **be done** by tomorrow.*

Uses of the infinitive

1 Infinitives are used after certain verbs.
  *I **can't afford to pay** the bill.*
  *I **hope to see** you again soon.*
  *I **didn't mean to hurt** you.*

  Here are some other verbs followed by the infinitive.

agree	attempt	choose	dare	decide	expect	help	want
learn	manage	need	offer	promise	refuse	seem	long

2 There are some verbs that are followed by an object + the infinitive.
  *He **advised me to listen** carefully.*
  *They **invited her to have** lunch.*

  Here are some other verbs like this.

allow	remind	
encourage	teach	someone to do something
order	tell	
persuade	force	

3 There are some verbs that sometimes take an object + the infinitive, and sometimes don't.
  *I want **to go** home.*
  *I want **you to go** home.*

  *I'd **like to help** you.*
  *I'd **like you to make** up your own mind.*

  Here are some other verbs like this.

ask	beg	
expect	would love	to go
help	would prefer	someone to do something
need	would hate	

Note

help can be used with or without *to*.

She helped me	tidy	up.
	to tidy	

4 The infinitive is used after *make*, *let*, and *allow*.
  *She made me **do** the exercise again.* (active – without *to*)
  *I was made **to stand** in the corner.* (passive – with *to*)
  *He let me **go** home.* (active – without *to*)
  *He allowed me **to go** home.*
  *I was allowed **to borrow** the car.*

  Let in this sense is not possible in the passive. **I was let ...*

5 The infinitive is used after certain adjectives.
  *It's **difficult to explain** how to get there.*
  *It's **impossible to get** through to her.*
  ***Pleased to meet** you.*
  *I'm **surprised to see** you here.*
  *You were **lucky to find** me.*
  *Dogs are **easy to train**.*
  *It's **good to be** back home.*
  *She's **nice to talk** to.*

  Note the pattern with *for*.

*It's difficult **for me to explain**.*

6 The infinitive is used after certain nouns.
  *It's **time to go**.*
  *It's a good **idea to ask** for help.*
  *I didn't agree with the **decision to close** down the factory.*
  *There's no **need to ask** for permission.*
  *My job gives me the **opportunity to travel**.*

7 The infinitive is used to express purpose.
  *I came here **to learn** English.*
  *I need more money **to buy** all the things I want.*

8 The infinitive is used after certain question words. See p 61.
  *I don't know **what to do**.*
  *Can you tell me **how to get** there?*

9 The infinitive can be used with *too* and *enough*.
  *I was **too tired to eat**.*
  *There were **too many people to get** in the house.*
  *It's cold **enough to snow**.*
  *There isn't **enough time to do** all the things I'd like to.*

-ing or the infinitive?

continue, start, begin

1 Both *-ing* and the infinitive can be used. The infinitive is more common.

He began	working / to work	when he was twenty.
She continued	ironing. / to iron.	

2 If the verb is in a continuous tense, we prefer the infinitive.
  *It's starting **to rain**.*

3 Certain state verbs are rarely found in continuous tenses. They are also rare in the continuous infinitive.
  *I began **to like** Joan more and more.* **I began liking ...*

like, love, hate, prefer

1 Often both *-ing* and the infinitive can be used with little difference of meaning.

I like	to get / getting	up early.
I love	to lie / lying	in the bath.

2 When *like* means *enjoy generally*, it is more usually followed by *-ing*.
  *I like **cooking**.*

  If the sentence is more specific, the infinitive is more common.
  *I like **to cook** a roast on Sundays.*
  *I like **to read** a book before going to sleep at night.*

3 When *like* means *think it a good idea*, it is followed by the infinitive.
  *I like **to pay** bills on time.*
  *I like **to go** to the dentist regularly.*

4 Used with *would*, these verbs are followed by the infinitive.
  *I'd like **to relax** for a bit.*
  *I'd love **to visit** you.*
  *She'd hate **to be** poor.*
  *We'd prefer **to travel** by train if possible.*

remember, forget, regret

1 After these verbs, the *-ing* form refers to an action that took place *before* the act of remembering, forgetting, or regretting.
  *I remember **having** some lovely holidays when I was a kid.*
  *I'll never forget **meeting** you.*
  *I regret **lying** to her.*

2 The infinitive refers to an action that takes place *after* the act of remembering, forgetting, or regretting.

*I must remember **to buy** my mother a birthday card.*
*Don't forget **to lock** all the doors.*
*I regret **to tell** you that you've failed.*

stop

1 The -*ing* form refers to an action that was in progress *before* the act of stopping.
*We stopped **playing** tennis because it got too dark.*
*Stop **looking** at me like that!*

2 The infinitive tells us why the action stopped, and what happened next. This is the infinitive of purpose.
*We stopped **to have** a break.*
*Have you ever stopped **to think** how much you spend on cigarettes?*

try

1 The infinitive refers to the goal, or what we want to achieve.
*I tried **to learn** Chinese, but it was too difficult.*
*We tried **to put out** the fire, but it was impossible.*

2 The -*ing* form refers to the methods used to achieve the goal.
*I tried **going** to evening classes.*
*We tried **pouring** on water, my husband tried **covering** it with a blanket, but it didn't work.*

3 Sometimes there is little or no difference.
Have you ever tried | ***driving*** / ***to drive*** | *in London?*

UNIT 8

Modal auxiliary verbs

Introduction

1 These are modal auxiliary verbs.

| can | could | may | might | shall |
| should | will | would | must | ought to |

They are used with great frequency and with a wide range of meanings.
They express ideas such as willingness and ability, permission and refusal, obligation and prohibition, suggestion, necessity, promise and intention. All modal auxiliary verbs can express degrees of certainty, probability, or possibility.

2 They have several characteristics in common.

• There is no -*s* in the third person.
He can swim.
She must go.

• There is no *do/does* in the question.
May I ask a question?
Shall we go?

• There is no *don't/doesn't* in the negative.
You shouldn't tell lies.
You won't believe this.

• They are followed by an infinitive without *to*. The exception is *ought to*.
*It might **rain**.*
*Could you **help**?*
*We ought **to be** on our way.*

• They don't really have past forms or infinitives or -*ing* forms. Other verbs are used instead.
*I **had** to work hard when I was young.*
*I'd love **to be able** to ski.*
*I hate **having** to get up in the morning.*

• They can be used with perfect infinitives to refer to the past.
*You should **have told** me that you can't swim.*
*You might **have drowned**!*
*She must **have been** crazy to marry him.*

Modal auxiliary verbs of probability, present and future

The main modal auxiliary verbs that express probability are described here in order of certainty. *Will* is the most certain, and *might/could* are the least certain.

will

1 *Will* and *won't* are used to predict a future action. The truth or certainty of what is asserted is more or less taken for granted.
I'll see you later.
*His latest book **will be** out next month.*

2 *Will* and *won't* are also used to express what we believe or guess to be true about the present. They indicate an assumption based on our knowledge of people and things, their routines, character, and qualities.
'You've got a letter from Canada.'   'It'll be from my aunt Freda.'
*Leave the meat in the oven. It **won't be cooked** yet.*
*'I wonder what Sarah's doing.'   'Well, it's Monday morning, so I guess that right now she'**ll be taking** the children to school.'*

must and can't

1 *Must* is used to assert what we infer or conclude to be the most logical or rational interpretation of a situation. We do not have all the facts, so it is less certain than *will*.
*You say he walked across the Sahara Desert! He **must be** mad!*
*You **must be joking**! I simply don't believe you.*

2 The negative of this use is *can't*.
*She **can't have** a ten-year-old daughter! She's only twenty-one herself.*
*'Whose is this coat?'   'It **can't be** Mary's. It's too small.'*

should

1 *Should* expresses what may reasonably be expected to happen. Expectation means believing that things are or will be as we want them to be. This use of *should* has the idea of *if everything has gone according to plan*.
*Our guests **should be** here soon (if they haven't got lost).*
*This homework **shouldn't take** you too long (if you've understood what you have to do).*
*We **should be moving** into our new house soon (as long as nothing goes wrong).*

2 *Should* in this use has the idea that we want the action to happen. It is not used to express negative or unpleasant ideas.
*You **should pass** the exam. You've worked hard.*
*You should fail the exam. You haven't done any work at all.

may and might

1 *May* expresses the possibility that an event will happen or is happening.
*We **may go** to Greece this year. We haven't decided yet.*
*'Where's Ann?'   'She **may be having** a bath, I don't know.'*

2 *Might* is more tentative and slightly less certain than *may*.
*It **might rain**. Take your umbrella.*
*'Where's Peter?'   'He **might be** upstairs. There's a light on.'*

3 Learners of English often express these concepts of future possibility with *perhaps* or *maybe ... will* and so avoid using *may* and *might*. However, these are widely used by native speakers, and you should try to use them.

could

1 *Could* has a similar meaning to *might*.
   *You **could be** right. I'm not sure.*
   *The film **could be** worth seeing. It had a good review.*

2 *Couldn't* is not used to express a future possibility. The negative of *could* in this use is *might not*.
   *You **might not be** right.*
   *The film **might not be** any good.*

3 *Couldn't* has a similar meaning to *can't* above, only slightly weaker.
   *She **couldn't have** a ten-year-old daugher! She's only 21 herself.*

Modal auxiliary verbs of probability in the past

All the modal auxiliary verbs above can be used with the perfect infinitive. They express the same varying degrees of certainty. Again, *will have done* is the most certain, and *might/could have done* is the least certain.

*'I met a tall girl at your party. Very attractive.'   'That**'ll have been** my sister, Patsy.'*
*It **must have been** a good party. Everyone stayed till dawn.*
*The music **can't have been** any good. Nobody danced.*
*Where's Pete? He **should have been** here ages ago!*
*He **may have got** lost.*
*He **might have decided** not to come.*
*He **could have had** an accident.*

Other uses of modal auxiliary verbs

Here is some further information about modal auxiliary verbs, but it is by no means complete. See a grammar book if you want more details.

Obligation and advice

1 *Must* expresses strong obligation. Other verb forms are provided by *have to*.
   *You **must** try harder!*
   *You **mustn't** hit your baby brother.*
   *What time **do** you **have to** start work?*
   *I **had to** work hard to pass my exams.*
   *You'll **have to** do this exercise again.*
   *We might **have to** make some economies.*
   *She's **never had to** do a single day's work in her life.*
   *I hate **having to** get up early.*

2 *Must* expresses the opinion of the speaker.
   *I **must** get my hair cut.* (I am telling myself.)
   *You **must** do this again.* (Teacher to student)

   Must is associated with a more formal, written style.
   *Candidates **must** answer three questions.* (On an exam paper)
   *Books **must** be returned by the end of the week.* (Instructions in a library)

   Have to expresses a general obligation based on a law or rule, or based on the authority of another person.
   *Children **have to** go to school until they're sixteen.* (It's the law.)
   *Mum says you **have to** tidy your room.*

3 *Mustn't* expresses negative obligation. *Don't have to* expresses the absence of obligation.
   *You **mustn't** steal. It's very naughty.*
   *You **don't have to** go to England if you want to learn English.*

4 *Have got to* is common in British English. It is more informal than *have to*.
   *I've **got to** go now. Cheerio!*
   *Don't have a late night. We**'ve got to** get up early tomorrow.*

5 *Should* and *ought* express mild obligation or advice. *Should* is much more common.
   *You **should** go to bed. You look very tired.*
   *You **ought** to take things easier.*

6 *Should* + the perfect infinitive is used to refer to a past action that didn't happen. The action would have been a good idea. The good advice is too late!
   *You **should have listened** to my advice. I was right all the time.*

Permission

1 *May, can,* and *could* are used to ask for permission.
   ***May** I ask you a question?*
   ***May** I use your phone?*
   ***Can/could** I go home? I don't feel well.*
   ***Can/Could** I borrow your car tonight?*

2 *May* is used to give permission, but it sounds very formal. *Can* and *can't* are more common.
   *You **can** use a dictionary in this exam.*
   *You **can't** stay up till midnight. You're only five.*
   *You **can't** smoke in here. It's forbidden.*

3 To talk about permission generally, or permission in the past, we use *can, could,* or *be allowed to*.
   *Children **can/are allowed to** do what they want these days.*

   I | **couldn't** / **wasn't allowed to** | *go out on my own until I was sixteen.*

Ability

1 *Can* expresses ability. The past is expressed by *could*.
   *I **can** speak three languages.*
   *I **could** swim when I was three.*

2 Other forms are provided by *be able to*.
   *I've never **been able to** understand her.*
   *I love **being able to** drive.*
   *You'll **be able to** walk again soon.*

3 To express a fulfilled ability on one particular occasion in the past, *could* is not used. Instead, we use *was able to* or *managed to*.
   *She **was able to** survive by clinging onto the wrecked boat.*
   *The prisoner **managed to** escape by climbing onto the roof.*

4 *Could* + the perfect infinitive is used to express an unrealized past ability. Someone was able to do something in the past, but didn't try to.
   *I **could have gone** to university, but I didn't want to.*
   *I **could have told** you that Chris wouldn't come. He hates parties.*

5 *Could* can be used to criticize people for not doing things. We feel that they are not doing their duty.
   *You **could** tell me if you're going to be late!*
   *You **could have done** something to help me instead of just sitting there!*

Request

Several modal verbs express a request.
***Can/could/will/would** you do me a favour?*

Willingness and refusal

1 *Will* expresses willingness. *Won't* expresses a refusal by either people or things. *Shall* is used in questions.
   I'll help you.
   *She says she **won't** get up until she's had breakfast in bed.*
   *The car **won't** start.*
   ***Shall** I give you a hand?*

2 The past is expressed by *wouldn't*.
   *My mum said she **wouldn't** give me any more money. Isn't she mean?*

Modal auxiliary verbs are also dealt with in Units 10 and 11.

UNIT 9

Questions

what and which

1 *What* and *which* are used with nouns to make questions.
What size *shoes do you take?*
Which of these curries *is the hottest?*

2 Sometimes there is no difference between questions with *what* and *which*.
What/which is the biggest city *in your country?*
What/which channel *is the match on?*
We use *which* when the speaker has a limited number of choices in mind.
There's a blue one and a red one. **Which** *do you want?*
We use *what* when the speaker is not thinking of a limited number of choices.
What car *do you drive?*

Asking for descriptions

1 *What is X like?* means *Give me some information about X because I don't know anything about it.*
What's your capital city **like**?
What are your parents **like**?

2 *How is X?* asks about a person's health and happiness.
How's your mother these days?

3 Sometimes both questions are possible. *What ... like?* asks for objective information. *How ... ?* asks for a more personal reaction.
'**What** *was the party* **like**?'   '*Noisy. Lots of people. It went on till 3.*'
'**How** *was the party?*'   '*Brilliant. I danced all night. Met loads of great people.*'
How *was your journey?*
How's *your new job going?*
How's *your meal?*

Indirect questions

There is no inversion and no *do/does/did* in indirect questions.
I wonder what she's doing. *I wonder ~~what is she doing~~.*
I don't know where he lives. *I don't know ~~where does he live~~.*
Tell me when the train leaves.
Do you remember how she made the salad?
I didn't understand what she was saying.
I've no idea why he went to India.
I'm not sure where they live.
He doesn't know whether he's coming or going.

Negatives

Forming negatives

1 We make negatives by adding *not* after the auxiliary verb. If there is no auxiliary verb, we add *do/does/did*.
I **haven't** *seen her for ages.*
It **wasn't** *raining.*
You **shouldn't** *have gone to so much trouble.*
We **don't** *like big dogs.*
They **didn't** *want to go out.*

2 The verb *have* has two forms in the present.
I **don't** *have*
I **haven't** *got*   *any money.*
But ... *I* **didn't** *have any money.*

3 Infinitives and *-ing* forms can be negative.
We decided **not to do** *anything.*

I like **not working**. *It suits me.*

4 *Not* can go with other parts of a sentence.
Ask him, **not me**.
Buy me anything, but **not perfume**.

5 When we introduce negative ideas with verbs such as *think, believe, suppose,* and *imagine*, we make the first verb negative, not the second.
I **don't think** *you're right.* *~~I think you aren't~~ ...*
I **don't suppose** *you want a game a tennis?*

6 In short answers, the following forms are possible.
'Are you coming?'   '*I think so.*'
                      '*I believe so.*'
                      '*I hope so.*'
                      '*I don't think so.*'
                      '*I hope not.*'

I think not is possible. *~~I don't hope so~~ is not possible.*

Negative questions

1 In the main use of negative questions, the speaker would normally expect a positive situation, but now expects a negative situation. The speaker therefore is surprised.
Don't *you* **like** *ice-cream? Everyone likes ice-cream!*
Haven't *you* **done** *your homework yet? What have you been doing?*

2 Negative questions can also be used to mean *confirm what I think is true*. In this use it refers to a positive situation.
Haven't *I* **met** *you somewhere before?* (I'm sure I have.)
Didn't *we* **speak** *about this yesterday?* (I'm sure we did.)
The difference between the two uses can be seen clearly if we change them into question tags.
You **haven't done** *your homework yet,* **have you?** (negative sentence, positive tag)
We've **met** *before,* **haven't we?** (positive sentence, negative tag)

UNIT 10

Expressing habit

Present Simple

1 Adverbs of frequency come before the main verb, but after the verb *to be*.
We **hardly ever** *go out.*
She **frequently** *forgets what she's doing.*
We don't **usually** *eat fish.*
I **rarely** *see Peter these days.*
We are **seldom** *at home in the evening.*
Is he **normally** *so bad-tempered?*

2 *Sometimes, usually,* and *occasionally* can come at the beginning or the end of a sentence.
Sometimes *we play cards.*
We go to the cinema **occasionally**.
The other adverbs of frequency don't usually move in this way.
~~Always I have~~ tea in the morning.

Present Continuous

1 The Present Continuous can be used to express a habit which happens often and perhaps unexpectedly. It happens more than is usual.
I like Peter. He's always **smiling**.
She's always **giving** *people presents.*

2 However, there is often an element of criticism with this structure. Compare these sentences said by a teacher.
Pedro always **asks** *questions about the lesson.* (This is a fact.)

*Pedro **is** always **asking** questions about the lesson.* (This annoys the teacher.)

3   There is usually an adverb of frequency with this use.
*I'm **always losing** my keys.*
*She's **forever leaving** the bath taps running.*

will and would

1   *Will* and *would* express typical behaviour. They describe both pleasant and unpleasant habits.
*He'**ll** sit in his chair all day long.*
*She'**d** spend all day long gossiping with the neighbours.*

2   *Will* and *would*, when decontracted and stressed, express an annoying habit.
*He **WILL** come into the house with his muddy boots on.*
*She **WOULD** make us wash in ice-cold water.*

used to + infinitive

1   This structure expresses a past action and state. It has no present equivalent.
*When I was a child, we **used to go** on holiday to the seaside.*

2   Notice the negative and the question.
*Where **did** you **use** to go?*
*We **didn't use** to do anything interesting.*

3   We cannot use *used to* with a time reference + a number.
*We used to have a holiday there for 10 years/three times.
But ...
*we **used to** go there every year.*

be/get used to + noun/-ing form

1   This is totally different from *used to* + infinitive. It expresses an action that was difficult, strange, or unusual before, but is no longer so. Here, *used* is an adjective, and it means *familiar with*.
*I found it difficult to get around London when I first came, but I'm **used to** it now.*
*I'm **used to getting** around London by tube.*

2   Notice the use of *get* to express the process of change.
*I'm **getting used to** the climate.*
*I'm **getting used to** eating with chopsticks.*

UNIT 11

Hypothesizing

First and second conditionals

1   First conditional sentences are based on fact in real time. They express a possible condition and its probable result in the present or future.
*If you **pass** your exams, I'**ll buy** you a car.*

2   Second conditional sentences are not based on fact. They express a situation which is contrary to reality in the present and future. This unreality is shown by a tense shift from present to past. They express a hypothetical condition and its probable result.
*If I **were** taller, I'**d join** the police force.*
*What **would** you **do** if you **won** the lottery?*

Notes

•   The difference between first and second conditional sentences is not about time. Both can refer to the present and future. By using past tense forms in the second conditional, the speaker suggests the situation is less probable, or impossible, or imaginary.

Compare the pairs of sentences.
*If it **rains** this weekend, we'**ll** ...* (Said in England where it often rains.)
*If it **rained** in the Sahara, it **would** ...* (This would be most unusual.)

*If there **is** a nuclear war, we'**ll** ...* (I'm a pessimist.)
*If there **was** a nuclear war, we'**d** ...* (I'm an optimist.)
*If you **come** to my country, you'**ll have** a good time.* (Possible)
*If you **came** from my country, you'**d understand** us better.* (Impossible)
*If I **am elected** as a member of Parliament, I'**ll** ...* (Said by a candidate)
*If I **ruled** the world, I'**d** ...* (Imaginary)

•   We can use *were* instead of *was*, especially in a formal style.
*If I **were** you, I'**d get** some rest.*
*I'd willingly help if it **were** possible.*

Third conditional

Third conditional sentences are not based on fact. They express a situation which is contrary to reality in the past. This unreality is shown by a tense shift from past to Past Perfect.
*If you'**d come** to the party, you'**d have had** a great time.*
*I **wouldn't have met** my wife if I **hadn't gone** to France.*

Note
It is possible for each of the clauses in a conditional sentence to have a different time reference, and the result is a mixed conditional.
*If we **had brought** a map (we didn't), we **would know** where we are (we don't).*
*I **wouldn't have married** her (I did) if I **didn't love** her (I do).*

Other structures that express hypothesis

The tense usage with *wish*, *if only*, and *I'd rather* is similar to the second and third conditionals. Unreality is expressed by a tense shift.
*I wish I **were** taller.* (But I'm not.)
*If only you **hadn't said** that!* (But you did.)
*I'd rather you **didn't** smoke.* (But you do.)

Notes

•   *wish ... would* can express regret, dissatisfaction, impatience, or irritation because someone WILL keep doing something.
*I wish you'**d stop** smoking.*
*I wish you'**d do** more to help in the house.*
*I wish it **would stop** raining.*

•   If we are not talking about willingness, *wish ... would* is not used.
I wish my birthday wasn't in December. (*I ~~wish it would be~~ ...)
I wish I could stop smoking. (*I ~~wish I would~~ is strange because you should have control over what you are willing to do.)
I wish he would stop smoking. (This is fine because it means *I wish he were willing to* ...)

should have done

1   *Should* + the perfect infinitive is used to refer to a past action that didn't happen. The action would have been a good idea. It is advice that is too late!
*You **should have come** to the party!* (But you didn't.)
*You **shouldn't have called** him a fool.* (But you did.)

2   It is also used to refer to an action that might or might not have happened in the past. This use is dealt with in Unit 8.
*It's 10.00. They **should have arrived** by now.*

UNIT 12

Noun phrases

Adding information to nouns

1   Adjectives come before a noun.
***red** roses   a **thatched** roof*
Two- and three-part adjectives are hyphenated before a noun.
*a **grey-haired** businessman*
*an **open-air** pool*
*a **three-year-old** girl*

2 Nouns can be joined to make compound nouns.
swimming pool   *parking ticket*
football boots   *traffic warden*

3 Relative clauses and participle clauses come after a noun. These are dealt with in Unit 6.
*a driving licence **which expires soon***
*a boy **licking an ice-cream***
*football boots **stuffed in a bag***

4 Phrases with a preposition come after a noun.
*a cottage **with** roses growing **round** the door*
*the road **down** to the beach*
*a man **with** a briefcase **in** his hand*

Articles

The use of articles is complex as there are a lot of 'small' rules and exceptions. Here are the basic rules.

a/an

1 We use *a/an* to refer to a singular countable noun which is indefinite. Either we don't know which one, or it doesn't matter which one.
*They live in **a** lovely house.*
*I'm reading **a** good book.*
*She's expecting **a** baby.*

2 We use *a/an* with professions.
*She's **a** lawyer.*

the

1 We use *the* before a singular or plural noun, when both the speaker and the listener know which noun is being referred to.
*They live in **the** green house opposite the library.*
***The** book was recommended by a friend.*
*Mind **the** baby! She's near the fire.*
*I'm going to **the** shops. Do you want anything?*
*I'll see you in **the** pub later.*
*'Where's Dad?' 'In **the** garden.'*

2 We use *the* when there is only one.
***the** world*   ***the** River Thames*   ***the** Atlantic*

3 We use *the* for certain places which are institutions. Which particular place isn't important.
*We went to **the** cinema/theatre last night.*
*We're going to **the** seaside.*

zero article

1 We use no article with plural and uncountable nouns when talking about things in general.
***Computers** have changed our lives.*
***Love** is eternal.*
***Dogs** need a lot of exercise.*
*I hate **hamburgers**.*

2 We use no article with meals.
*Have you had **lunch** yet?*
*Come round for **dinner** tonight.*

But ... *We had **a** lovely lunch in an Italian restaurant.*

Determiners

Determiners that express quantity are dealt with in Unit 4.

each and *every*

1 *Each* and *every* are used with singular nouns. *Each* can be used to talk about two or more people or things. *Every* is used to talk about three or more.

Every/each time I come to your house it looks different.
Each/every bedroom in our hotel is decorated differently.

2 In many cases, *each* and *every* can both be used with little difference in meaning.
We prefer *each* if we are thinking of people or things separately, one at a time. We use *every* if we are thinking of the things or people all together as a group.
***Each** student gave the teacher a present.*
***Every** policeman in the country is looking for the killer.*

Adding emphasis

Word order and the passive

1 An unmarked word order is where all the parts of a sentence are in a 'non-special' order.
The company presented Kevin with a gold watch on his retirement in 1995.

2 This order can be altered to bring different elements to a stronger position in the sentence.
***On his retirement in 1995**, the company presented Kevin with a gold watch.*
***In 1995**, the company presented Kevin with a gold watch on his retirement.*

3 Using the passive shifts the focus of attention onto the object of the active sentence.
*On his retirement in 1995, **Kevin was presented** with a gold watch.*

Often, *by* + the agent is not used in passive sentences. On the occasions when it is, it is in a strong position in the sentence.
*On his retirement, Kevin was presented with a gold watch **by the chairman of the board**.*
*A country's food is largely influenced **by the climate**.*
*Entertainment on board ship will be provided **by the well-known singer and comedian, Gary Weeks**.*

Emphatic structures

Sentences can be reordered and introduced by certain structures to make the important information stand out.
***What I like about London is the fact that** it never sleeps.*
***What annoys me about Gerald is** his arrogance.*
***The thing that annoys me about Gerald is** his arrogance.*
***It's people like you who** spoil things for everyone else.*

Emphasis and speaking

1 We can use our voice to stress the important part of a sentence.
'Where did you get that car from?'   *'**Peter** gave it to me.'*
'Did he sell it to you?'   *'No, he **gave** it to me.'*
'I want it.'   *'Tough. He gave it to **me**.'*

2 If we want to express a contrast on the idea expressed by the verb, we stress the auxiliary. If there is no auxiliary, we add *do/does/did*.
*She told me to clean my room, but I **have** cleaned it.*
'Don't get angry.'   *'I **am** angry.'*
'Why weren't you at the party?'   *'I **was** at the party.'*
'What a shame you don't like ice-cream.'   *'I **do** like ice-cream.'*
'Why didn't he give you a present?'   *'He **did** give me a present. Look.'*

Acknowledgements

The authors would like to express their sincere thanks and appreciation to the following people who have all helped in the production of this book:

The students in our class at International House, London, who tried the book out with us and gave us valuable feedback. We had a lot of fun together: Annick Montoulieu (France); Naohiro Nobuta (Japan); Lori Eidelsztein (Argentina); Kaori Sato (Japan); Shirlei Bortoleto (Brazil); Gonul Kartal (Turkey); Son Ke-Young (Korea); Andrei Nissen (Brazil); Selma Rio Goncalves (Brazil); Fernando Borges D. Furtado (Brazil); Luiz Henrique Coelho Baeta (Brazil); Zofia Przednowek (Poland).

Justin Baines for his clever and witty maze; Guy Heath for his suggestions for the vocabulary in Unit 7; Richard Carrington, Paul Gillingham, David Griffiths, and Sarah Rosewarne for their research and recordings of people in all walks of life; Natalie Hodgson, Jo Devoy, Tom and Sue Higgins, Megan and Kate Soars for agreeing to be interviewed; Fiona Goble for her short story *Things we never said*.

Everyone at OUP for their unfailing encouragement, support, and enthusiasm: Sylvia Wheeldon (Managing Editor), Elana Katz (Senior Editor), Sally Lack (Production Editor), Jane Havis (Designer), Sara Gray (Art Editor), Peter Marsh (Audio Producer), Pearl Bevan (Senior Design Project Manager). They were a great team!

The publisher and authors are very grateful to the following teachers and institutions for reading and/or piloting the manuscript, and for providing invaluable comment and feedback on the course:

Beyhan Aytekin; Alex Boulton; Danuta Domaradzka; David Doyle; Tim Herdon; Robert Fenlon; David Horner; Bernie Hayden; Amanda Jeffries; Frank Lajkó; Mike Mansell; Antonio Marcelino; Roger Marshall; David Massey; Szilvia Mándli Portöro; Iain K. Robinson; Michael John Sayer; Martin Toal.

Language Centre of Ireland, Dublin; Eckersley School of English, Oxford; European Language Schools, Vigo; Révai Miklós Gimnázium, Gyòr; International House, Budapest; József Attila Gimnázium, Budapest; Escola d'Idiomes Moderns, Universitat de Barcelona; TÖMER, Ankara; Facultad de Idiomas, Universidad Veracruzana.

The authors and publisher would like to thank the following for permission to reproduce extracts and adaptations of copyright material:

Sean Blair for extracts from his article 'Icy Hell' from Focus, February 1997.

Jess McAree for extracts from the article 'Does the black box still do its job?' from Focus, July 1996.

Ewan MacNaughton Associates on behalf of the Telegraph Group Limited for extracts from Michael Schmidt: 'The Woman who made £17m from only £5' Daily Telegraph, 13 June 1996; Charles Laurence; 'I'll marry you, but only if we can …' Daily Telegraph, 14 February 1996.

Robert Matthews for adapted extracts from his articles 'The hundred weirdest mysteries known to science' from Focus, August 1996 and September 1996.

News International Syndication on behalf of Times Newspapers Limited for extracts from Peter Millar: 'I am become Death, the destroyer of worlds' from The Sunday Times Magazine, 16 July 1995, © Times Newspapers Limited, 1995.

The Observer for extracts from 'King of the Eccentrics' from The Observer Magazine, 17 January 1993, © The Observer, 1993.

Pan Books for use of 'The Third Twin' by Ken Follett.

Reed Books for extracts from Nigel Blundell: 'The World's Greatest Mistakes' (Octopus, a division of Reed Consumer Books Ltd).

Solo Syndication for extracts from Stewart Payne: 'Living History' Evening Standard 18 July 1994; Mary

Greene: 'Money - has it become the eighth deadly sin?' Daily Mail Weekend, 12 June 1995; Melissa Jones: 'The Great Escape' Daily Mail Weekend, 11 May 1996; Chris Parker: 'There's no place like our home' Daily Mail Weekend, I June 1996: Giles Minton: 'Does tourism destroy everything it touches?' Mail on Sunday, 19 May 1996; Tanya Reed: 'You can't come into Harrods dressed like that' Mail on Sunday, 18 August 1994.

Nicola Tyrer for extracts from her article 'They have nine TV sets …' from the Daily Telegraph, 26 October 1995.

The Week for extracts from 'The man who could own 100,000 Ferraris' from The Week, 22 February 1997.

Fast Car words and music by Tracy Chapman © 1988 EMI April Music Inc/Purple Rabbit Music, USA, reproduced by permission of EMI Songs Ltd, London WC2H 0EA.

Hello Muddah, Hello Fadduh words and music by Allan Sherman and Lou Busch © 1997 Warner Bros Music Corporation, 50% Warner Chappell Music Ltd, 50% unknown publisher.

Waiting at the Church words by Fred W Leigh, music by Henry E Pether © 1906 Francis Day & Hunter Ltd, London WC2H 0EA, reproduced by IMP Ltd.

Every endeavour has been made to identify the sources of all material used. The publisher apologizes for any omissions.

Illustrations by:

Veronica Bailey pp 64, 110; Jon Berkeley p 61; Neil Gower pp 89, 106; Emily Hare pp 99, 108; Lorraine Harrison pp 42, 43; Jane Havis pp 12, 15, 34, 66, 79, 107; John Holder pp 31,32, 33; Ian Kellas pp 8, 13, 22, 26, 27, 37, 38, 47, 49, 54, 58, 60, 68, 71, 74, 76, 77, 79, 80, 87, 88, 89, 94, 95, 97, 98, 100, 108 (Tom), 114, 115, 118, 127; Anne Magill, The Inkshed p 96; Ian Mitchell pp 72, 73; Sarah Perkins, The Inkshed p 51

Handwriting by Kathy Baxendale pp 6, 7, 14, 15, 68, 86, 115

Studio photography by:

Mark Mason pp 6, 7, 14, 15, 18, 24, 25, 29, 30 (Thomas Hardy novels), 35, 39 (coins), 40, 52, 53, 55, 56, 57, 68, 70, 77, 86, 90, 101 (money), 115

Location Photography by:

Maggie Milner p 47

Haddon Davies pp 69, 78 (woman in bed), p 111

The publisher would like to thank the following for their permission to reproduce photographs and copyright material:

Ace Photo Agency p 10 (H Hoffman/Family); Associated Press p 125 (Napalm Attack, Vietnam); Axiom p 16 (Traveller); BBC Picture Archives p 82 (Clapper board - Pride and Prejudice) (filming lights - Pride and Prejudice) (Mr Darcy - Pride and Prejudice) (Clapper board 744 - Pride and Prejudice) (Making of Pride and Prejudice); Bridgeman Art Library p 119 Sistine Chapel Ceiling (1508–12): Creation of Adam, 1511 (detail of Adam by Michelangelo Buonarroti (1475–1564) Vatican Museums and Galleries, Vatican City, Italy); Bubbles Photolibrary p 95 (Elizabeth, head and shoulders); Collection japonaise/Magnum Photos p 122 (Kikuchi/devastation by first explosion of the atom bomb); The J Allen Cash Photolibrary p 104 (The Taxman - male office worker on phone); Comstock p 75, p 90 (Man eating Hot dog); Corbis UK Ltd p 84 (Marlee Martin holds Oscar), p 112 (Romantic Couple); Daily Mail p 103 (P Davies/divorced mother with 4 kids); Dewynters p 85 (Phantom, Jesus, Cats); Greg Evans p 11 (M Wells/Family), 15 (girl), 66,67 (G Balfour/Restaurants, G Balfour/Shaftesbury Ave, G Balfour/Berwick St Market); Mary Evans Picture Library p 16 (D Livingstone), p 30 (T Hardy); Jimmy Gaston pp 72, 73, B Sell, Reuters, p 81 (Jane Austen); Genesis Photolibrary p 125 (First man on the moon); Getty Images p 10 (Rockies), p 11 (B Marsden/Greek Scene), p 19 (L Gordon/Cave Painting, C Ehlers/Grand Canyon, O Soot/Machu Picchu), p 41 (W Jacobs/Arab Market), p 70 (Evacuee), p 72 (K Hutton/domestic scene), p 95 (B Torrez/Nicole, head and shoulders),

p 109 (K Fisher/Holly Harper - Magazine Editor), p 105 (P Tweedie/homeless people huddled together on pavement), p 100 (Two girls on beach, black and white image), p 116 (old sepia print of great aunt with baby); The Ronald Grant Archive p 36; Robert Harding Picture Library p 39 (female portrait); Tom & Sue Higgins p 45; Natalie Hodgson p 24; The Image Bank p 14 (T Schmitt/Sao Paulo), p 16 (M Schneps/Map), p 17 (J F Podevin), p 19 (C Brown/Petra), pp 20, 45 (abstract), p 49 (K Philpot), p 56 (Durham), p 67; Jonathan Knowles p 80 (Man on phone); Pictor Uniphoto p 14 (male portrait), p 28 (Harrods), p 41 (Stock Market), p 47 (Rotterdam), pp 50, 62 (Antarctica), p 95 (George, head and shoulders); Popperfoto/Reuter I Waldie, Reuters, p 120 (Princess Diana arrives at the Royal Albert Hall), p 81 (Emma Thompson with Oscar), p 125 (JFK's assassination), p 125 (Blériot over England), p 126 (The young Elvis); Pictures Library p 15 (Basle), p 30 (Hardy's cottage), p 45 (fish & chips), p 66 (New Year); Popperfoto p 58 (A Bolante/Reuters); Quadrant p 63 (black box); Rex Features p 59, D Cooper, p 85 (Jesus Christ Superstar), J Witt, p 125 (release of Nelson Mandela), R Wallis, p 125 (collapse of the Berlin Wall), p 85 (Tim Rice), p 102 (Chrissie Lytton-Cobbold), p 125 (Diana, Princess of Wales - funeral procession); Science Photo Library p 121 (The first atomic bomb), Los Alamos National Laboratory, p 121 (detonation of the world's first atomic bomb); Tom Scott p 9; Robert Stigwood Organisation Ltd p 85 (Evita); Solo Syndication p 28 (Gilly Woodward), p 99 (K Towner/Rosemary Sage), p 104 (The Miser); Still Pictures p 21; Sygma p 62 (D Hudson/Mangle-Wurzle); Telegraph Colour Library, I McKinnell, p 92 (Starfield (illustration), S J Benbow, p 105 (Male homeless person), p 91 (Planets/Stars); Victoria and Albert Museum p 70 (paper).

The publishers would like to thank the following for their help and assistance:

Jonathan Altaras Associates; Browns Restaurant, Oxford; Oxford Antique Trading Co.; Bank of England.

Oxford University Press, Great Clarendon Street, Oxford OX2 6DP

Oxford New York

Athens Auckland Bangkok Bogotá
Buenos Aires Cape Town Chennai
Dar es Salaam Delhi Florence Hong Kong
Istanbul Karachi Kolkata Kuala Lumpur
Madrid Melbourne Mexico City Mumbai
Nairobi Paris São Paulo Shanghai
Singapore Taipei Tokyo Toronto Warsaw
and associated companies in
Berlin Ibadan

OXFORD and OXFORD ENGLISH
are trade marks of Oxford University Press

ISBN 0 19 435 800 3 International Edition
ISBN 0 19 436 176 4 German Edition
Bestellnummer 48 209

© Oxford University Press 1998

First published 1998
Fifteenth impression 2001

Printing ref. (last digit): 6 5 4 3 2 1

Typeset by Oxford University Press

Printed in China